AutoCAD VBA Programming
TOOLS AND TECHNIQUES

John Gibb and Bill Kramer

Miller Freeman Books

San Francisco

Published by Miller Freeman Books
55 Hawthorne, Suite 600, San Francisco, CA 94105

 Miller Freeman
A United News & Media publication

Distributed to the book trade in the U.S. and Canada by
Publishers Group West, 1700 Fourth Street, Berkeley, CA 94710

Cover Art: Robert Ward
Cover Design: The Visual Group
Interior Design and Composition: Brad Greene

Library of Congress Cataloging-in-Publication Data

Gibb, John W.
     AutoCAD VBA programming: tools and techniques / by John Gibb and Bill Kramer.
           p. cm
     ISBN 0-87930-574-6 (alk. paper)
     1. Computer graphics. 2 AutoCAD. 3. Microsoft Visual Basic for applications.
     I. Kramer, Bill, 1958. II. Title
T385.G5217 1999
620'.0042'02855369—dc21   99-43360
                                     CIP

Printed in the United States of America

99 00 01 02 03 04   5 4 3 2 1

Dedication

My Dad always taught me to look at things in a different way. That has helped me all through my programming career and as a consequence, I'd like to dedicate this work to his memory. I will always feel his presence.

Bill Kramer

I wish to dedicate this book to the memory of my friend John Keith and my cousin Christopher Etheridge. Thanks to John for his humor and creative talent and Christopher for his youthful enthusiasm. Both left us much too soon.

John Gibb

Acknowledgments

I would like to thank my girlfriend Margaret, her sons Brian and Bob
and my mother for their unwavering support despite my frequent lapses
of memory during the writing of the book. Sometimes focus is good for
writing but hard on the ones you love. Thanks for your patience.

I would also like to thank Application Developers, Andy Baron and Mike
Gunderloy for the use of their command line material as the basis for the
command line workaround material. A special thanks to Bob Verdun
and my colleagues at CFI for their patience during the time it took to
write this book.

John Gibb

My heartfelt thanks go to my family and friends for continuing to put up
with my eccentric hobbies and interests. Without their support I would
not be able to do many of the things I enjoy doing including the writing
of books and articles about computer programming. I'd also like to
thank the readers of books like this since it is because of them I must
learn more and am ever challenged to come up with new ideas. You all
have no idea how much energy and contagious enthusiasm that
provides!

Bill Kramer

Preface

Search though you may, you won't find two more qualified people to co-author a book on VBA and AutoCAD than Bill Kramer and John Gibb. Both have written several books plumbing the depths of programming as a science and an art. Both have explored AutoCAD and AutoLISP since their inception and both are much sought-after programmer-consultants by a wide range of science and engineering firms.

When issue No. 1 of *CADENCE* was published in 1986, Bill Kramer launched a column titled "AutoLISP Concepts," that over the years has transformed into his current "Programmer's Toolbox" and that stands as the longest running column in *CADENCE*'s 14-year history. With the advent of VBA capabilities in AutoCAD Release 14, Kramer expanded his "how to" programming tutorials to include frequent explorations of the intricacies of Visual Basic for Applications. John Gibb, too, has been a frequent contributor to *CADENCE* and both have helped countless programmers boost their knowledge of AutoCAD, AutoLISP and VBA through courses at Autodesk University, among other venues.

A graduate of Ohio State University's College of Engineering where he studied computer science and astronomy, Kramer first "got into" computers with a DEC PDP-8 in 1975 teaching himself assembler code. He programmed his first microcomputer, a Z-80-based system with 32K RAM and two 160K disk drives, using BASIC and assembler languages. In 1985 he launched Kramer Consulting and began developing applications for general CAD systems and AutoCAD in particular, including an NC programming system called NC-AUTO-CODE that he has supported ever since its first customer ship in 1986. Kramer has taught AutoCAD as an adjunct professor at Franklin University for several years and frequently offers sold-out classes in programming through Autodesk University.

As an Autodesk certified instructor, John Gibb has himself spent a fair amount of time sharing his vast programming knowledge with students at the Moraine Valley Autodesk Training Center. With a background in topology and utility mapping, space planning and facilities management systems, he has devoted 12 of his 15 years as a programmer to AutoCAD-related applications. An author of three books and numerous journal articles related to AutoCAD, Gibb is currently a senior applications developer with Computerized Facility Integration.

Gibb and Kramer share a keen ability to comprehend the black art of programming science and render it palatable. Both are noted for their sense of humor. But you *can* tell them apart in a crowd. Bill is the tall one —a former basketball player and current eclipse chaser who almost doesn't need a telescope to practice his craft. John's the one with the pony tail.

As a team, Gibb and Kramer bring unparalleled programming knowledge and experience to customizing AutoCAD with VBA. Updated to include capabilities introduced with AutoCAD 2000, this book is destined to become a de facto standard for AutoCAD programmers. Although aimed at those with advanced-intermediate and expert-level ability, there is much here as well for others who are new to programming science who would like to use VBA to maximize their AutoCAD productivity.

As authors, lecturers and consultants, Gibb and Kramer are *best of class*. They are also decent human beings. Read this book—you won't be sorry you did. And when you attend the next Autodesk University, take a class with them, or just stop them in the hallway to chat. They'll love it and likely keep you just a bit longer than you may have planned. But when you're done, you'll be all the richer for it.

—Arnie Williams, Editor in Chief, *CADENCE* magazine

Table of Contents

Introduction

Why another book about VBA? John and I first started talking about writing a book together some time ago. As programmers and teachers of others how to program, we found that we had many similar experiences. One of which is that you can never have enough examples of how to do various things. Both of us used books written by others as well as ourselves as sources for examples in both writing new code as well as teaching others to program. Another thing we felt that many books provided was a variable perspective on how to get the job done. That is, different ways to think about how to solve problems with programs and obtain improved productivity.

And while we were discussing the merits of books and the logistics of writing one together, an opportunity was presented by Miller Freeman Inc to author one about VBA – Visual Basic for Applications. Both of us had extensive experience in BASIC and programming in general thus we thought it would be fun to put one together. We were right. It was fun and we both learned a lot from each other along the way. And to increase the amount of pleasure, we switched systems along the way. We started working with VBA in AutoCAD Release 14 and ended up in Auto-CAD 2000 by the time we finished. The book is written for both versions however there are features in the newer AutoCAD VBA that will not work in the earlier one. We tried to point those out when we reworked the chapters after getting the newer AutoCAD release.

Writing a book about a subject as broad as VBA means that we jumped around a little here and there between chapters. We tried to build on knowledge learned from earlier chapters as the book progresses but at times it may seem like we shifted subjects in an extreme manner. That was so we could fill in more of the foundation of knowledge needed for the next step. The following paragraphs demonstrate this fact as they briefly explain the chapters in the book.

In chapter 1, we start with a basic introduction of what VBA is and how it fits into AutoCAD. Because many readers of this book are new to VBA, we wanted to get the terms defined that make up the "VBA Talk". We also wanted to help clarify the differences between VBA, AutoLISP, and Visual BASIC from Microsoft.

Chapter 2 jumps feet first into a simple project. This chapter was intended for those readers who prefer to take a look around the software first and then learn more about the details. The VBA environment is explored in a hands-on fashion to provide a feel for what it is like to write programs using this tool.

From our experiences in teaching VBA, both of us have learned that it is important to understand what objects are all about and how they relate to programming. Although simple in concept, object-oriented-programming is a new notion to many just learning VBA and other newer programming systems. In chapter 3 we introduce objects and how the AutoCAD object database is connected together. This chapter serves as a foundation for further details into the objects VBA programmers manipulate.

Chapter 4 drills into the AutoCAD object looking at the way everything is connected and introducing the main features found in the model. In chapter 5 we take a detailed look at manipulating collections of objects such as selection sets or groups of entities in a drawing. Chapter 6 explores the tables found in the drawing such as layers, line types, dictionaries, and so forth. These chapters combine to provide a look at the entire AutoCAD VBA object system and how you work with it from a general point view.

Many books about VBA finish after explaining the object model, but since this book is focused towards AutoCAD application developers we wanted to go further into some of the areas students have wanted to see.

In chapter 7 there is a discussion about how to interface with other automation servers such as Microsoft Excel. Examples are provided that show how easy it is to interface with these other tools in the computer system. We also look at extended data and how one can use that feature of AutoCAD's customization to yield tremendous benefits.

Project management for programming is important and chapter 8 provides information about how to work with more than one project at a time to save time in the development effort. And while on the subject of saving time, chapter 9 shows how to make use of the tools provided in the Windows environment itself. Virtually all of the time saving, operator friendly, aspects of Windows of that you want to use are available through the Windows API library. The only problem is that you have to find them and this chapter shows you how to do just that.

A list of samples, examples, and useful utilities is found in chapter 10 where John provides a long list of routines from his personal toolbox. John's earlier books on AutoLISP contained many of these utilities and he translated them to VBA making them available with this work.

In chapter 11 we took a more serious look at VB versus VBA. They are not the same, but they share a lot of the same attributes. For programmers looking to export their knowledge of VBA to VB this chapter serves as a guiding light to what can be done. At the same time, those programmers experienced with VB but wanting to learn about VBA will find useful information in this chapter as well. And as long as we are talking about experienced, we chose to share some of our experiences in chapter 12 where we investigate several possible pitfalls and provide tips we have learned along our journey. That leads into chapter 13 with a discussion of programming style to make your programs easier to read and work with in the future.

In the last chapter we look at creating your own objects through two examples. Most beginner VBA programmers do not venture this far and that's why we saved it for the last chapter. If you are serious about doing wonderful things with AutoCAD VBA, then defining your own objects is a very powerful tool to use. And the best way to explain it is to show two useful examples.

You should not think of this book as your only reference for VBA, there is an extensive help library included in the system. This book will help you understand that help library even better by having a strong foundation of VBA know-how behind you. In addition, the attached CD has more examples and even more information about other aspects of the AutoCAD system such as plotting.

We hope you are able to learn about VBA and enjoy it as much as we do through this book. The fun of getting the computer to do something special that you programmed is tremendous. It is also contagious as you learn new tricks and tidbits along the way. Keep on programmin'!

—Bill Kramer and John Gibb, November 1999

CHAPTER ONE

The AutoCAD VBA Environment

I ntended for programmers new to Visual BASIC for Applications (VBA), this chapter explores how VBA relates to other programming solutions inside AutoCAD. We will present a comparison of VBA, Visual LISP, and AutoLISP for readers familiar with the AutoLISP language and associated methods of AutoCAD customization. We will also introduce the various components of the VBA programming environment and give an explanation of how to start VBA inside AutoCAD.

AutoCAD Programming Solutions

AutoCAD is one of the most open architecture-designed CAD/CAE/CAM systems with a large variety of programming options on the market. The base AutoCAD package (not AutoCAD LT, but regular AutoCAD) comes with five interpretive programming languages that can be used to customize the system. There are also libraries for use with other programming systems that will create new objects and interfaces with the system.

The five programming languages found inside AutoCAD are as follows:

• a script file option containing AutoCAD commands that are played into AutoCAD in the order typed in the file;

- a menu programming system that allows users to select commands with optional user input.

- a menu statement language containing variables and elementary logic called DIESEL.

- a complete language system based on the LISP language;

- a complete language system that is an implementation of the BASIC language.

All of these programming options are provided with the standard AutoCAD package. They are not all provided with AutoCAD LT—only scripts, menus, and DIESEL can be found in that environment.

The LISP-based language called AutoLISP (and Visual LISP) allows you to develop new commands that you can easily integrate into menus. This permits the operator to incorporate advanced program logic of his or her own design into the custom menu system. The operator may also enter these new commands at the command line. AutoLISP has been available to AutoCAD developers for a number of years and contains multiple options for accomplishing the various tasks involved. Input options for AutoLISP include the command line as well as a dialog box–based interface. The dialog box interface must be programmed in a separate text file called a Dialog Control Language (DCL) file. The DCL file structure is simple to work with and does not provide as complete control over the dialog box layout as found in the Visual Developer Environments from Microsoft and other developers.

AutoCAD 2000 enhances AutoLISP considerably in the form of Visual LISP. Visual LISP provides greatly enhanced routines for accessing the drawing system. It also provides a vehicle for distributing applications in a compiled format that runs up to four times faster than AutoLISP. There are some differences between AutoLISP and Visual LISP in regards to ActiveX support and other systems related features, but for the most part if you know AutoLISP, you know Visual LISP. The "Visual" part comes from the full-screen text editor provided with Visual LISP that makes programming in AutoLISP much easier. Visual LISP is a significant improvement over AutoLISP and brings more power to that language than ever before.

The BASIC language system found inside AutoCAD is Visual BASIC for Applications. VBA is provided through a cooperation between Autodesk and Microsoft: it's a Microsoft product that Autodesk has licensed for use. The reasons for this generous gesture on Autodesk's behalf is that Visual BASIC is a very popular programming language and it better provides for an integrated programming environment. Of course, Microsoft is also quite interested in this venture as well since Microsoft makes the easiest to integrate tasks for VBA to work with. Developers and users of AutoCAD will find that this joint development tool represents a powerful feature for the creation of enhanced productivity utilities.

VBA is a superior development tool for creating dialog box–based interfaces. The Visual Development Environment is very flexible and provides the type of tools needed to create good-looking applications. There are several other features, covered later in this chapter that make it a powerful choice for developers.

How AutoLISP Differs from VBA

The primary difference, other than language structure, between AutoLISP (including Visual LISP) and the VBA language option is that AutoLISP runs from the command line or menu system. Solutions based on VBA are more interactive in nature and make extensive use of dialog boxes. Even though AutoLISP is capable of working with dialog boxes, VBA is far superior in that regard. Using the dialog box editor, you can quickly design new dialogs. The code window is just a click away from the dialog box editor window, so you can develop user interfaces quickly. Lastly, the controls or dialog box components found in VBA are better than those found in the AutoLISP DCL. Each of these components (controls in VBA terms) has many properties that the programmer can control during both run and design time. Programmers who use Visual BASIC will be able to build dialog-based interfaces significantly faster and better than those who build with AutoLISP.

Another primary difference between the two languages has to do with how they interface with other programs in a computer. VBA is simply much better at talking to other Windows programs than AutoLISP. Through a standardized process-to-process communications system, VBA is able to initiate other programs, control the programs, and pass data back and forth. Of course, the other programs must be able to respond to the requests from VBA, and not all Windows-based programs are capable of this task. To find out if a particular program can be interfaced through VBA, check for VBA automation support or ActiveX support in the product description. All of the Microsoft Office 97 products respond very well to VBA automation. Visual LISP supports ActiveX type interfacing as well, but not as elegantly as VBA automation and certainly not as well documented as in many references. You can learn more about ActiveX and how to use it to control word processing as well as spreadsheet applications in other texts. Some examples of interfaces to other programs are presented in later sections and on the associated media of this book.

It is important to note that you can expand AutoLISP through the ObjectARX (AutoCAD Runtime eXtension) to provide interfaces to other Windows programs. However, this involves using compilers and other system development tools that are not provided with AutoCAD. This sort of expansion is more for advanced programmers who are comfortable working with more than one computer language at a time. It is not recommended for developers who want to get the job done quickly so they can return to the design work that creates real income. In addition, more coding may be required to make the interfaces work. And this involves not only more time, but more effort on behalf of the programmer. On the plus side, expanding AutoLISP in this manner does open the door to working with products that do not directly support VBA automation but offer some other interface options.

VBA provides a fast, easy-to-program solution for interfacing Auto-CAD with other programs such as the Microsoft Office 97 productivity suite. From these you can integrate a word processor, spreadsheet system, or database directly with the AutoCAD drawing. And you do not need to purchase any additional compilers to get the job done: VBA is more than capable of working with these other packages. You just have to spend the time to program it the way you want it.

Another area where VBA is different from AutoLISP is in file handling. VBA provides a greater array of options for reading and writing data files. VBA's file input and output options include sequential text, random access records, and binary data. Through interfaces to Access 97 it can work with a variety of database structures. AutoLISP works with sequential text files, and through a library of functions it can also work with a variety of database systems. Thus VBA provides more options for file accessing, which can be an important aspect in building integrated applications from tasks that have traditionally been independent. An example would be a coordinate geometry system that stores data about points in a direct access binary data file. AutoLISP would have a difficult time (except through ObjectARX expansion) working with this data, while there is a chance that VBA could read and work with the numeric data stored in the file.

AutoLISP and VBA programming styles differ greatly when it comes to object manipulation and creation. VBA programs use functions that are related to the entity object definitions in order to perform the edit operations on a particular entity. AutoLISP can either use the command system of AutoCAD or directly change the data found in the entity objects based on programmatic control. Visual LISP provides a library of functions that also access the objects in the same manner as VBA through the ObjectARX interface. VBA also provides a pipeline to the command processor of AutoCAD—however, there are some good reasons not to use it.

It's a good idea to avoid using AutoCAD's COMMAND system for manipulating objects in the drawing. The simple reason is speed of execution and application control. A classic example of the speed is found in the Explode function that is associated with the block reference and other complex objects. Instead of using the EXPLODE command in AutoCAD to explode a block insert, VBA would first get the block reference object and then run the associated Explode function. This executes significantly faster than sending the object entity name to the command processor following the EXPLODE command. AutoCAD must first interpret the command name just sent, then check the object to make sure it is of the correct type to explode, and then call the same function being called when the Explode method is called for the object.

Using methods instead of commands may sound complicated at first, but it really isn't when applied in a programming context. Both VBA and AutoLISP applications programmers must decide whether to use the familiar COMMAND-based sequences or to gain the speed of execution by accessing the objects directly.

We have presented a comparison table of VBA and AutoLISP data types below. As seen in the table there are numerous data types in VBA that are not supported in AutoLISP. At the same time, there are several AutoLISP data types specific to AutoCAD entity handling that are handled as objects and collections of objects in the VBA environment. It is through this use of objects that VBA is different from AutoLISP when working with AutoCAD data. All other data manipulation in AutoLISP is supported in VBA, plus a lot more. VBA is better suited to data processing applications than AutoLISP as a result of this expanded data type support.

While AutoLISP provides a data type specific to working with the AutoCAD database such as entity names and pick sets, VBA works through the object system. Objects in AutoCAD are exposed to VBA, and that makes their properties and methods available for manipulation. This calls for some different thinking when it comes to working with Auto-CAD customization in VBA as compared with AutoLISP. Again, it cannot be stressed enough: although VBA is a powerful tool in the customization of AutoCAD, it is not always going to be the best solution. Sometimes just a simple menu macro can be more productive to an operator than a fancy dialog box–based application. It is always important to maintain the perspective of the operator when writing software that customizes a package such as AutoCAD.

Table 1.1: Comparison of data types between AutoLISP and VBA

Data type	AutoLISP	VBA
Boolean	Nil or non-nil binding	Boolean 1 byte binary data
2 byte integer	Integer	Integer
4 byte integer	None	Long integer
4 byte floating point	None	Single precision real
8 byte floating point	Real	Double precision real
Currency, money counting	None	Currency
Date and Time	Julian days as real numbers	Date/Time 8 byte value
String of characters	String	String
Entity name	Ename data type	Object
Selection set	Pickset data type	Collection
List	List	Array, Collection, Object
Point List	List	Array of real numbers

Visual BASIC versus Visual BASIC for Applications

Just what are the differences between Visual BASIC and Visual BASIC for Applications? For the most part, not too many. If you already know VB, then working with VBA is easy with just a few adjustments. For now, the important difference to keep in mind is that VBA runs inside AutoCAD while VB runs outside AutoCAD. This means they communicate with the AutoCAD system in different ways—and more importantly for many programmers, at different speeds. VBA is faster than VB when it comes to manipulating entities inside AutoCAD.

So does that mean you should not consider purchasing Visual BASIC? The answer to that question is really up to you and where you plan to go with the language.

If you intend to use VBA as a primary development engine, then we highly recommend purchasing one of the Visual BASIC editions. When you install any of the Visual BASIC editions (Standard or Professional), you get more controls available to your applications development. In addition, the programming talents learned from VBA can be applied in Visual BASIC to develop applications completely outside of AutoCAD to solve other design and engineering problems.

On the other hand, if your intent is to use VBA only when it is the "best" solution to the problem at hand, then purchasing Visual BASIC is not really called for. Perhaps the only exception would be to gain the use of a control that is not provided in VBA such as the communications module opening the door to RS-232 serial communications via a modem. This control is provided in the Professional edition of Visual BASIC and is not found in the VBA environment. Of course, not everyone will need that control, either!

Chapter 11 is devoted to the subject as well as the issues involved in porting applications from one environment to the other. VBA and VB are not identical in the way they work. For instance, they have different approaches to starting a form due in part to the fact that they use different forms development and management systems.

Essential VBA Vocabulary and Concepts

As with any computer language system, the VBA environment has unique terminology. These terms will be used freely throughout this book. Thus, if you are new to the visual development environment or new to Visual BASIC, you will need to become familiar with these terms.

These first terms relate to general Windows programming. They are used frequently to describe how something takes place in the computer environment or how a program can talk to some other program.

Windows: The rectangular areas on the display where you communicate with the user. Each window will have an ID that identifies it to the system, and it is through that ID that you talk to a specific Windows task. AutoCAD typically has two windows: the graphics window and the text window. If you run more than one copy of AutoCAD at a time, then there may be more than the two windows in the system. Note that VBA talks only to the first one found, and this can be a problem when you open multiple windows of AutoCAD at once.

Events: The variable processes that take place as the computer runs. Events include actions such as keyboard input, mouse clicks, interface requests, process messages, and so forth. Anything that can happen in the computer is essentially an event. Most of the programming done in VBA is in response to events that the user initiates. When the user clicks the mouse while it is pointing to a button in one of your programs, an event-related task of your design is started. You program just what this event does, and it is through a series of event handling tasks that an application is created. Programs can cause events to happen that make other programs respond in some way. These messaging events are how VBA communicates with other programs, including AutoCAD.

Messages: When an event occurs, messages are used to relay information about the event to the various processes that might be interested. Most incoming messages relate to the operating system such as the changing of a window's disposition. Depending on the application, user-initiated and system-initiated messages may be the only messages a program needs to handle. Other messages are from one program to another. For most applications you will write, these messages are outgoing, as your program is making a request of another program to do something. Messages are typically in the form of code numbers. About the only exceptions occur when user input is involved and strings are passed as part of the message. As such, message transmission tends to be quick in the computer and is not as encumbering as it may sound.

IDE: This stands for the Integrated Development Environment and is used to reference the editor, project explorer, object browser, properties window, and other programmer information windows. The IDE is a rendition of the Microsoft Developer Studio that is used for other language systems such as C++ and FORTRAN. If you already program in the studio environment then you already are familiar with many of the windows in the IDE.

The next few terms relate to the VBA IDE.

Forms: The windows designed by your programming efforts are forms, and you will use the form editor to develop the appearance of your forms. For the majority of VBA applications there will be a primary form that the user will interface with by selecting button options and other items. Applications can have multiple forms or multiple dialog boxes, and your program controls which ones are active or visible at any given time.

Controls: The individual items in a dialog box are called controls. There are several types of controls available in VBA, including buttons, text displays, icon or bitmap buttons, lists, pop-up lists, and so forth. All the most common items found in a dialog box are available to VBA developers. When you are in the form editor, the control toolbox should be visible. This toolbox contains buttons for each of the primary controls. To use one, select the button, then locate on the form where you want the control to be placed.

Properties: This term is used to describe the set of data associated with an object such as a form or a control or some other program object. In VBA program development, you manipulate the properties of the controls in a dialog box where you can change their values as needed by an application. When we are talking about objects, the properties are the data elements associated with them. For example, an Arc object in Auto-CAD would have properties for the center point, radius, and angles. By changing the properties, you change the way the object will be displayed or will work with the system.

Project: A program in VBA is a project, and the project window will display all of the components in a given project. When VBA inside Auto-CAD is first started, the only component in the project is the AutoCAD drawing that is currently active. As forms and modules are added to the project, they appear in the project window display. Projects are stored in DVB files in the hard drive of the computer.

Module: Projects contain forms and modules. The forms are the dialog box and associated code while modules are just code with no dialog boxes. Modules are typically used to house standard routines from a productivity library or to hold code and data that is accessed by more than one form.

Objects: Objects are containers that house both program code and data. Generally, the data elements are called properties, and the program code elements are called methods. The best way to think of objects is as a set of data that uses routines to manipulate that data. Other programs can use some of the routines while others are privately held inside the object for internal use only. Objects are capable of being cloned into new objects that share the same properties and methods. Software libraries often make use of the cloning or inheritance aspect of objects to build a tree of different yet related objects. Because of this cloning, objects can also use the same name as other objects to reference information or routines that are unique inside that object. The subject of object-oriented programming can fill a book by itself and is beyond the scope of this text. However, you will become familiar with the concept of object-oriented programming just because that is how things are accomplished in VBA as far as working with AutoCAD. In VBA, the object browser is used to explore the objects available. When an object is selected, its properties and methods are displayed for further reference. This makes programming in objects very easy, and as we explore the development environment further you will see that object programming can be quite easy.

Methods: This term is applied to the subroutines and functions that are inside an object. When looking for a particular function that performs a particular activity, you start by looking for the object that controls those aspects of the system. Once you identify the proper object, the method can be found along with the properties. For example, to change the start point of a Line object in AutoCAD, the StartPoint method is

11

used. This method can be found in the object definition for a Line entity called acLine. AutoCAD methods and objects tend to start with the characters *ac*, making them easy to identify in the code as well as when searching the object browser.

Collections: A collection is a group of common objects that can be referenced as a singular item. For example, a project contains collections of modules and user forms. More important to the task of customizing AutoCAD is the fact that groups of drawing objects are manipulated as collections. When working with a selection set in VBA, you are working with a collection.

Getting Comfortable with the IDE

The first thing you will encounter as you learn VBA is the IDE. The IDE is a collection of windows that combine to form a complete programming system, including an editor for the program text, a forms or dialog box editor to build the interface, a project component browser, and other tools to make the programming task easy. For some, their first impression of the IDE is that it is a bit overwhelming because so much information is presented at once. It appears to be a very complex tool to use, but that is far from the truth. All you need is to spend a little time working within the environment to become comfortable with the elements inside.

The situation is not unlike learning to drive a car for the first time. At first, the controls are foreign, and you're not sure which are important and which are not important. But after spending a little time behind the wheel in driver education, you become comfortable with the feel of the vehicle, and you learn how to scan the dashboard for critical information. The VBA IDE is much the same. There are windows displayed that you may not need to use in your programming efforts, at least not all the time. But because they are presented when you first start the system, most think they must be important and become concerned when they don't understand what they see. Because of the complex display, many beginners get the feeling that the system is complex and difficult to use.

These windows can be hidden most of the time, brought forward when needed, and pushed to the background when not. So, like learning that the battery gauge in a car does not require constant checking, there are windows that you do not need to see all the time as you write programs in VBA.

Starting the VBA IDE

The start-up procedure for the IDE inside AutoCAD varies slightly depending on which version of AutoCAD you are running. As of the writing of this book, there are two approaches to starting the IDE. The different approaches depend on the exact version of AutoCAD in use.

VBA first appeared in AutoCAD Release 14 as a preview edition. Installation of the preview edition was optional, so not all AutoCAD R14 installations will have VBA installed. You need to make sure you have VBA installed if you are still running the original Release 14 product of AutoCAD. To install VBA from that version, get the original AutoCAD distribution CD and use the Windows Explorer program to locate the VBA setup program. When loaded, VBA will appear as a pull-down menu entry. Selecting the editor option from that menu entry starts the IDE.

An updated version of AutoCAD Release 14 (called Release 14.01) and AutoCAD 2000 both contain VBA as a normal part of the system installation. In order to have VBA not installed, you must select a custom installation and remove the mark for the VBA components. As a consequence, most AutoCAD Release 14.01 installations contain VBA. Start the IDE in this environment by typing the command VBAIDE at the command line of AutoCAD.

The difference between VBA in AutoCAD R14 and AutoCAD 2000 is that the newer version (AutoCAD 2000) contains many more methods and properties that allow access deep into the AutoCAD system. There are also more objects available in the newer version.

Another way to start the IDE is when you're loading a VBA project into memory. The VBALOAD command is used to load a project, and there is a toggle on the dialog box for file selection that indicates whether the editor should be started after the project has been loaded. The existing project will be displayed when the IDE starts up.

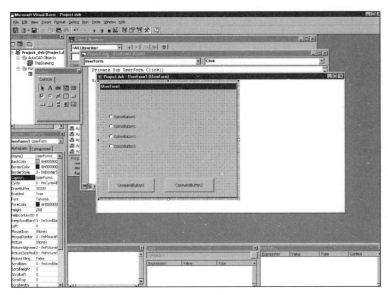

Figure 1.1: VBAIDE in AutoCAD

When started with a project already loaded, the IDE will present a full-screen development environment containing multiple windows as seen in figure 1.1. Select the one you want to work with by picking it from the Windows pull-down menu or by selecting the proper icon in the toolbar menus shown. When starting with no existing VBA program in memory, the IDE presents a blank work area with the project explorer and properties windows visible. Use the menu Insert options to start the definition of a code module or input form. The next chapter contains a tutorial walk-through to create a simple program in VBA and can be used to learn the basics behind programming in this environment.

What's in the IDE?

As we mentioned before, there are numerous windows in the IDE, and at first they may not appear all that friendly. But it does not take long

14

before you will be comfortable navigating your way through complex programs of your own design. The IDE was written by programmers, for programmers, and as such it serves as a very powerful tool in the development of applications. So let's look at the various components in the IDE and get a general feeling as to what they are for and how to use them.

Project Explorer: (Figure 1.2) This window presents a tree diagram showing the modules and forms that are part of the current project. The Project Explorer provides one method for getting around in your program code. To get to a particular module, select it in the hierarchy, then select the view code or form button. When you're writing code, you won't use the Project Explorer too often, so it can be hidden to make more space for the code window.

The Project Explorer becomes more and more useful as your projects grow in complexity through the addition of more forms and code sections. As the need comes up, you can restore it to the screen for navigating about your project.

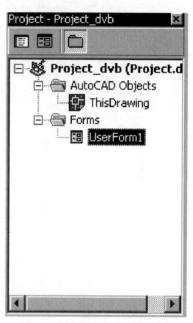

Figure 1.2: Project Explorer

User Form Windows: The dialog boxes of an application are defined in user form windows. Generally you start development of a new application by opening a new user form window and then placing the controls for that window into the grid displayed. You can quickly jump to the code window and the code specific to an event by double clicking on a control while in the user form window. Designing new forms is very easy, and it is tempting to get "creative" in how you present something. Chapter 13 has been devoted to programming style, and we recommend that you adopt standard styles for a variety of reasons.

Properties Window: (Figure 1.3) The details about whatever object is currently highlighted will be shown in the Properties window. Details

Figure 1.3: Properties window

include the name of the object, the color or display disposition of controls and forms, captions, and numerous other features. You'll use the Properties window the most when you are working on the design of a form for user input. During coding it will seldom be referenced, except to see what possible values a property might take. Like the Project Explorer, it can be removed from view to make more room for the code window.

Each object on a form has a variable number of properties, and the list will change as you select the different controls. These represent the control properties that can be set at design time when you are creating the program for the first time. For some controls, there are additional properties that can be added while the program is running. When referencing a property in the help system, make sure to note if it is run time changeable.

Code Window: Program entry and review takes place in the code windows: there is a code window for each user form that has code associated with it. Entering code into a new program is aided in the code window by the system. When you reference an object such as a control in a form or an AutoCAD data entity, the editor will prompt you through the various levels of the object to get to the property or method you need. And as you debug your programs the system will show you the code that caused a problem in the code window related to the user form or module in which the problem occurred.

The Object Browser: (Figure 1.4) Start the Object Browser window by selecting the Object Browser button, by selecting it from the View menu, or by pressing the function key 2. The Object Browser is a tree structure display that shows all the objects known by the VBA system. This is where you go "shopping" for an object when you are not sure of the name or when you are looking for a method (function) to perform a particular task. The Object Browser links to the help system through the function key 1 that facilitates the learning of the object library. Although there are many objects in the library it does not take too long to learn the important ones.

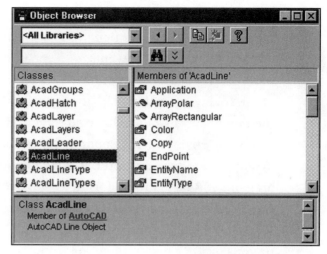

Figure 1.4: Object Browser

Developing Applications with VBA inside AutoCAD

The steps involved in developing applications using VBA start with properly identifying that VBA is a proper, if not the best, solution for the job. Although VBA is a very flexible programming solution, it does not provide a method for adding new commands to AutoCAD, and this may present a problem for the developer. Instead, VBA applications revolve around dialog boxes and interfaces to AutoCAD and other programs. So the first step in developing a VBA application is to develop the user interface.

The user forms editor and toolbox are used to define the dialog box or user form. Select a control from the toolbox, then locate on the form grid where you want it to be and how big you want it to be. You'll then reference the properties window to change the captions or colors or whatever other properties need to be modified to fit the application. As you define the controls, you can enter the code window to define what happens when the control object is picked, clicked, changed, or some other event takes place related to the control object.

17

A key aspect to keep in mind when writing programs in VBA is that the programs are event oriented. That means you program modules that respond to events. The events your modules will respond to are usually user driven—caused by a mouse click or keyboard activity. Hence most of the code you write will be to respond to these events and to process the input values when instructed to do so by the user. Unlike other programming environments you may be used to working in, there is no main program that controls the flow of events. At least there is no main program you have to write. When you run your program, you actually run a dialog box manager that looks at the form design, paints it on the screen, and handles the essential program setup sequences. You are responsible for programming the setup and processing modules that pertain only to the data you are manipulating. The remaining activities that take place in the Windows environment are controlled by the VBA processing system. If you have ever programmed or looked at the process involved in developing a Windows application the hard way, you will greatly appreciate all that VBA does to aid in your application development.

The common structure of a VBA program is to simply collect data in a dialog box and then process the data when a button is pressed. Generally, there is a dialog box setup stage where default data is placed into the controls. Keeping the data in the controls is a great way to store the data in your program. When the user changes the value, your program can test to see if the data change is proper in the context of the application. That way, the data in the control is always something that can be used, and no more code may be needed to check the value for accuracy and usability. If a module needs to know what the value of a particular user input variable is, the control is accessed to get the current data value.

In most VBA applications there is at least one button that performs a process with the input data. There may be more than one button for more complex applications, but there will be at least one. That way the user can input all data, review it on the screen, then press the activation button to process the data into output. There should also be an abort or exit button in case the user needs to run some other task inside AutoCAD and return to your program.

The next chapter will walk you through the process of how to write a simple program in VBA that actually does something useful. If some of these concepts in programming seem difficult to you, go through the next chapter carefully and observe how easy programming in VBA is once you get used to it. The hardest thing for most programmers learning VBA is the idea of saving data in the input dialog, even though the dialog may not be visible on the screen. But this is a natural way of programming, once you become familiar with objects and the tactics involved in object-oriented programming.

CHAPTER TWO

VBA Application Jump-Start

In this chapter we are going to jump right into the VBA programming environment and develop an application program. The program is not advanced, but it does serve as a good example of the power of VBA inside AutoCAD. It also gives programmers who are learning the VBA system a chance to try out the features in the programming environment by following the step-by-step procedures.

Description of the Application

The program to be developed is the start of a bill of material counting routine. Specifically, it will count block references in the drawing and report them in a list box as seen in Figure 2.1. When the list members are selected, the block references are highlighted in the drawing.

This application demonstrates a number of aspects of how VBA applications handle things inside AutoCAD. It also shows the true power of VBA inside AutoCAD and how objects can be used to keep the coding at a reasonable level. The application shows objects of all kinds in use, ranging from dialog box objects to AutoCAD objects.

As a teaching tool, this program involves a form for user reporting and input. It also involves blocks and the manipulation of the block table.

Selection sets, filters, basic user input, and string handling are also demonstrated in this simple example. Programmers learning how to develop applications using VBA should attempt to build the same problem by following the instructions below.

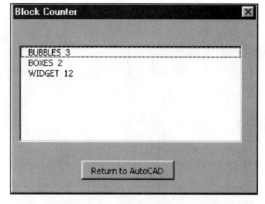

Figure 2.1: Block Counter macro running

Start Your IDE

Get started by loading AutoCAD 2000 into the computer, then starting the VBA developer environment with the command **VBAIDE**. When using AutoCAD R14, you will be required to first install the VBA system before the VBAIDE command environment will be available. VBA is not supported under earlier releases of AutoCAD.

Design the Form

The development of many VBA applications will start with a dialog box or form. Forms are easy to build inside VBA using the visual tools provided. A form is an object, and the items that go inside the form are also objects, but they are called components more often than not.

Figure 2.2: Toolbox controls

- Using the pull-down menus, go to Insert then select the UserForm option.

- A rectangle will appear on the screen that contains grid points.

- There will also be a toolbar shown of control options as in figure 2.2.

The toolbox contains the components that can make up a screen. As you move your mouse over each and

21

Figure 2.3: CommandButton selection

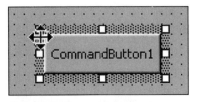

Figure 2.4: Placing CommandButton in grid

Figure 2.5: Properties dialog

hesitate, a highlight box (tool tip) will appear telling you the name of the object as in figure 2.3.

The dialog box in Figure 2.1 contains two controls (objects). The button is a control, and so is the listbox.

• Select the CommandButton option from the toolbox controls.

• Locate a point on the grid to place the button as in Figure 2.4.

If you make a mistake or want to move the button on the grid, just select it and drag it to a new location. You can also resize it and change the corners as needed by your application. The control just inserted will behave like most Windows objects do. You can change its location and size with the pointing device only. Now let's change the information inside the control object. That is, we will change some of the properties of the CommandButton to suit our needs. You cannot change these properties with a mouse alone, so you will have to do some keyboard work.

• Select the properties dialog box as in figure 2.5.

• Pick the Caption property within the list shown. You may have to scroll the list to get to the property you want.

• Using the keyboard, type a new caption value— "Return to AutoCAD."

Notice that as you type the command button will change as well. The text you are typing will appear in the CommandButton in the form design window. You can resize the CommandButton as needed so that the text fits.

22

The components of a dialog box are considered objects. We will discuss objects in the next chapter, but an important thing to keep in mind when programming them is that they contain properties. Another term might be *variables*, but it really goes much beyond that notion.

First Lines of Program Code

Now let's add the program code for the CommandButton object. Although the button is fairly smart about being a button, it does not know what we want when the button is selected. That is where coding comes into the game. We are going to write a routine that reacts to the button being pressed. To do that, we need to define the program sequence and tell the system about the linkage to the button. Sounds complicated, and it is inside the computer, but not at the VBA development level.

- Double click the Command-Button we just created in the grid screen.

- A text editor window (see Figure 2.6) should open up with the subroutine CommandButton1_Click() already started.

- Start a new line before the End Sub statement and type "End" so that the source code matches the listing below.

Figure 2.6: Text Editor Window

```
Private Sub CommandButton1_Click()

    End

End Sub
```

That's it for this button command. All we want it to do is terminate the program and return to AutoCAD.

23

Jumping from forms directly to the text editor is one of the features of VBA (and VB) that make them an easy programming environment for dialog box– (form-) based applications. Double clicking the form component will open the text editor window at the click event routine for that component. The name of the function is predetermined by VBA for linking purposes. If you change the name, the function will not run when the button is clicked. The function and control names are linked so that a change to either one must be reflected in both to maintain the linkage. But the VBA editor makes it easy to keep everything straight as it writes that part of the code for you. That helps prevent typographic errors that keep a routine from functioning properly.

Now we shall return to the forms editor to change some more properties and add some more controls. You can "hack" together an application quickly in VBA by defining a control, then defining the primary event reacting code associated with that control.

Form Properties

Properties in the various objects provide a great deal of programmability to the system without writing any code. The dialog box (form) and controls have a large number of variable properties associated with them that make customization a breeze for an applications programmer. The next step in our programming tour will be to change the form properties so that the appearance of the form is more of what we need for the application. Specifically, we are going to change the name of the form object to be more meaningful to our application, and we are going to change the title text that appears at the top of the dialog box.

- Now return to the form design by selecting the pull-down menu item Window.

- Next select the UserForm option.

- You can also select the View Object icon in VBA to bring the forms editor to the front.

It is time to give our form a name and a better title. We can do that by changing the properties of the form object.

- To view the properties, if they are not already visible on the screen, select anywhere on the form (grid or title bar), then press the right mouse button. The Properties window option is in the list. Select on the form—not on the Command-Button—to make sure the properties showing are for the UserForm as in figure 2.7.

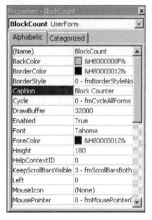

- In the Properties window, select the (name) property at the start of the list.

- Type in the name, "BlockCount." This is now the name of the form object.

- Select the Caption property.

- Type in the new caption, "Block Counter."

Figure 2.7: Properties for UserForm

Add a List Box Control

The form for the application we are building requires one more control to be inserted—a list box. A list box is a control in which we can insert a list of text that will be displayed on the screen. List boxes have some interesting properties that we will explore later in Chapter 12. They are worth investigating with some additional experiments on your own, too.

- Select the ListBox icon from the control toolbox as in figure 2.8.

- Show a point by locating the upper left corner. You can resize the list box as needed to match the needs of the application.

Figure 2.8: Selecting a list box control

You can manipulate both control objects in the form using the pointing device. By picking the object (with a single click), you can move and resize the control into position. This is the most visual feature of building a visual interface and can be a lot of fun as you see what different controls look like together.

Checklist

At this point in our program design, we have the following defined:

1. A form named BlockCount

2. Two controls on the form, a button, and a list box.

3. The controls are named CommandButton1 and ListBox1. These are the default names assigned when the objects were defined.

4. A function named CommandButton1_Click that is attached to the BlockCount form.

Programming the Starting Sequence

The next step in the program is to write the code that manipulates all these objects. We have already done a substantial amount of programming, but by using VBA, all that work is in the background, and we simply defined objects using the pointing device. Because objects know how to handle themselves, this is surprisingly easy. But there are a couple of concepts to understand before we get too much further.

When a typical VB program starts, a form is loaded and the Form_Load function is generally the first one run. That's because a user typically starts a VB program at the operating systems level. As such, the user expects the program to do something on the screen as a result. Rarely will you develop a VB program that does not involve a dialog box.

VBA is different in that regard. You start macros when you run a VBA program. There can be any number of macros defined in a module that you load and start. Every VBA program will contain at least one macro in a module. The macro is what you run from AutoCAD, and it is not expected to always have a dialog box or form. The Form_Load function does not exist in VBA as a consequence.

When you run a VBA macro, the form or dialog box (if any; there does not have to be one) is initially hidden from view. You must transfer control to the form from the macro before it becomes visible and the user can input and output. The form is an object, and as such there is a method or subroutine that you can run to activate the object. In the case of a form it is the Show method.

The Show method will cause the form to be displayed on the screen in front of the AutoCAD window (and all others). Computer control is transferred to the form until it is closed via the Hide method or it ends through some other method. Your application must provide some place to do these things in order to end. Never-ending programs can be a nuisance to the operator.

Global Variable Declarations

With all this in mind, let's code the macro for the block counting application.

- Select the Insert pull-down menu.

- Pick the Module option.

- A text editor window with the new module will be displayed.

- Type the code shown in the following listing. It should go into General—Declarations.

Figure 2.8: Text editor banner

```
Global SS As AcadSelectionSet

Global BLKS As AcadBlocks

Global BLK As AcadBlock

Global Grps(0 To 1) As Integer

Global Dats(0 To 1) As Variant

Global Filter1, Filter2 As Variant
```

This code sets up some variables that will be used in the program. We are declaring these variables as global so we can re-use them in various subroutines within our application. The variable "SS" is declared as a selection set object. We will use this object to locate the block inserts inside the drawing. We will use BLKS as a pointer to the blocks collection where the block table can be found. BLK is a block object, which contains information such as the name of the block, base point, and much more. Two arrays are defined, Grps and Dats, to hold the filter information for building the selection set. Because of the way variables are passed to AutoCAD from VBA (and VB), variants are used for the filters. Filter1 and Filter2 are the variants used.

Note how VBA tries to help you along when you're typing in the program code above. Although some may question the value of this feature, when you are typing long AutoCAD names, it's a real time saver. To select the highlighted item from the automatic pop-up list, just press the Tab or Enter key. You can use the pointing device to highlight the name desired.

We will discuss table collections, selection sets, filters, and other details in much more detail in subsequent chapters. This example is meant to give you a flavor of the programming environment.

Counting Blocks Macro

Now it is time to write the macro that starts the entire process. The macro is to be titled BlockCounter—this is where we'll find some more program code typing.

- While still in the text editor, after typing the Filter1 and Filter2 variant declaration, type Sub BlockCounter () and press the Enter key.

- The End Sub statement will automatically be added and the header above the code should be changed to General—BlockCounter.

- Now type in the code that appears in the following listing. Be careful to get it right! Program code must be exact, as computers do only what we tell them to do.

```
Sub BlockCounter()

  Grps(0) = 0: Dats(0) = "INSERT"

  Grps(1) = 2: Dats(1) = ""

  On Error Resume Next

  Set SS = ThisDrawing.SelectionSets.Add("SS")

  If Err.Number <> 0 Then

    Set SS = ThisDrawing.SelectionSets.Item("SS")

  End If

  SS.Clear

  Set BLKS = ThisDrawing.Blocks

  Dim J As Integer

  J = BLKS.Count - 1

  For I = 2 To J

    Set BLK = BLKS.Item(I)

    Dats(1) = BLK.Name

    Filter1 = Grps

    Filter2 = Dats

    SS.Select acSelectionSetAll, , , Filter1, Filter2

    Out$ = BLK.Name & " " & Str$(SS.Count)

    BlockCount.ListBox1.AddItem Out$

    SS.Clear

  Next I

  While 1 = 1

    BlockCount.Show

  Wend

End Sub
```

Let's look at each line, one at a time, to understand what is going on here. All the variables we are going to be using have been defined as global in the previous section. The goal of the routine at this point is to build a list of all the blocks in the drawing. That list is to be displayed, along with the count of the number of insertions for each block.

```
Grps(0) = 0: Dats(0) = "INSERT"

Grps(1) = 2: Dats(1) = ""
```

In order to obtain a count of the number of insertions for each block, we will build a selection set. In VBA a selection set is a collection of entity objects. When creating selection sets, a filter can be applied that will cause only specific objects to be selected. In this application we are looking for "INSERT" objects. The first two lines of the function establish the group codes and string settings for the filter. The name of the block (associated with group code 2) will be filled in as we loop through the block table in the drawing.

We construct filters by using two arrays that must be dimensioned to the exact size that will be required to house the filter elements. These two arrays are passed to the selection set function in AutoCAD via a pair of variant variables. Variants are multiple byte pointer variables that specify data type and other contents. They make it easier for the receiving program to decipher what has been sent as a parameter. As a result, we use variants quite often when passing information between applications written in different programming languages.

```
On Error Resume Next

Set SS = ThisDrawing.SelectionSets.Add("SS")

If Err.Number <> 1 Then

    Set SS = ThisDrawing.SelectionSets.Item("SS")

End If

SS.Clear
```

The next step in the program is to define a selection set object. This operation merely sets the room aside for a selection named "SS". The variable name of the object (SS) matches the name of the selection set for our own convenience—it is not a requirement of the system. Since we don't know if that selection set has anything in it, the next operation is to clear it just to make sure. The add() method will add a new name to the selection sets collection if it does not already exist in the list. If the name already exists, an error will result. By setting the error recovery mode active in the program the error will not cause the program to fail. Instead, the object is opened using the item() method. The Clear method of the selection set object clears out any entity object references that may have been in the selection set.

```
Set BLKS = ThisDrawing.Blocks

J = BLKS.Count - 1

For I = 2 To J
```

The next step in the program is to start into a loop to look at all blocks stored in the drawing. The block table is stored in what is called the blocks collection, which is accessed through the current drawing object. The first statement above obtains the blocks collection object. ThisDrawing is the current drawing, and the dot following it symbolizes a property or method. The property being used is Blocks.

Notice how the BLKS variable now can be used to obtain information about the blocks collection. In the second statement above, the BLKS.Count reference obtains the count property. The count is the number of block objects in the blocks collection.

We start a For loop to iterate through the collection. Access into the collection is by index, meaning that it is zero-based. Index 0 gets the first element, 1 gets the second, and so forth. The loop starts with the third element in the blocks collection. The first two blocks are Model Space and Paper Space, and these blocks are not inserted into the drawing— they are the drawing. The For loop will iterate until the number of blocks in the table minus one has been reached. The minus-one portion of the loop control is for the index value of the last element in the block table. To illustrate, if there are five blocks in the table, including Model and Paper Space, the loop will iterate three times (index values 2, 3, 4).

```
Set BLK = BLKS.Item(I)

Dats(1) = BLK.Name
```

The BLKS object is the table or collection of block names. To get the details on a particular block we can access this table by name or by index number. The result of accessing the table is a block object (BLK). The name of the block is a property of the block object, and the program assigns it into the data array for the filter.

```
Filter1 = Grps
Filter2 = Dats
SS.Select acSelectionSetAll, , , Filter1, Filter2
```

The variants Filter1 and Filter2 are assigned to the arrays (Grps and Dats). This must be done after any changes to the arrays, as the variant linkage needs to be refreshed before they are used in the parameter call to the selection set building functions.

SS.Select will build a selection set. In this case, it has been instructed to look at all objects in the drawing and use the filters to determine which ones are of interest. The filter used in our example looks for "INSERT" objects with a specific name.

```
Out$ = BLK.Name & " " & Str$(SS.Count)
BlockCount.ListBox1.AddItem Out$
```

We obtain the value to be added to the list box by taking the name of the block and concatenating it to a string created from the size of the selection set just created. The property name Count was used for the selection set collection as well as the blocks collection. This is a feature of object-oriented programming called *polymorphism*, and it is used extensively in VBA object control inside AutoCAD.

The name of the list box is derived from the name of the object that houses it. The form we created is called BlockCount. Inside that form we created a list box object named ListBox1. To get to the list box, we have to declare this hierarchy to VBA through the mechanism demonstrated above. AddItem is a method (subroutine) associated with list box objects. It will add a new string item to the end of the list box.

List boxes in VBA are different from list boxes in other AutoCAD programming systems using DCL. The list boxes of VBA retain the data so that they can be retrieved directly from the list box itself. List boxes and other controls serve as data containers for applications, even when they are not on the screen as in this case. The BlockCount form is still hidden, as far as the system is concerned, while this section of code is running. We are simply loading up the contents, and when we are ready, we will turn on the form for the user to see.

```
    SS.Clear

Next I
```

Before going on to the next block in the block table, the selection set (SS) is cleared. The Select() method will add objects to the selection set each time it is run. Existing objects in the selection set remain while the new ones are added; hence it is important to remember to clear the selection set with each iteration.

At the completion of the loop we are ready to start the dialog box (form) to display the blocks and their respective counts. The list box contents have been loaded, and all that remains is to set the computer focus to the dialog box.

```
While 1 = 1

    BlockCount.Show

Wend
```

A While loop with an always true test of 1 = 1 (one equals one) inside of which the BlockCount form is activated via the Show method. When Show is run for a dialog box, the program calling Show is stopped and will not continue until the dialog box is hidden or unloaded. When you want a dialog box to go back and forth to the AutoCAD screen there are a couple of tactics you can employ. This is only one example.

Test Run the Main Macro

The test macro is now ready to test run. Create a drawing with some block inserts in it. The size of the drawing should not matter—just make sure you save any critical drawings before testing new program code.

- Point to any part of the macro just typed in.

- Select the Run pull-down menu.

- Pick the Run macro option.

A list box should appear with the block names and counts—as long as everything has been typed in correctly.

VBA allows for modular testing of the program code, which is what just happened in the test run. The application has not yet been completed, as there is still more programming to do. But the ability to test code in modules is very handy for programmers who work in busy environments—like most.

List Box Reactor Function

The next step is to add the program response to the operator selecting one of the blocks in the list box. Our program is going to highlight the block inserts for the list box member selected by the operator.

In order to do that, we need to build a response function for the list box. Like the function created for the CommandButton, the code for the list box response will be located in the form.

- Select the Window pull-down menu option.

- Pick the BlockCount UserForm option.

- The BlockCount form should be displayed along with the control toolbox and properties windows.

- Double click anywhere inside of the list box.

- The code editor should now be shown with the function name ListBox1_Click ready to be filled in.

- Type in the code as seen in the following listing. Lines that start with a single quote (') do not need to be typed as they are comments to help you understand what the program code is doing.

```
Private Sub ListBox1_Click()

  LL$ = ListBox1.List(ListBox1.ListIndex)

  While Mid$(LL$, Len(LL$), 1) <> " "

    LL$ = Mid$(LL$, 1, Len(LL$) - 1)

  Wend

  While Mid$(LL$, Len(LL$), 1) = " "

    LL$ = Mid$(LL$, 1, Len(LL$) - 1)

  Wend

  Dats(1) = LL$: Filter1 = Grps: Filter2 = Dats

  SS.Clear

  SS.Select acSelectionSetAll, , , Filter1, Filter2

  BlockCount.Hide

  SS.Highlight True

  LL$ = ThisDrawing.Utility.GetString(0, "Press Enter")

  SS.Highlight False

End Sub
```

This program module contains some code that is a little tricky for most beginners. The module starts when the operator clicks on or selects one of the list box members. Our goal is to display the block insertions for that member by highlighting them.

```
  LL$ = ListBox1.List(ListBox1.ListIndex)
```

This line of code extracts the highlighted selection from the list box. ListBox1 is the name of the control (object) in the form. There are two properties we are going to use from the list box. The first accessed is the ListIndex, which is the integer index (base 0) into the list of the currently selected item in the list. The second property of interest is the List property that contains the list in the form of an array of strings. By obtaining the list index first, then passing that to the list access property, we obtain the value of the selected member in the list. The selected member is stored as a string in variable LL$.

35

```
While Mid$(LL$, Len(LL$), 1) <> " "

    LL$ = Mid$(LL$, 1, Len(LL$) - 1)

  Wend

  While Mid$(LL$, Len(LL$), 1) = " "

    LL$ = Mid$(LL$, 1, Len(LL$) - 1)

  Wend
```

Our list box contents consist of the block name followed by a count of the number of insertions found in the drawing. This section of code removes the count and trailing spaces from the string (LL$). Suppose we have a block named WIDGET and it has been inserted twelve times in the drawing. The value in LL$ would be WIDGET 12.

Because block names can have embedded spaces in them, we must start at the back of the string (LL$) and remove the numeric characters, then the spaces. We cannot start at the front of the string and work our way forward until we encounter a blank. The first While loop in the code segment will iterate until a blank is found; thus, it would remove the 12 from the example cited. The second While loop then removes characters until a nonblank character is encountered. The string manipulation going on inside the loops is standard Visual BASIC string manipulation making use of the Mid$ (middle or partial string) and Len (length of string) functions.

```
Dats(1) = LL$: Filter1 = Grps: Filter2 = Dats

SS.Clear

SS.Select acSelectionSetAll, , , Filter1, Filter2
```

As in the initial block counting function, a select set is created given the name of the block in a filter. Because the group code and data list has already been created, and is defined as a global variable, this module can simply fill in the missing data for what it wants. The string (LL$) is placed in the data list and then both the filter variants (FILTER1 and FILTER2) are re-established. The selection set is cleared of any residual objects and rebuilt using the Select function (method).

```
BlockCount.Hide
```

This statement causes the form (dialog box) to be hidden. When the current function finishes, control will be returned to the macro that performed the Show function for the dialog box. If the Hide function were not present, control would return to the dialog box system when the function terminates. The use of Show and Hide is a slick way to control dialog boxes in VBA. A calling program starts the dialog box with a Show, and when the dialog box wants to return to the calling program, one of the call back functions performs a Hide operation. Note that in the Button1_Click (above) function the End statement was used. This resulted in both the dialog box being hidden and the program terminating. Control was not returned to the macro containing the Show function call.

```
SS.Highlight True

LL$ = ThisDrawing.Utility.GetString(0, "Press Enter")

SS.Highlight False
```

The block inserts found for the particular block name are highlighted with the Highlight method. This method contains a single parameter, true or false. When true the objects are highlighted. When false the highlight mode is turned off for the objects.

Between the two highlight statements, our program pauses for the user. You can think of the utility object as a set of functions for performing user input and output at the AutoCAD command level, thereby providing access to the traditional interfaces for users.

Test the Program

Now it is time to run the program again. Let's hope everything has been typed in correctly and the program will run without syntax errors. If a problem is encountered, use the VBA debug option to highlight the offending statement and check it carefully. If it is okay, check the preceding statements to see if one of the variable references is fouled up in some way. Lastly, check the global definition and make sure the names are all the same. Otherwise, know that it worked for us and proceed with confidence in that fact when testing it.

In order to test the full functionality of the routine, create a simple drawing containing a few insertions of several different blocks. To run the macro inside the VBAIDE, select the module source code for display using the window options or project browser and place the cursor inside the macro BlockCounter. Then type F5 or select the run option from the pull-down menu.

Save the program by selecting the diskette icon or by picking the File/Save option in the pull-down menu system. Use a name like Block-Counter to save the file so you can pick it out easily when reloading.

Final Test

As a final test of the code, leave the current drawing and start or load another. Then type the VBALOAD command and load your macro (named BlockCounter). Next type the command VBARUN and select the block counter macro from the available list. The function should run without any difficulties inside the drawing. If problems are encountered or you want to make revisions, use the VBAIDE command to view the program code again.

There are better ways to load and run a VBA program. You can auto-mate the task in a menu selection or bury the start-up process in an AutoLISP routine. We discuss handling multiple projects and program start-up considerations later in this book. For now, you have written your first VBA program and are well on your way to learning how to fully automate your design system.

CHAPTER THREE

Understanding the AutoCAD Object-Oriented Database

O bject-oriented programming (OOP) is a buzzword in computer programming circles. In this chapter we will discuss what it means and how you use it in relation to AutoCAD customization. We will devote the beginning sections of the chapter to objects and object-oriented programming practices. Toward the end of the chapter we will pay specific attention to how to use VBA to accomplish the interface.

Object-Oriented Programming Introduction

Object-oriented programming provides a tool by which applications developers can exploit complete software mechanisms already written and fully tested by other programmers. In VBA, we use tools provided by the programmers at Autodesk who created AutoCAD. The primary advantage of this module-based programming is that once a module is written and fully tested, we can use it with the knowledge that the component is fully functional in its own way. The key to successfully developing such modules for use by others is to identify the confines of the activities it performs. That is—what the module does, can do, wants to do, should do, and so forth.

An applications programmer can use these software mechanisms, called objects, to accomplish tasks inside a software environment such as AutoCAD. AutoCAD provides an extensive interface system that allows programmers to directly access the drawing database and drawing editor environment. A computer application such as AutoCAD can offer various depths of access into itself. The depths of access are often referenced as the amount of exposure that a program provides to an environment. The ActiveX/VBA interface grants very good exposure into AutoCAD's objects, especially into the database, which is exactly where the majority of industry-specific applications want to concentrate.

At first glance, an object as viewed by a programmer is a set of related functions that can be called from a program. These functions make something happen inside the related system. For AutoCAD objects, that something in the system may be as mundane as changing the color of an entity object—or it may be as complex as calculating intersections between two curved entity objects. The manufacturer of the objects, such as Autodesk, defines the functions in an object. The functions that are found inside an object are called methods and events. We will be discussing these in greater detail as we explore the AutoCAD object system.

Not only do objects consist of functions, they also contain data items called properties. Every object has properties, and AutoCAD operator/programmers will find most of the entity object properties pretty obvious. AutoCAD entity objects all have a layer property as well as an optional color and linetype property. As you get more specific and look at a particular entity object, you will find additional properties available, such as points, sizes, angles, and scaling factors.

Many experienced programmers will recognize the object concept as being the same as libraries of related functions. These functions share a common variable space that contains detailed information about the object. Although object-oriented programming and the use of objects go a lot deeper than this notion, the general idea is a good starting place conceptually.

The good side is that object-oriented programming is powerful, and if the systems are set up correctly for the developer, they can greatly reduce application development time.

What's an Object?

Let's start by getting a handle on the term *object* and what it means in relationship to computer program development. We also need to get comfortable with some terms related to objects and object-oriented programming.

So exactly what is an object? Technically speaking, an object is a software container package that holds both properties (data) and methods (functions). Objects are container packages in that the data and functions all exist together. You cannot get at a piece of the object without having the whole object available. How the computer keeps track of everything is not that important at this point. What is important to realize is that although this may seem like a terrible burden, it is actually not too bad for modern computers. And besides, these tools are meant to make the programmer more efficient! One thing that experienced programmers will notice immediately is that an object can be referenced in whole with a single variable. When dealing with complex objects, that can be very nice indeed.

An important feature of objects is that you can rely on them. By having an entire object together in the system, it can keep track of itself. What this means is that an object can have integrity. Integrity in this case includes allowing only specific changes within a set of rules as defined for the object. This way you don't end up with a circle without a radius value or a line with only one data point. When you create one of these graphical objects successfully, they contain all the elements needed to be functional in the context of AutoCAD. The integrity features of objects can impact the amount of time it takes to program an application. An object will not let you put bad data in or do something that it doesn't want to do.

41

The concepts behind objects are not new in computer science. In fact, they have been around for several decades, and several variations on the concept can be found in most modern computer systems such as the Apple Macintosh and Microsoft Windows. Until recently the problem has been that computers need a lot of memory to work with large object-based systems. Modern computers sport more main memory than the disk drives of machines a decade ago, so object-style programming has become the norm. With the advent of CD distribution for larger media (no more installing twenty-plus diskettes for a larger application), objects have really become the popular way to develop advanced programs.

The Management Features of Objects

Object programming is attractive to computer programmers and managers because it re-uses working code. And should that piece of code stop functioning for whatever reason, it can be modified to work properly once again. This preserves past work in a better fashion and allows newer applications to be built on solid foundations.

Not too long ago it was discovered that entire applications had to be rewritten as the technology evolved. Programs changed from having no user input except from a card reader to being interactive. Then they changed again from being sequentially interactive to being event driven. This happened because computers got better and faster. Thirty years ago it was a dream to have a video system capable of what is found in a typical home computer on the market today. The problem is that it costs a lot of money to have working programs rewritten to take advantage of the improved technology. And that is considering only the input aspect of the application—it does not incorporate the evolution of output devices and processors.

From a management point of view, objects provide a nice way to preserve your work through multiple generations of hardware. Applications based on objects will be portable so long as the objects are available. A rebuild of the application based on the improved or modified object libraries is all that will be needed in many cases. The key to identifying the items that would make good objects is understanding what objects are all about.

Object Concept Example

Objects were invented to model real things, so we will use a real world example to explain the theory of objects. Take a public transportation system such as a bus or train. There is a lot going on here. First, someone has to build buses and trains. Then someone has to learn how to drive them. And, of course, someone else develops a schedule to keep track of them. Drivers need to be dispatched, the engines maintained, and so forth. Fortunately, as users of the public transportation "object," we don't need to be concerned about all this. We have a completely different viewpoint of public transportation. We simply pay for the right to ride, get on board, then get off at the desired destination.

Now here are some interesting things about the public transportation object. From the users' point of view, there are common terms, such as the fact that you "ride" in both objects. The idea of a ride is the same for both: you sit (or stand) and are conveyed from one location to another. If you had never been on a train, but had been on a bus, you might learn about train riding in terms of bus riding and hence be able to accomplish the task with little instruction. That is one of the principles behind objects. To the user of a group of common objects, the terminology remains the same.

As you learn the AutoCAD database in terms of objects, this will become an important feature since all the objects use common terminology to get things done. For example, there is one function name used to set the layer name for any object that has a layer property. There is also a single function name used to calculate the intersection of one object with another.

Should the train system become obsolete due to an improved technology, such as airplanes, the usage of the object can be substituted. Instead of getting a train ticket and taking a train ride, you would get an airplane ticket and take an airplane ride. The fact that the technology got you to a destination farther away or got you there faster than the previous version is a benefit to using the newer technology. If you were writing computer programs directing people to take public transportation, you need only replace the object "train" with "airplane," and the system is updated to use the newest stuff.

Another way of using objects for new technology is simply to rebuild the object around the newer ideas, such as when jet aircraft replaces propeller airplanes. The term *airplane* is used for both, so from a user point of view, taking an airplane ride could result in being in either a jet or a propeller airplane. As newer technology is adopted, the names can be the same and the functionality and features change. In a computer, this could be the same as having data on the local drive or out on a fast network. Data is still accessed in the same manner, but behind the scenes the amount of work for the computer has changed considerably.

The use of the public transportation object includes buying a ticket, boarding, riding, and disembarking. These are the public functions of the object and are available to all members of the public. As mentioned before, there is a lot involved in setup, maintenance, and ongoing operations of the public transportation system. The functions that happen behind the scenes, such as driving, scheduling, and making repairs, are the private functions of the object. Users have no access to the private functions of the object, which serves to protect all the other users who use the same object. After all, would you want one of your fellow passengers to announce that he or she is going to fly the plane? Unless that passenger was a pilot, that could be a disaster! Private functions and data control help maintain the integrity of the objects. When riding the bus or airplane you trust the integrity of the system. The same is true in using computer objects such as the AutoCAD object library—your application trusts that certain things will happen.

Grouping all of the different transportation options as a single object, the transportation object, allows us to work with their common properties and methods. Each transportation option supports the common concepts of getting a ticket, embarking, riding, and disembarking. The differences that exist in the implementation of the different options are of no consequence to the user. The details that are different, such as the cost of the ticket, the speed of travel, number of fellow passengers, and so forth are unique to each individual transportation object. Objects borrow from other objects in a tree growth–like fashion. In other words, an object shares all of the same features as an object located closer to the trunk or roots of the tree.

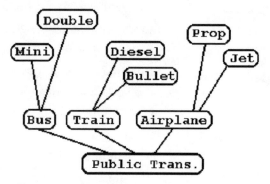

Figure 3.1: Public transportation object

In Figure 3.1, all the objects share the features of the public transportation object. That means you can buy a ticket, take a ride, and so forth. In addition, the Propeller and Jet objects share similar properties because they are both airplanes. That is, they both fly, and it's required to get a special license to operate the airplane. Having an operator license for a plane does not qualify one for operation of a bullet train, however. Similar objects on the same tree branch can often trade features, but you cannot trade features across different branches.

There are many reasons why objects are attractive to the people who use computers. Managers of large computer systems like them because they allow for growth and migration to different technology. The supplier of the objects has to update only the system-related objects to upgrade the system. And they are of interest to the users because they allow them to move to the same new technology in a comfortable fashion, using language with which they are already comfortable. The public transportation object shows that object-level thinking allows for easy migration to newer technologies and helps keep code up-to-date.

Because objects are models of real world ideas and concepts, operators can use them at a further distance from the systems aspects of the computer. They don't have to be computer scientists to work with the computer in creative ways. Instead, using objects that model the way a designer works allows the same designer the opportunity to create new applications without being an expert computer programmer. That is not to say that VBA objects can be used by nonprogrammers to create advanced applications, but it does say that the level of technical knowledge required of the programmer is not that great.

Here is another quick example of an object and associated functions. The PLOT command in AutoCAD outputs the drawing to the output device. The output device can vary tremendously from a pen plotter to an ink jet printer to some other technology. As output devises have improved, the command has still been to PLOT the drawing. Should you be a CAD operator who has stepped through a time warp from ten years ago you will still know how to PLOT a drawing in AutoCAD. You might be surprised at how many things have improved in the meantime, but you would also find those things you are familiar with from the older version of the software.

Computer Science Description of Objects

Objects have specific meanings in computer science, so we will now take a quick look at the concepts underlying objects and object-oriented programming from that perspective. For the most part, there are three features that make up an object-oriented programming system:

- encapsulation of properties and methods;
- inheritance of properties and methods; and
- polymorphism across objects.

These terms sound very impressive and complicated, but they are very straightforward.

Encapsulation of properties and methods means that an object combines both data items (properties) and subroutines (methods). In addition, objects can contain references to other objects. Encapsulation means that all these related items could be referenced using a single name. It also means that data in an object is maintained by the object and that external program modules cannot access the information in an object without the entire object being available.

Inheritance of properties and methods means that objects that are derived from parent objects contain the same elements as the parent objects. This is seen in the airplane object in which both the propeller and jet airplanes inherit the ability to fly because they are of the airplane object class. Inheritance helps save programming time by sharing program features between similar modules. It also aids in establishing and maintaining a hierarchy of objects.

Polymorphism, which means *many forms*, is applied to programming in the messaging system. To a programmer, it means that objects that share similar characteristics also share similar messaging formats. That is, you can send the same message to different objects to get the results unique to that object. Using the airplane example again, both propeller and jet airplanes will fly. Hence you could issue the order from the control tower for a plane to take off, and it doesn't make any difference as to what mode of propulsion it used. Through polymorphism, objects use the same name to accomplish related tasks such as obtaining the layer name of an entity object or computing the intersection between two objects.

How Objects Are Stored in a Computer

The next question often pondered by experienced programmers is how an object exists in the computer. Without getting too technical, it works as follows: Inside the system, an object is defined as a pointer to a block of memory. The block of memory can be any reasonable size and as a user of the object, you generally have no control over the actual details. The developer of the object defines the majority of the contents of this block of memory, including the properties for the object along with pointers to the functions that handle the properties. These functions are specific to the object at the detail level required.

47

There are some functions found in the object library that the system requires and uses to manage the object. These required functions include a description of what the object is in terms of a general classification. That classification is used to determine which additional sets of functions are available for a given object. Classifications are objects, so they are blocks of memory containing pointers to functions, object definitions, and so forth.

When a program is running, it finds the object code for these object functions in a Dynamic Link Library (DLL) for that object. DLL files are another form of executable code for a computer to use. DLL program files are created using languages such as C++ and Pascal and are binary files containing computer codes ready to run through the processor system. A DLL file can contain multiple object library definitions: they are typically grouped by common usage. Most of AutoCAD is made up of DLL files that are brought in and out of memory as needed by your drawing and edit session. So, objects work in a program by tracing down through these object chains to find the location of the function to run. (We are obviously skipping a lot to provide an overview of how objects work inside a computer, but a general understanding of the concepts is all that matters to really work with them. Creating them is another book altogether.)

To access an object, programmers commonly provide the highest level object first with a connector (a decimal point in the case of VBA) to the next part of the object chain. For example, if we have an object that is a line in the current drawing, we would reference it by first getting the AutoCAD drawing object, then an AutoCAD table object (block definition, paper space, model space), then the instance of the particular entity. This may seem like a lot to go through just to reference a line, and it is. Fortunately, VBA provides a shortcut for getting this done by knowing that we are working with the current drawing and thus not requiring a specific reference to that item. Additionally, the VBA language provides fast ways to access objects that are all part of the same table with keywords such as "Use". There are more shortcuts regarding entity objects manipulations that we will discuss in later chapters.

About Creating New Objects

VBA has access to objects as defined by other systems such as AutoCAD. However, it does not provide a facility to create a new object type based on the objects in the other system. This does not mean that you cannot create new entity objects in a drawing or a spreadsheet. You can create new entity objects based on existing objects inside AutoCAD with ease, then manipulate or access them with a powerful set of methods (functions).

What the restriction does mean is that you cannot define a new type of entity object such as a hybrid circle with a line through the middle of it. Suppose you wanted to name this new object a CirLin and allow normal AutoCAD manipulation of the object via grip points and property changes for color and layers. VBA does not supply the required tools to create a new object in that manner. Instead, AutoCAD supplies a facility for VBA developers to do such things through the block mechanism, where combinations of existing graphic objects can be defined and then manipulated together.

Defining new object classes may not be important to the majority of AutoCAD applications developers. But it bears mentioning at this time as we introduce the notion of objects. Should you find yourself in a situation in which you need to define new objects from the existing objects in AutoCAD, your best choice is to investigate the ObjectARX and Visual LISP development systems from Autodesk. ObjectARX is a C++ language library that permits even more extensions to be added to AutoCAD and is the primary development tool for new features inside AutoCAD at Autodesk. Visual LISP is a greatly improved version of AutoLISP with ObjectARX support built in.

The AutoCAD Object Tree

Like the public transportation object, AutoCAD is an object in the eyes of the VBA programmer. There is a tree structure that defines all of the primary items needed by programmers when working with AutoCAD drawings. The tree trunk is the AutoCAD application object, which defines a single instance of the AutoCAD drawing system in the computer. There are properties in this object, including the location of the window on the screen and other items of importance to the running of the program. If you are working with more than one instance of AutoCAD at a time in the computer, the application object can be used to help identify which one you are running inside.

AutoCAD works with one active drawing at a time. In VBA programming terms, that is the active document property of the application object. The document object contains numerous properties and methods that relate to the drawing. If you want to perform activities that occur across the entire drawing, such as purging unused blocks and layers, the document object is the area where such functionality can be located.

Figure 3.2 shows a general view of the AutoCAD object tree. A complete diagram is available online while running VBA inside AutoCAD via the help mechanism. The Object Model display in the help file for ActiveX automation contains hyper links to detailed descriptions of the contents of the various objects found in an AutoCAD drawing. Figure 3.2 shows a highly simplified version of this diagram, but it is helpful in showing the hierarchy of the AutoCAD object system.

The AutoCAD application object is where it all starts. The next level up the tree trunk is the document object collection, then onto the current or active document. The active document contains all the objects that make up the drawing, including the tables (collections) and entity definitions. There is a direct connection between the document object and the Paper Space and Model Space objects. This direct link bypasses the block table, allowing faster access into the Model and Paper Space objects. That linkage exists to save time when accessing these two entity collections since they contain the majority of the drawing detail information. The block collection contains the references to the entity groups where the individual entities can be discovered for a given block.

This structure may appear complicated, but it is very simple to navigate. The next pages introduce each of the major levels involved in

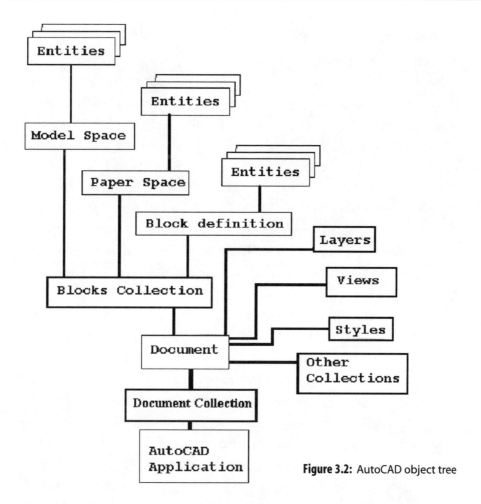

Figure 3.2: AutoCAD object tree

the AutoCAD object tree. With a little practice, getting to what you want in the object tree will be simple. Most of the time application programs need to access the entities in Paper and Model Space, or they need to get to the tables. When other tasks are required, the object tree can be referenced to find the details involved. Because of the way objects are addressed in VBA, it is best to have an understanding of the object tree for whatever system you are interfacing into. Other programming system interfaces (such as Word and Excel) will have their own object model that will also be tree-based. Once you have worked your way through any one of them you will see how they are all very similar in structure.

The Document Object

AutoCAD as an application works with multiple drawings at a time, and those drawings are called *documents*. Generally we are concerned only with the active document or the one that the user is currently manipulating. Inside the object tree, the applications object connects to the document collection that contains individual document objects. Document objects consist of the details about the drawing such as the file name, directory path, and so forth. There are methods (subroutines) at the document object level for saving that drawing as well as importing DXF, BMP, and EPS files into the drawing. In general, anything you can think of that relates to a drawing in relationship to the operating system is defined as a method in either the document object or documents collection.

The two areas of interest that programmers most often reference at the document level have to do with obtaining pointers to the collection objects and drawing file manipulations. But there is also a set of functions available in the document object that are of interest to programmers writing highly interactive solutions. These are called *events*.

The document object is where we first encounter events in the object model of AutoCAD. An event is a function you define that is called by AutoCAD when something of interest is happening. For AutoLISP programmers who have used dialog boxes in the past, these are just like the call back functions that are invoked by the dialog box manager when the user performs an activity on the linked dialog box components. For experienced VB programmers, these events are just like the ones programmed for handling the various conditions of a dialog box.

The event functions are notified when the specific event is taking place inside the computer. Your VBA program can be aware of events such as the saving of the drawing or the start and end of a command sequence. You cannot stop the event from happening, you can only react to it in some fashion. We will be discussing events in more detail in later chapters. VBA has extensive event exposure inside AutoCAD and can be programmed to handle the majority of application issues. But it is not quite as sophisticated as ObjectARX, in which new object classes can be defined and reactors attached to them as well.

Collection Objects

Within the document object one finds a host of collection objects. Collections are all of the tables used in an AutoCAD drawing. Tables include information such as layers, blocks, dictionaries, styles, extended data application names, and so forth. New items are added to the collections (tables), and specific members selected at this level in the object database. Once a specific member has been selected, it can be manipulated or removed from the collection.

From the document object, an object pointer is obtained to the collection of interest. Given the object pointer of the collection, the Count property will tell our application how many members are in the collection, and the Item() method can be used to go to a specific block by name or index number. There are several examples of scanning and reading the AutoCAD drawing tables that will appear in later chapters.

In the multiple document interface mode of AutoCAD, the various documents that are open are stored in a collection accessed through the application object. In VBA there is a faster way to get to the current document object that we will see in the next chapter.

The Block Collection Object

Let's focus on one particular collection object, the block collection. The block collection is where you will find the block definitions. A block definition is a collection of entity objects that detail the individual entities that comprise the block. To get to the entities in a block, start at the document level and go to the collection level. Next, select the specific block instance you are interested in viewing, then use a loop to step through the objects in the collection. New entity objects can be added by using the appropriate Add method for the type of entity object involved. The Add methods are found associated with the block object.

To remove a block description from the collection of blocks, the Delete method is used at the block level. You add new blocks with the Add method at the block collections level. Sometimes this confuses programmers who feel the delete function should be at the collections level. The reason it is not located there is so that AutoCAD can check the usage flags of the block definition before attempting to purge it from the drawing.

There are two special entity collections that can be accessed from either the block collection or directly from the document object. These are Model Space and Paper Space. As new entity objects are added to a drawing, they are added either to Model Space, Paper Space, or to a block definition. Nothing is drawn on the screen until it has been added to either Model or Paper Space. Entity objects added to a block will not become visible until the block is inserted into one of the two display spaces. Many of the example programs found in this book demonstrate the techniques involved in adding entities to drawings and block definitions. It can look a bit odd at first, but once you get used to the object tree hierarchy, it is pretty easy to get the job done.

Entity Objects

Last in the AutoCAD object tree are the entity objects. Entity objects are the specific entities such as a line or an arc. Each entity object houses the specific data and methods required when working with the entity. The line object contains data for the start and ending points, arcs contain center points, radius and angle values, and so forth. You can modify these object properties through methods that will check the input for validity before making any assignments.

The entity objects contain several methods that do not change or manipulate the properties of the object but are intended for use with other entity objects. These methods provide very useful computations such as determining the intersections between two objects or performing system tasks such as making copies of the current object. Because the polymorphism concept is at work in all of these entity objects, the methods all have the same name, making it easy to learn the complete library with a little effort.

If you are familiar with the AutoLISP language and how it works with entities, you will find the object methods of VBA to be much better. As an example, instead of digging through entity lists looking for extended data or a specific group code, you can use a method to access or set the specific data. The method GetXdata is a great example of this feature. With a single call, an array containing all the Xdata for an object or just the specific Xdata related to an application can be retrieved and stored into an array for easy processing by a VBA program. Compare the two code segments below that demonstrate accessing a line object and changing the starting point to a value of 1,1,0.

In the AutoLISP version, given an entity name as a symbol EN, the following expression will retrieve the starting point of a line.

```
(setq PT (cdr (assoc 10 (entget EN))))
```

While the above example looks simple enough, look at the opposite situation, in which we want to update the starting point given a new point in the symbol PT. Once again, the entity name is provided in the symbol EN.

```
(setq EL (entget EN)
      EL (subst (cons 10 PT) (assoc 10 EL) EL))
(entmod EL)
```

Although this code is not long, it is confusing. We are substituting the value of the starting point using a group code to get the data we want. As a consequence, unless you use this format every day, you will most likely spend a lot of time referencing the group code lists and so forth when reading programs that have multiple entity changes going on.

Now let's look at the same situation in VBA. This time, the entity name is supplied as an object referenced by the variable EN.

```
Dim PT as Variant
PT =  EN.StartPoint
```

It is that simple. And there is little doubt as to what we are retrieving with this statement. Unlike the AutoLISP code, for which one must know that group code 10 is associated with a point, this version uses the natural language name *StartPoint*. It is just as easy to set a new start point. The following line of code will set a new start point for the same entity and give a variant containing a point list.

```
EN.StartPoint = PT
```

As seen, the object level interface found in VBA is much more readable and offers programmers a common language to work with when developing custom AutoCAD applications. Note how the names used are the same; they just appear on different sides of the equal sign. This makes the VBA interface very easy to learn as many of the entities use the same names and structures to work within the objects.

Learning about Objects in VBA

The object browser (Figure 3.3) provides a tool in the VBA IDE for learning about the various objects in the AutoCAD database as well as objects in other attached libraries. Start the object browser inside the VBA IDE by selecting the Object Browser button, by pressing the function key F2, or by selecting it from the View pull-down menu.

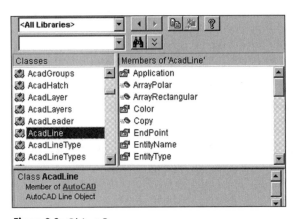

Figure 3.3: Object Browser

The object browser presents a list of all the objects defined to the system. It provides a visual key as to the different types of objects and what they are made of. At the top of the display window is a pop-up list that contains all of the libraries that are currently attached to your project. You can select the class with the list box on the left, then see a listing of all the members of the class in the list box to the right. This is the fastest way to view all the elements that a library has to offer.

The object browser makes use of various icons or glyphs to aid you in identifying the components found in a library. Once you learn these icons you can navigate the object browser faster as you begin to look for a specific type of information. The glyphs that appear in the object browser window are described below:

Figure 3.4: Class Symbol

Figure 3.4 is the symbol for class definition. A class is another term for an object. Objects contain both methods and properties. Classes appear in the left list box along with enumerated lists and modules. When you look at the object browser, you will notice that all of the classes and components defined for AutoCAD start with the letters *acad*. For the most part, we are interested in classes (objects) when programming VBA solutions. The classes are where we find the individual objects that make up the entities our applications will want to manipulate.

Figure 3.5: Module Definition Symbol

Figure 3.5 is the symbol for a module. A module is typically a collection of constants that are global to a library. The names for the constants can be used instead of the values to make your code more readable. In other cases a module will be just a set of subroutines that are not tied into an object but exist for general usage. An example of a module group would be a series of functions for converting strings and numbers. Modules of subroutines tend to be general purpose in nature.

Figure 3.6: Enumerated Object Symbol

Figure 3.6 is the symbol for an enumerated object list of numbers. Essentially, this is a list of whole numbers (integers) where each entry is unique and has an associated name by which it may also be referenced. Enumerated objects are often employed to define a selection of options such as the style of the mouse cursor or options for the display of a form.

Figure 3.7: Method Symbol

Figure 3.7 is the symbol for a method within an object. Methods are subroutines and functions. To use one you must include the name of the object (unless it is implied—more on that later) before the method name and separated by a decimal point. You will notice as you explore the various objects in the object browser that many of the AutoCAD objects share the same name. This is polymorphism at work!

Figure 3.8:
Data
Property
Symbol

Figure 3.8 is the symbol representing a data property. Properties are the variable values associated with an object. For example, the start and end points of a line are properties, as is the layer name. Property values in a class (object) can be declared as public or private. Only the public properties can be changed in an object through programmatic control. Private properties do not show up in the browser under normal circumstance. The only time you will see private properties is when your program creates them for a custom object of your own design.

Figure 3.9:
Read Only
Property
Symbol

Figure 3.9 is the symbol representing a property that is read-only and cannot be changed. These properties are for reference only and contain data such as the area of an enclosed geometry object (circle, ellipse, polyline, and so forth). Not all of the read-only properties are marked in this manner, however, and this can lead to occasional confusion. For example, the ObjectID property is read-only, but is not marked with this glyph.

Figure 3.10:
Event
Function
Symbol

Figure 3.10 is the symbol for an event function. Events are functions called by AutoCAD when something of interest happens inside the system that directly affects the object. Events use a standardized naming system allowing AutoCAD to keep track of those applications that need to be notified when something occurs. Events are found at several levels inside the AutoCAD object system and can be used by VBA applications to seamlessly integrate into the AutoCAD environment.

The object browser represents a very powerful development tool for programmers who are learning a new system. As you begin to explore other environments such as the Microsoft Office productivity suite or an updated AutoCAD library, the object browser becomes a valuable tool to learn what is inside the library.

CHAPTER FOUR

The AutoCAD Object Model

I n this chapter we will introduce and explore the AutoCAD object model as seen from the perspective of VBA. The object model is structured to allow a program to navigate easily through the entity objects and groupings of data. Starting at the topmost object level, this chapter examines the AutoCAD object system, looking at the important objects—including their methods and properties—along the way. The purpose of this chapter is to introduce the complete AutoCAD object hierarchy in terms of how VBA sees it.

Methods, Properties, and Events

In VBA there are three aspects of any object that are of interest: methods, properties, and events. Learning a new object library can be somewhat daunting, especially one as robust as the AutoCAD object library. Online help files and the object browser are valuable tools for finding more information about objects and what they have in them. As the AutoCAD VBA object library evolves, new objects and new methods and properties for existing objects can be found in the object browser.

Let's start by getting some terminology straight regarding object libraries. As mentioned before, objects have methods, properties, and events. An understanding of these terms is important as we explore the library contents.

All objects will have some **methods** with which an application program can manipulate the object. Other words often associated with method are *subroutine* or *function*. Methods will accomplish a variety of tasks ranging from the extremely simple to the complex. Many of the methods are for manipulating or changing the object properties.

All objects will have some **properties** or data elements that can be accessed to learn about the details of the object. Another word often associated with properties is *variables*. Some objects contain properties that are actually other objects or collections of objects.

Several AutoCAD objects also have **events** associated with them. Events are functions tied to an object that will be called by AutoCAD when something of interest takes place. There are events for when the drawing is changed, saved, or opened; when a command starts or ends; or when a specific object is changed. Events are closely tied to AutoCAD, so the names are specifically defined by the system. There are also special programming procedures associated with events that we will explain in more detail later in this chapter.

As we walk through the AutoCAD object library we will be introducing the methods and properties of the various objects and collections.

Exploration of the AutoCAD Object Tree

As we drill down into the object tree of AutoCAD, we will present an abridged list of the methods and properties for each of the primary objects. It is not feasible to list them all in this book, as the list is extensive and is still being appended with future releases of VBA. A complete list is available in the online help system for AutoCAD VBA, and we strongly recommend exploring that tool further to learn more or to search for a specific item of interest to your application. The names of the objects in the tables will help in locating more related objects. We will focus on the objects that are most commonly employed in applications development based on our experiences in developing programs for a wide variety of clients.

We are now going to explore the AutoCAD object tree (refer to figure 4.1) in the following order. Starting with the application object, we will quickly move down to the active document object. The next step is into the utility object, where a library of very useful functions can be found. Also within the docu-

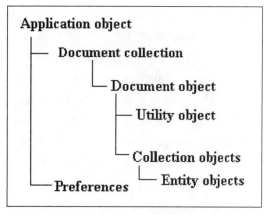

Figure 4.1: Exploring the object tree

ment objects are the collection objects. The collection objects contain all the tables for the drawing, such as the layer and block tables. Chapter 5 explores collections in more detail: this chapter exposes only the basic operations of collections. Within collections are the entity objects, and they are explored next in the chain. After looking at some specific entity objects to learn how they are structured, the next step is back to the root of the tree and on to the preference object. This object contains the drawing setup and controls information for the edit session.

Getting to the Application Object

We will start off with a confusing notion as to accessing the information. The application object, although closer to the root of the AutoCAD object tree, is accessed through the document object. You might think, when working with an object tree structure, that you would start at the root of the tree. But that is not the case in VBA, and the reason makes sense when you step back and think about it for a minute. Because VBA applications run inside AutoCAD, with an open drawing, there is always a current drawing available. That drawing or document object is known as ThisDrawing to the VBA system. ThisDrawing is a library symbol in VBA.

To get to the application object, access the application property of the document object. This may seem repetitive because the words *application* and *object* are used twice, but they refer to two different things that happen to have the same name. One way to think about this is that the application property is just a pointer to another area in memory. The application object is what is stored in that area of memory. Remember that objects are containers of both data and procedures. The data elements are called properties when discussed in terms of objects.

```
ThisDrawing.Application    'the application object
```

The Application Object

From the application object a program can control several aspects of AutoCAD, including the loading and unloading of other drawings, ARX modules, and control elements of the Windows display screen as related to the AutoCAD application object.

Let's take a look at some of the methods and properties of the application object. Remember that at this level we are controlling the AutoCAD application, and many of the changes will be reflected in all documents that are currently attached (open) to the application.

Method n	What it does
GetInterfaceObject	Connects to other ActiveX servers. Given a name of the server such as AutoCAD Application, this method will return a pointer to the application object of interfaced application.
ListARX LoadARX UnloadARX	Provides ARX application support from VBA. A program can load and unload ARX modules as well as check a list to see exactly which ARX modules are currently loaded.
RunMacro	Runs a VBA macro. Can be used to load and run another VBA project from within the current project.
Quit	Exits the drawing and drawing editor. This function will run properly only when the operator is not in the middle of another command.

Method n	What it does
StartUndoMark EndUndoMark	Groups operations by setting undo markers in the active drawing. The AutoCAD undo mechanism will treat all operations that occur between the two function calls as a single operation.
Update	Updates the object on the display. This method can be used with a singular entity object or applied to the entire drawing. It is the same as a redraw or regeneration of the object when applied to drawing objects.
ZoomAll ZoomCenter ZoomExtents ZoomScaled ZoomPickWindow ZoomWindow	Provide display control in the current view port of the current drawing. Only one drawing is considered the current or active drawing even though multiple drawings may be open at one time. It would be wasteful to duplicate the actions of these methods for each document object.

Most of the properties associated with the application object relate to the Windows operating system and how the application appears on the screen. Although you can adjust some of these settings, we recommend that they be used for reference purposes only. Many of the properties are read-only to keep the system integrity level high.

Property	What it does
ActiveDocument	Points to the document object that is the current open drawing. Also pointed at with the name ThisDrawing in the VBA environment.
Caption	Displays the caption above the primary window of AutoCAD. This is a read-only property that you cannot change.
Documents	Access to a collection of documents currently available for access in the AutoCAD application. The currently active document will be included in this list. Your application can open more than one drawing at a time and obtain information in one for another by traversing the documents collection.

Property	What it does
FullName Name Path	FullName returns the complete path and file name where ACAD.EXE is located. Path returns only the path value and is used most often when seeking other files that are located relative to the AutoCAD program files. Name provides just the drawing name without the directory information. These properties are useful when seeking the AutoCAD main program for other directory-related activities.
Height Width	Gives the height and width of the main application window in pixels.
Left Top	Gives the distance from the left or top edge of the display to the left or top edge of the application window in pixels.
LocaleID	Identifies the current AutoCAD application when talking with other Windows applications.
MenuBar MenuGroups	Links to the menu objects for pop-up menus and the menu bar. Pop-up menus are part of the menu groups. In a typical application, menu groups are first loaded and then the individual menu pop-up is accessed for insertion into the menu bar.
Preferences	Provides access to the various drawing setup and access preferences. There are several levels of preferences in the application object that access all of the same data that is found in the Preferences tabbed menu.
VBE	Provides access to the VBAIDE object and its data values. The most common use of this property is to see if a project (VBA program) is currently loaded in the VBAIDE.
Version	Gives the current AutoCAD version as a string. This is the same value found in the ACADVER system variable of AutoCAD.
WindowState	Controls whether or not the AutoCAD application object is visible on the display. The settings of this property are acMin, acMax, and acNorm, which stand for minimized, maximize, or normal.

Many of the properties just listed are object points or collections. The application object is the root of the tree, so most of the connected data elements are objects. You'll use the application object to get to other objects inside the system that are of specific interest to a program.

The other properties are used to communicate to other programs inside Windows, including the operating system. These values are accessed if you need to interface with another program that is outside of the AutoCAD, such as a word processor or spreadsheet software system.

The following is a VBA program example that shows how to traverse the object tree to get at one of the Preferences settings. In this case, we want to see if the screen menu is being displayed. If so, we will send a quick message to the user asking why it is on. (Using this property, you can turn the screen menu on and off, although that would not be recommended except in cases where it was absolutely required. The MenuBar and MenuGroups objects provide a much better way of dynamically manipulating menus for the operator's selection.)

```
Dim prefs As AcadPreferences

Set prefs = ThisDrawing.Application.Preferences

If prefs.Display.DisplayScreenMenu then

    MsgBox "Why do you have screen menus on?"

End if
```

The first step is to establish the variable prefs as an object. The type of object it is mapped to is the AcadPreferences object. A value is then set into prefs that is a link to the Preferences object off the application object. Note that we use ThisDrawing to get the application object; from there we go down to the preferences. DisplayScreenMenu is a property of the Display preference object and is a Boolean. It will return true if the screen menu is active.

```
Dim prefs As AcadPreferences
Set prefs = ThisDrawing.Application.Preferences
if prefs.D
```

Figure 4.2: Automatic Typing by Visual Basic

If you are just learning VBA, don't worry that there is a lot of typing involved in creating programs. The editor (VBAIDE) provides a fast typing mechanism for object trees. When you properly dimension (Dim) an object type, the system will display the properties and methods in a popup list for quick selection as seen in figure 4.2.

After typing the first character or two of the property or method you are after, the menu scrolls down to the area you are looking for. You can then select the remainder of the word with the mouse. Portable computer users with the pointing device near the keyboard report that this is a really great feature. You can use keyboard strokes to select the value desired as well and press the Tab key when you're satisfied with your selection. This method of code input greatly enhances the speed and accuracy of the coding.

Accessing the Document Object in VB

VBA runs inside AutoCAD; when the AutoCAD drawing editor is active, there is always a current drawing. The current drawing (or document) is defined as an object with the name ThisDrawing in the VBA environment. ThisDrawing is essentially the trunk of the object tree with the application object being the root. Programs can control opening, saving, and other file-based operations of the AutoCAD system using the associated methods. This is not the case when writing applications in Visual BASIC (VB) and using the ActiveX interface options.

When programming in VB (not VBA), which is running outside of AutoCAD, the program must first establish a link to the AutoCAD application, and from there to the active document. In VB, you must first reference the AutoCAD object model before your program can make use of the AutoCAD objects. Under the Projects menu you can find the References option. Inside the References command is where the reference to AutoCAD's object model is defined.

The following code example demonstrates how VB can interface to the drawing by setting a global variable for the document object (acadDOC) after the AutoCAD object library has been referenced into the project. This variable has been dimensioned as an object in a global section of the program. After you have made this assignment, you can explore the object tree by referencing that object variable in the same manner that ThisDrawing would be used in a VBA program.

```
On Error Resume Next

Set acadAPP = GetObject(, "AutoCAD.Application")

If Err Then

    MsgBox "AutoCAD not running"

    Err.Clear

    'your program should launch AutoCAD now or simply terminate

Else

    'AutoCAD is running

    'Variable acadDOC is an object dimensioned in a global module

    Set acadDOC = acadAPP.ActiveDocument 'same as ThisDrawing

End If
```

Note that most program samples provided in this book are for VBA. If you want to take advantage of the interface through ActiveX only with VB, the appropriate object assignments must be made to link with the active document and application.

The Documents Collection

The majority of applications deal with the currently active document. For that reason, the shortcut to ThisDrawing is provided in VBA. If an application needs to get to another document that is open in the multiple document mode of AutoCAD 2000, the documents collection is accessed. Drawings in the documents collection are accessed by an index value (zero-based) or the name of the drawing (including the extension .DWG).

Programming for multiple document mode requires that you know which open drawing is of interest. You access open drawings in the documents collection by using an index number or the name of the drawing. The name of the drawing is the same as the one that appears in the

Name property of the document object. This property contains the file name without the path name attached.

For example, if a drawing is open and in the drawings collection, the following code would access it and make it the active drawing.

```
Dim DWGS As AcadDocuments

Set DWGS = ThisDrawing.Application.Documents

Dim ADWG As AcadDocument

On Error Resume Next

Err.Clear

Set ADWG = DWGS.Item(DrawingName)

If Err.Number <> 0 then

  'drawing name not in collection

 Else

  If ADWG.Active = False Then ADWG.Activate

End If
```

In the code segment above, the first step is to establish a link to the AutoCAD documents collection. Variable DWGS is defined as an instance of the documents collection and then set to the actual value. This process of defining an object and setting it will be repeated for the majority of linkages you will be building in VBA.

Given the documents collection object, the Item method is employed to obtain the document. The name of the document is used as the index into the collection. In the next chapter we will explore collections in more detail. The code contains an error trap to test if the Item method was successful. If it is not, an error will result, and if the error trap is not enabled, the program will crash. After clearing the error buffer, the Item method is run and the result placed in the DWG variable. DWG had been dimensioned earlier as a document object. An IF test immediately follows to see if the error handler ran into something undesirable. If so, the drawing requested was not in the open documents list. Otherwise, the active property of the document is checked to see if this is the active document. If not, the activate method is used to make the current document.

The document object is explained in greater detail in the following section. Let's get back to the document collection object and how we would use it. In a commercial or extensively implemented application, a program needs to operate in both single and multiple document modes. In order to learn this we must check the AutoCAD application preference settings.

The following code segment shows how to check for multiple document mode, then how to open a drawing in multiple document mode under VBA control.

```
Dim APS As AcadPreferences

Set APS = ThisDrawing.Application.Preferences

If APS.System.SingleDocumentMode = False Then

        Dim DWG As AcadDocument

        Set DWG = ThisDrawing.Application.ActiveDocument

        ThisDrawing.Application.Documents.Open (Nam)

        ThisDrawing.Application.ActiveDocument = DWG

End If
```

The AutoCAD preferences are obtained to check the SingleDocument-Mode property. When this property is true, single document mode is active and the document collection object contains only the current drawing. When it is false, the default state for AutoCAD 2000, multiple drawings can be opened.

The code module saves the current drawing information in variable DWG and opens the drawing supplied in variable Nam. Nam is a string containing the name of the drawing to be opened. We are saving the current drawing object so that we can reset the active drawing after opening the new one. To open a drawing under the control of VBA, the Open method is used from the documents collection. Open will get the drawing from the disk and create a new window for displaying it inside

AutoCAD. It will then set that drawing as the current drawing. The next line of code then sets the current drawing back to the one saved in DWG.

Once a program has obtained a document object it can manipulate the components of that object. Components from one drawing can be copied or compared with components from other drawings if needed by the application.

Drawings are opened in a different fashion in single document mode. To open a drawing in single document mode, the open method is still used, but this time with the current document object and not the documents collection. The difference is important. The current document object will be replaced when the Open method is applied. If you attempt to add a new member to the documents collection when in single document mode, the request will not be completed. Lastly, it is recommended that the current drawing be saved before a new one is opened, as any changes since the last save of the current drawing will be lost when the new drawing is loaded.

Most applications involving VBA and AutoCAD 2000 will operate in the multiple document mode. It is unlikely that single document mode will be encountered except when working with third-party software that has not been updated to work properly under the latest platforms.

Document Object Methods

From the document object, all other objects inside a drawing are accessed. For example, if you were interested in getting to the layer table, you would use the ThisDrawing.Layers property to obtain the link to the layer collection object. The individual layer names and their respective properties are each found inside the layer collection.

The following is a partial list of methods that you can access with the document object. File accessing and global drawing settings are the primary activities that take place within these methods.

Method	What it does
Activate	Makes This Drawing the current document when in multiple document mode.
Close	Closes the drawing.
Export Import	Outputs and inputs drawing information in DXF, WMF, BMP, SAT, or EPS type files. These file formats are used by other applications for storing graphic data.
GetVariable SetVariable	Retrieve or set the value of a specified AutoCAD system variable.
HandleToObject	Converts a handle (string) into an object reference. When you're reading handles from an external database and want to locate the associated object, you will use this function extensively.
LoadShapeFile	Loads a shape file into the current drawing. Shape files are used in custom linetypes and as a possible substitute for blocks. This method loads the entire shape file for access by other commands.
New	Starts a new drawing based on a template drawing in single document mode. For multiple document mode, the Add method should be used from the documents collection.
Open	Opens an existing drawing in single document mode. For multiple document mode, use the Open method in the documents collection.
PurgeAll	Purges the tables in the current drawing.
Regen	Regenerates the current drawing in the graphics window.
Save SaveAs	Saves the drawing to the disk using the current name or another name.
SendCommand	Sends an AutoCAD or AutoLISP command to the command processor for that document. The document will be made the current document if it is not already when this method is run.
Wblock	Writes the contents of a block definition to the disk.

Document Object Properties

The following table lists some of the properties or data elements that are defined at the document level. Not all of the properties are in this table.

These are simply the most popular ones used among applications developers. You can find a complete list in the online help files supplied with AutoCAD for VBA ActiveX automation. The properties of the drawing object contain a varied set of information. Data ranges from file naming of the current drawing to collection linkages, allowing the programmer to dig deeper inside the drawing to get at information such as layer names, entity details, and block definitions.

Property	What it does
Active	Flags to indicate if this is the active document in multiple document mode.
ActiveLayer ActiveLinetype ActiveSpace ActiveTextStyle ActiveUCS	Pointers to the objects that are the current settings for the drawing system.
ActiveSelectionSet	The active selection set in the drawing is one currently being built by a command in progress or as a result of selecting objects as in the use of grips. This is a reference to a collection of entities.
Application	Controls the AutoCAD windows. This is a read-only value that provides a bridge to the upper level of the program. All objects in the ActiveX/VBA interface have an application property. The application object is actually higher in the AutoCAD object tree than the document object and this property provides a link back to it.
Blocks	Returns the blocks collection object for the drawing. This is a read-only value that is used to get at the block table objects.
Dictionaries	Returns the dictionaries collection object for the drawing. This is a read-only value that accesses the user-defined dictionary table.
DimStyles	Returns the dimension styles collection object for the current drawing. This is a read-only value that is used to access the dimension style table.
FullName Name Path	Gives the complete name, just the drawing name, or just the path name of the drawing with directory path. You can set the value of FullName prior to using the SAVE method.

Property	What it does
Groups	Returns the groups collection object for the current drawing. This is a read-only value that is used to get at the group objects.
Layers	Returns the layers collection object for the current drawing. This is a read-only value that is used to get at the layer table objects.
Limits	Controls the display of the drawing grid and zooms all options. The drawing limits can be set and referenced as a variant containing the upper and lower corners as 2D points.
Linetypes	Returns the linetypes collection object for the current drawing. This is a read-only value that is used to get at the linetype table objects.
ModelSpace	Returns the model space collection for the current drawing. This is a read-only value that is used to get at the entity objects in model space.
PaperSpace	Returns the paper space collection for the current drawing. This is a read-only value that is used to get at the entity objects in paper space.
Plot PlotConfigurations	The Plot object contains the methods for generating the output while the PlotConfigurations object contains the details of what to plot. Access to the plotter information is related to the drawing.
ReadOnly	Tells an application if the current drawing is read-only or not. This is a read-only property.
Saved	Tells an application if the current drawing has any unsaved changes. This is a read-only property flag.
TextStyles	Returns the text style collection object for the current drawing. This is a read-only value that is used to get at the text style table objects.
Utility	Returns the utility object for the drawing. The utility object contains a library of useful functions for communicating with the AutoCAD user. We will explore this object in detail at the end of this chapter.

There are many more properties associated with the document object; these are just a few of the more commonly used ones. The document level contains the methods and properties that apply to the entire document as well as the collection objects that contain the details of the drawing.

Document Object Events

Events are functions that AutoCAD calls when something of interest to a particular object is taking place. The document object is where the majority of events take place that relate to the command system and the drawing database itself. Programming events do require that you follow specific procedures; if you are not careful, it is easy to cause AutoCAD to enter into an infinite loop—meaning that the system is locked up from the user's perspective.

Let's start into events by looking at how you code an event related to the document object. Because there are specific naming requirements associated with these events, there is an easy way to access them in the VBA development editor (VBAIDE).

Event functions are defined in the ThisDrawing object. To access the code window for the event functions, take the following steps in the VBAIDE window for an active project.

- Double click on the ThisDrawing object reference in the Projects window.

- The code window should be displayed for the ThisDrawing object.

- Select the left side pop-up list (objects) at the top and pick the AcadDocument choice.

- The right side pop-up list now contains the names of the events that can be defined. Select the name of the event function you want to program and that subroutine will be started in the code window.

The names of the events cannot be changed and must be used as supplied. This is how AutoCAD knows what module to run as a particular event happens. There are functions for a wide variety of events inside AutoCAD at the document level.

Note that multiple projects may be responding to a single event and that the order of the projects being called by AutoCAD is not always the same. The calling sequence is based on who was loaded first; if your program needs to control that aspect of the event system, it must also control the loading procedure of any projects that may contain events. The developer should consider the fact that multiple projects may be running when creating a new application project and create the code accordingly.

One aspect to keep in mind when programming event routines is that an application program is only notified of the event. An application does not have the option of terminating the event. Sometimes that is referred to as No Veto Power. What an application program can do is perform some action counter to the activity just taking place.

For example, suppose there are some entity objects that cannot be changed in the drawing for your application to function properly. You could then program the document-related ObjectModified event to check if the entity being changed is one of interest to the application. If it is, then a copy of the entity can be made that stays in place, and the entity being changed can be further changed to remove any indicators that may have been stored with the object. To do this, you must keep a copy of the object data somewhere in the program. When the ObjectModified event takes place, the object has already been changed, and saving the object pointer will get you the new data. If you want to change it back, you must retrieve those values from a saved location.

One thing to watch for when coding applications that make extensive use of object manipulations inside of events is that the actions cause the events to be called again. In the earlier example, changing the objects back to the saved values would result in the ObjectModified event being called again with the same object. This is how infinite loops get started inside AutoCAD's reactors—your program changes the object that the system is reporting has been changed. Unless you are careful, you will have to shut down AutoCAD—and maybe even the computer—to recover.

The following list contains some of the more popular events associated with the document object in VBA. There are quite a few event triggers in AutoCAD VBA, and you can use the object browser to locate others that may be of interest to a given application.

Function	What it means
Activate Deactivate	Called when the document has been activated or deactivated as the current document.
BeginClose	The Close operation has just started for this drawing. Now is the time to save any global variables that may need saving.
BeginCommand EndCommand	AutoCAD has just started or finished a command. The command name is supplied as a parameter to these functions. When using these, remember that transparent commands may get in the middle.
BeginLisp EndLisp LispCancelled	An AutoLISP expression is about to be evaluated, has just finished evaluation, or has finished due to a cancel request. Happens only when the expression is started from the Auto-CAD command level (typed in or activated by a menu).
BeginOpen EndOpen	A drawing is being opened into the drawing editor. If your program uses an external data file for variable information, it should be loaded at the same time the drawing is being loaded. The EndOpen is called after the drawing has been opened and the editor is ready.
BeginPlot EndPlot	The PLOT command is about to start or has just finished for this document.
BeginQuit	The operator has selected an exit option and the drawing editor is terminating. Your program should clean up anything left open at this point.
BeginSave EndSave	The operator has selected a save option and the drawing is in the process of being written to disk. These events are handy if you want to have your program save its data to disk at the same time AutoCAD saves the drawing.
ObjectAdded	A new database object has been inserted into the drawing. Anytime any kind of entity object is added to the drawing, this event function will run.
ObjectErased	An entity object has been erased in the drawing. This event will be called for each entity object that is to be erased. The object ID number (a long integer) is supplied as a parameter to the event function. You cannot do much with this number, as it no longer represents a valid object. However, you can compare it with a saved value to determine if the object just erased was critical to your application.
ObjectModified	An entity object has been changed in some manner. The parameter to the event is the entity object so that an application can check the values or update associated information. Be careful not to end up in an infinite loop by modifying the object back to some other state!

Event-based programming is much stronger in the ObjectARX environment, in which event reactor functions can be set up for a much larger set of possibilities. However, by using the document level events, you can do a surprising number of applications.

Event Programming Example

The following is a simple example of event programming. The application is to keep track of the time spent working in a window. When the window is no longer active, the system will report how much time was spent there.

```
Dim Time_Start

Dim Dwg_Name As String

'

Private Sub AcadDocument_Activate()

  Time_Start = Timer

  Dwg_Name = ThisDrawing.FullName

End Sub

'

Private Sub AcadDocument_Deactivate()

  MsgBox "Time Spent in " & Dwg_Name & " was " & Timer -
Time_Start

End Sub
```

There are two functions involved here: the Activate and Deactivate events. When the window is activated, the Activate event will be called. At this time, we will save the current value of Timer, a VBA function that returns the number of seconds since midnight. We will also save the drawing name for future reference in the program. The drawing name is saved in the variable Dwg_Name. The full name of the drawing is obtained from full name property of the current drawing object.

The second function in this example is the Deactivate event. This function is called when the current drawing window is no longer current. This event will occur when the user selects a different drawing in the AutoCAD MDI environment. (Note that when you are working in the VBAIDE, leaving AutoCAD to return to the editor seems to trigger this event too.)

As just seen, event-based programming can offer some powerful tools in the development of AutoCAD utilities to fill in the holes missing for your specific application. Event-based programs tend to be small so that they don't get too much in the way. In fact, the use of a message box in an event that occurs frequently can really slow down an application—making them perfect for programmers to use when debugging advanced projects!

Utility Object Functions

Now let's look at some more useful programmer functions that can be found inside the document object. These methods are associated with the Utility object of a document. The Utility object houses the functions and does not contain any data properties of interest.

To get to the utility functions, you'll access the Utility property of the current drawing, ThisDrawing. The functions in the utility object include user input via the graphics system as well as conversion of data not available in VBA. These functions will seem like old favorites for Auto-LISP programmers, as they are almost identical in both languages. For those programmers just learning AutoCAD and VBA, these functions allow direct access to the AutoCAD interface for point selection, command line input (instead of using forms), and for converting AutoCAD data from one format to another.

Because AutoCAD is an interactive CAD system, all programming interfaces for the system must be able to communicate with the AutoCAD input and output system directly. The Utility object's methods provide the tools needed to talk to the user through the traditional AutoCAD interface methodologies from VBA. That is, the user can select a point, pick an object, or type in a response to a question appearing in the command line area of the display.

The functions shown in the table below are for converting data from one format to another. Most of the conversion utilities deal with angles and points in ways that normal BASIC does not.

Function	What it does
AngleFromXAxis	Accepts two points and calculates the angle relative to the X-axis of AutoCAD.
AngleToReal	Conversion utility: takes strings containing angular values and turns them into real numbers. The resulting value is in radians.
AngleToString	Conversion utility: takes real numbers representing angular values in radians and creates strings.
CreateTypedArray	Conversion utility: takes a set of values, all of the same data type, and creates a variant array. This utility is used to prepare data for some of the other methods in VBA that may want a variant array typed argument.
DistanceToReal	Conversion utility: takes strings containing distance values and converts them to real numbers.
PolarPoint	Calculation routine: returns a point variant that has been determined relative to an existing point. The distance and angle to the new point are supplied as parameters.
RealToString	Conversion utility: takes real numbers and converts them to strings.
TranslateCoordinates	Utility: converts points in one system of coordinates to another system of coordinates. This function is very useful when working with objects that have been defined on an alternative UCS (user coordinate system). The points from those objects can be run through the translation function to obtain points in the world coordinate system.

Although the functions just listed are very handy when you need them, the majority of application developers moving from AutoLISP to VBA will find the following functions to be essential in developing interactive programs.

Function	What it does
GetAngle	User input function: prompts the operator for the input of an angle value. The result is a real number containing the angle input in radians.
GetCorner	User input function: prompts the operator the input of a point relative to another point. The second point is meant to be the opposite corner of a bounding box. This function is used to accept user input when rectangular selection windows are involved.
GetDistance	User input function: prompts the operator for the input of a distance value. The result is a real number.
GetEntity	User input function: prompts the operator to select an entity object on the screen. Two different variables that are supplied as parameters to the function will return with the entity object and point variant where it was selected. A third parameter is the optional prompt.
GetInput	Retrieves the actual value input when optional input is enabled through the use of the InitializeUserInput method.
GetInteger	User input function: prompts the operator for an integer value. The result is an integer.
GetKeyword	User input function: prompts the operator for input from a set of possible values defined in the InitializeUserInput method.
GetOrientation	User input function: accepts an angle and returns the value as a real number containing radians. The difference between GetAngle and GetOrientation is that the latter does not pay any attention to the ANGBASE system variable setting in AutoCAD while the former does.
GetPoint	User input function: accepts a point and returns a variant array.
GetReal	User input function: prompts the operator for input of a real number value. The result is a real number.
GetString	User input function: prompts the operator for input of a string. The result is a string.
InitializeUserInput	Function: prepares the user input system enabling features such as keyword options and the setting of input flags. Input flag options include settings for not accepting negative numbers, zero values, points outside the limits, no null input, and the acceptance of strings for traditionally non-string input functions.
Prompt	Outputs a string to the command line of AutoCAD.

To use the utility functions you must first connect to the utility object. You'll do this through the document object. For example, to request a real number from the operator using GetReal() the following statement could be used.

```
Dim MyVal as Double

MyVal = ThisDrawing.Utility.GetReal("Enter a real number: ")
```

When the code above is run, the prompt "Enter a real number: " appears at the AutoCAD command line and the user is given the option to enter a numeric value.

The required format to call this routine may seem a bit odd to Auto-LISP programmers who are used to simply running the (getreal) subr to achieve the same results. The difference is in the language environment. VBA typically uses forms or dialog boxes for user input and for reporting information to the user. AutoCAD VBA goes a step further by allowing interfaces to take place at the command line and on the graphics screen. Consequently, the function GetReal() is not a normal VBA command that would also be found in other implementations of Visual Basic. GetReal() is something that is supported only by AutoCAD. You'll add this to VBA by adding an object with supporting methods. As such, the object tree must be defined to direct VBA where the function is residing in the system.

The With statement can be used to reduce the amount of coding involved in the utility object. The following example demonstrates the With statement in use with the utility object for a series of user input.

```
With ThisDrawing.Utility

Dim myVal As Double

myVal = .GetReal("Enter a real number")

Dim MyStr As String

MyStr = .GetString(1, "Enter a string")

Dim MyInt As Integer

MyInt = .GetInteger("Enter an integer")

End With
```

The With statement comes from Visual BASIC and is used to reduce the amount of typing required when working with the same object over and over again. In the example code above, the With statement establishes a reference to the Utility object of the current drawing. Thereafter, any methods called from the Utility object will have to include only the dot (.) at the front to be associated with the object already linked. This practice can save a lot of typing when dealing with a series of accesses into the same object.

You'll choose the Utility object for input in VBA depending on the type of input you are requesting from the user. Sometimes a dialog box is best, and sometimes it is not. Generally, when you are looking for point or entity object related input, the Utility object functions are better than having the user type in the object or point related data. A good example would be a function that requests the operator to select two objects and then supply a numeric value. There is no reason to display a dialog box for just the numeric value and the selection of the objects (via a command button). Such an interface simply gets in the way of the user, and a series of simple Utility function calls are all that is needed.

If your application has a dialog box showing when the utility object function is referenced, the user will possibly be confused. The dialog box should go away for the time that the graphical input is taking place. Dialog box objects (forms) have a method called Hide that can be used to turn off the dialog box. When Hide is executed, the dialog box will no longer be visible on the screen until the Show method is used.

The following code segment demonstrates the basic principle of hiding the input form and getting point input. After the point input, the dialog box is restored. In this example, the dialog box form is named MyInput-Form. The X and Y values from the point selected will be placed in two text box controls named PtX and PtY.

```
MyInputForm.Hide

Dim Pnt As Variant

Pnt = ThisDrawing.Utility.Getpoint(,"Select a point")

MyInputForm.PtX.Value = Pnt(0)
```

```
MyInputForm.PtY.Value = Pnt(1)

MyInputForm.Show
```

Collections of Objects

A collection is defined as an ordered set of data items that can be referenced as a singular unit. From an AutoLISP programmer's perspective, a
collection is a lot like a list. There are several collections used in the
AutoCAD automation interface. Although collections do not have to
contain all the same data types for each member, the AutoCAD collections tend to be made up of object references. For example, the blocks
collection contains only block objects, and the text styles collection contains only text style objects. Another way to think of a collection is that
it is an array of references to other data containers.

Something many programmers just learning VBA and AutoCAD find
confusing at first is that many of the collections and objects have the
same name. The only difference is that collections are the plural version
of the name. Thus, the Blocks collection contains Block object references. In the multiple document interface (MDI) of AutoCAD 2000, the
documents that are open are stored in the Documents collection. Each
member of the document collection is a Document object reference. The
concept of collections in Visual Basic is important to understand since
the majority of the AutoCAD object model consists of collections.

All of the table items in AutoCAD are stored as collections of objects.
This includes the blocks, layers, linetypes, views, view ports, dimension
styles, registered application names, text styles, and dictionaries. When
you want to programmatically add a new member to a collection, use
the collection object method Add to add the object to the set. The Add
method has a single parameter that is the name of the object to add.

For example, the following code snippet will add a new layer named
MyLayer to the current drawing. When adding MyLayer, it will set the
color to blue and the linetypes to "DASHED". The linetypes must be
loaded before this code will function properly. If not, the linetypes
change will cause an error.

```
Dim MyLayer As AcadLayer

Set MyLayer = ThisDrawing.Layers.Add("MyLayer")

MyLayer.Color = acBlue

MyLayer.Linetype = "DASHED"
```

Note the use of the constant acBlue to designate the color value. A complete list of constants can be found in the <globals> class inside the Object Browser. In most cases, you can figure out what the name of the constant will be once you learn the basic method behind the naming scheme. To illustrate, the remaining color codes are acRed, acYellow, acCyan, and so forth.

The uses of most of the named constants found in the object browser are pretty obvious. But if you are not sure, select the member item: at the bottom of the object browser, the value of the constant will be shown along with a quick description of how it is intended to be used. Press the F1 key for even more information about the constant and how to use it.

Returning to the collections—collections are used in AutoCAD for more than just tables of common information. They are also used when working with groups of entity objects such as those found in the block references, Model Space, Paper Space, selection sets, and entity groups. The same basic strategies are employed in these cases as well. Entity objects are added to the Model Space collection or Paper Space collection or to a block definition collection. When an application wants to access an entity, it can do so through the collection methods as applied to any of the entity collections.

The following tables are available for all collections in the AutoCAD VBA environment. There are not as many methods and properties associated with collection objects as there are with the objects we've looked at thus far. The reason is that collection objects are a general object used to house other objects that will have more properties and methods as you drill deeper. Think of collections as a list containing reference pointers to the individual items that in turn contain all the details about themselves.

Method	What it does
Add	Adds a new member to the collection of choice. Remove a member using either the Delete or RemoveItems methods defined in the object members.
Delete	Deletes a member from the collection. This is <u>available only in the view ports collection</u>. In all other AutoCAD collections, the delete function is found in the data objects. That is, to delete a layer, you first access the specific layer object, then the delete() method applied to that object. This will remove it from the collection.
Item	Retrieves a member given its index value, which can be a number or a string.

Properties	What it's for
Count	An integer containing a count of the objects in the collection. This value is read-only.

The Item method is used to retrieve collection members. It works on all manners of collections, ranging from tables to selection sets. When referencing an item from a collection, you can use either an index value (an integer) or the name of the collection member being sought. Names are applied only when working with objects that have names such as the block table or text style table. On the other hand, a selection set collection does not contain names and can be referenced only by an index number. We will explore collections in much greater detail in Chapters 5 and 6. The important thing to keep in mind right now is that you use collections to drill deeper in the object hierarchy.

Entity Objects

Each entity in the AutoCAD database is an object and has a set of methods and properties that are specific to the control of that object. There are many methods and properties that share the same name and accomplish the same feats from one entity to the next (this is polymorphism at work). There are additional methods and properties that are unique to each object.

As with any object in VBA, gaining access to the methods and properties of an entity object requires that a pointer be established to that particular item. A pointer to an entity object can be obtained in a number of fashions as seen in the following quick examples.

When an entity is created through the appropriate add method, the result returned is an entity object pointer. The first code example creates a line object from (1,1,0) to (5,1,0), saving the entity object pointer in the variable (Obj).

```
Dim Obj As AcadLine

Dim P1(0 To 2) As Double

Dim P2(0 To 2) As Double

P1(0) = 1#: P1(1) = 1#: P1(2) = 0#

P2(0) = 5#: P1(1) = 1#: P1(2) = 0#

Set Obj = ThisDrawing.ModelSpace.AddLine(P1, P2)

'Variable (Obj) now contains line object.
```

In the example above the first step is to define the data elements. There are three variables defined. Obj is defined as an AutoCAD Line object. The variables P1 and P2 are defined as arrays of double precision numbers. After placing the initial values into the P1 and P2 arrays, the AddLine method is used to create a new line object in model space. Afterward, the variable Obj can be used to access the line object just added to the drawing database.

Moving on to another way of obtaining entity objects, a selection set is a collection of entity objects. The same is true of block definitions as well as Model Space and PaperSpace. This means that an entity object can be obtained using the Item method and the index or offset into the collection where the object of interest can be found. The following code shows how to obtain an entity object from the ModelSpace collection. The first member is at offset 0.

```
Dim Obj As Object

Set Obj = ThisDrawing.ModelSpace.Item(0)
```

Another way to obtain an entity object is to have the user show it on the screen. The following code segment requests that the user "Pick an object" from the drawing. Note that as user activity increases, so must the error-checking in the program code. If the user does not pick an object and the error handler is not enabled, the program will crash. By enabling the error handler as shown below, your program can respond as required when user input does not follow what was expected.

```
Dim Uobj As Object

Dim Pnt(0 To 2) As Double

On Error Resume Next

ThisDrawing.Utility.GetEntity Uobj, Pnt, "Pick an object: "

If Err.Number <> 0 Then

    Err.Clear

    MsgBox "Entity not selected."

  Else

    'Entity object now in variable (Uobj).

End If
```

Another way to get an object is to have the handle (a string) or Object ID (a number) and convert it to an object. These two approaches work best when interfacing with external databases (handles) and when conversing with some ObjectARX modules.

Given the object pointer, an application program can use the associated methods and properties to manipulate the entities.

Because entity objects are all derived from the same general object handling system, there are many methods and properties that are common to all entity objects. The following tables list those that are common.

The first table contains those methods that are related to performed edit type operations on the entity objects.

Method	What it does
ArrayPolar ArrayRectangular Copy	Copies the object multiple times or a single time.
Erase	Erases the object.
GetXData SetXData	Retrieves and sets extended data attached to an object.
Highlight	Highlights the object.
Mirror Mirror3D	Creates a mirrored image of the object given two points that define the axis of reflection.
Move	Moves the object to a new location.
Rotate Rotate3D	Rotates the object.
ScaleEntity	Scales the entity given a base point and scaling factor.
Update	Regenerates the object in the display.

Geometry methods associated with entities are very powerful tools for application developers. These are the same routines used inside AutoCAD to solve the basic problems of CAD manipulation.

Method	What it does
GetBoundingBox	Returns two points describing a rectangular boundary around the object that is parallel to the world coordinate system.
IntersectWith	Determines the points where the current object intersects with another object.
TransformBy	Applies a transformation matrix to the object to combine rotation, axis shift, and scaling operations.

Many of the methods have parameters associated with them that you can quickly learn while typing them into the VBAIDE. As a properly dimensioned object is filled in with the IDE, the parameters of the methods are prompted for as needed. Even more information is available via the online help too. Programming has never been so programmer friendly!

Property	What it's for
Color	Entity object color value as an integer.
EntityName	Same as the class name of the object. This value contains a descriptive type name used to identify what kind of object is in use. The result is stored in a string and can be used when accessing custom objects. For most AutoCAD objects, the EntityType property should be referenced instead.
EntityType	Integer code value indicating what type of AutoCAD object this reference represents. The integer code values have named constants that can be used in VBA. The entity name (in English) has the characters *a* and *c* appended at the front. For example, the constant for a circle entity can be referenced in the VBA code as acCircle.
Handle	The entity handle that can be used to interface with external databases. Each entity object is assigned a handle that remains unique from one drawing session to the next making this string value perfect for indexing from other databases back into AutoCAD.
Layer	The layer name for the object.
Linetype	The linetypes name for the object.
LinetypeScale	Scale factor for the linetypes.
ObjectID	Like the handle, but a long integer instead of a string. Used when communicating with ARX applications.
Visible	Controls the visibility of the entity object. Setting an object to visible means that the layer controls whether the operator can see it or not. When set to not visible, the object does not appear on the display.

Curved Entity Objects

Certain entities are considered curved objects in AutoCAD. These objects include lines, arcs, circles, polylines, lightweight polylines, ellipses, leaders, rays, splines, and xlines. All of them describe objects that involve curvilinear geometry. This means that they have many common properties and methods that two or more will share. Keep in mind that these common items are the result of polymorphism, and as a consequence they are really different routines for each type of object. But from the VBA programmer's perspective they are the same because they essentially solve the same problem.

The list presented below is by no means complete. There are methods and properties that exist for specific entities. In addition, not all curved objects will support all of the methods and properties presented.

Method	What it does
AddVertex	Adds a new vertex to a lightweight polyline.
AppendVertex	Appends a new vertex point to a polyline object.
GetBulge	Gets the current bulge value at a given index in a lightweight or traditional polyline.
GetWidth	Gets the starting and ending width value at a given index in a polyline.
Offset	Calculates an offset and creates a new object that is the result of that offset.
SetBulge	Sets the bulge factor at a given index location.
SetWidth	Sets the starting and ending width value at a given index.

Property	What it's for
Area	The area enclosed by the object. Not applicable on objects without area, such as lines.
Center	Center point for arcs, circles, and ellipses.
Closed	Indicates if a polyline or lightweight polyline object is closed or open.
Coordinates	The points of a polyline or lightweight polyline object.
EndAngle	End angle for an arc or ellipse.
EndPoint	End point for an arc, line, or ellipse.
StartAngle	Start angle for an arc or ellipse.
StartPoint	Start point for an arc, line, or ellipse.
Thickness	Extrusion thickness of 2D objects. Also included in the text, solid, shape, and other objects.

Each of the entity objects will have some methods and properties that are unique to that particular entity object. Working with lines and other simpler objects in VBA is pretty easy once you get a feel for the naming

systems used in the AutoCAD object
library. Remember that because of polymorphism, most of the names are the
same, which makes learning the system
that much easier.

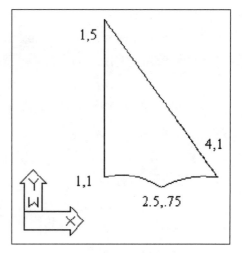

Figure 4.3: LWPOLYLINE example output

The lightweight polyline object in Figure 4.3 is a 2D polyline. A polyline is a
series of connected coordinates with
optional bulge factors. Bulge factors
describe arcs. You calculate them by taking the included angle of the arc (in radi-
ans), dividing it by 4 and then computing the tangent value. The resulting
tangent value is set to a negative value
if the arc direction is clockwise. The result is called the bulge factor and
is found in both lightweight and regular polylines. Although this mechanism may seem complicated, it is elegant in that only a single number is
needed, in addition to the two points to define an arc. An arc of any size
(up to, but not including a full circle) can be stored in this manner.
When accessing a polyline object and obtaining the bulge factor, the
included angle is found by computing the arc tangent of the absolute
value of the bulge factor and multiplying that result by 4. If the bulge
factor is negative, the arc's direction is clockwise. If the bulge factor is
nonnegative, the arc is counterclockwise.

The next program segment shows how to create a lightweight polyline
object and apply bulges to it. The code will generate the triangular-like
shape shown in Figure 4.3. In the listing, note the use of the colon character (:) to allow more than one logical line of code to appear on the
same physical line in the source file. This sort of programming style can
improve readability of the source code by shortening the number of lines
to read. More about programming styles for source code layout will be
covered in Chapter 13.

```
Dim Obj As AcadLWPolyline
Dim P1(0 To 7) As Double
P1(0) = 1#: P1(1) = 1# 'Vertex 0
P1(2) = 1#: P1(3) = 5# 'Vertex 1
P1(4) = 4#: P1(5) = 1# 'Vertex 2
P1(6) = 2.5: P1(7) = 0.75 'Vertex 3
Set Obj = ThisDrawing.ModelSpace.AddLightWeightPolyline(P1)
Obj.Closed = True
'add 35 degree included angle at 2nd to last segment
Obj.SetBulge 2, 0.15
'add 45 degree included angle at closing segment
Obj.SetBulge 3, 0.2
```

When creating a polyline or lightweight polyline object, the initial points are supplied in a single array. For a lightweight polyline, this array must be a multiple of 2 in size. Each two real numbers represent an X,Y coordinate. Regular polyline objects use an array with a size that is a multiple of 3, as the Z ordinate value is also included in the points.

Complex objects such as polylines require more than just the Add method to fill in the object with the remaining details. The Add method simply gets the object started. Additional properties are then set and other methods run to complete the details for the complex entity object. The entity will be generated on the screen whenever the Update() method is run for the object (or a parent to the object).

In the case of a new object (like the above code), the object will also regenerate whenever the AutoCAD graphics screen gets the focus. This is important to remember when you are writing code and wondering why the graphics don't show up as they are created. When that sort of inter-action is required of an application, the focus needs to be forced back to AutoCAD each time you want the graphics displayed. This will greatly slow down a function that is creating many entity objects, so we don't recommend it in the majority of cases.

Text Entity Objects

There are three basic text objects in AutoCAD drawings. Basic text, multiple line text (MLINE), and attributes. The text objects contain properties specific to the text information as seen in the following table. Setting these properties will cause the text to change in appearance the next time the object is updated on the screen.

Property	What it is
Height	The height of the text object characters in drawing units.
HorizontalAlignment	The text horizontal alignment generation flag. One of the following values (constants in AutoCAD VBA): acHorizontalAlignmentLeft, acHorizontalAlignmentCenter, acHorizontalAlignmentRight, acHorizontalAlignmentAligned, acHorizontalAlignmentMiddle, acHorizontalAlignmentFit.
InsertionPoint	The base point of the text.
ObliqueAngle	Text generation slanting angle in radians.
Rotation	Text object rotation about the insertion point in radians.
ScaleFactor	Text generation scale factor for the width scaling. Does not change the text height, only the character's scale along the X-axis.
StyleName	The text style name for the object. Text styles contain the font and other text generation assignments.
TextAlignmentPoint	Depending on the alignment used, the text alignment point will take on different values. If aligned right, this point is the anchor point on the right side. If centered, the point is the center text.
TextGenerationFlag	Integer code—0 if no special generation flags are set. Other optional settings are the constants, AcTextFlagBackward, and acTextFlagUpsideDown.
TextString	The text string.
VerticalAlignment	Specification of the vertical alignment generation flags for the object. The vertical options are much like the horizontal ones but they specify the vertical aspects of the text generation. The options are acVerticalAlignmentBaseline, acVerticalAlignmentBottom, acVerticalAlignmentMiddle, or acVerticalAlignmentTop.

Text manipulation in VBA is very easy. The following example code segment will retrieve the system date and file name, building a single string that is output in the drawing at the set position (1,1). The text height is set at 0.2, completing the required input to the AddLine method. Each of the Add methods will have specific parameter requirements that represent the barest essentials required to create the object. For the text object, that includes the text string, an insertion point, and a text height value.

```
Dim Atext As AcadText

S$ = ThisDrawing.FullName & "   " & Now

Dim Pt(2) As Double

Pt(0) = 1#: Pt(1) = 1#: Pt(2) = 0#

Dim Ht As Double

Ht = 0.2

Set Atext = ThisDrawing.ModelSpace.AddText(S$, Pt, Ht)

Atext.Layer = "TEMP"
```

After the object is created, you can manipulate it by changing the properties as shown above. In this case, the layer name of the object was changed to be "TEMP" which must exist in the drawing when the program module is run. If you attempt to use a named item such as a layer or linetypes name that has not been loaded or defined to the drawing, an error will result. In most cases, your application will have created layers and loaded linetypes before creating new objects. Error checking under these circumstances is not required—however, it is not a bad idea. After all, the user could have purged the specific layer you are using between execution of the layer create and initial layer usage in the modules. Your application environment will dictate what level of error checking is required.

Preferences

Now let's shift back to the Application object at the root and go to the Preferences object. The Preferences object deals with system settings that are not saved in a drawing but may be specific to an individual user or edit session. Applications will reference the preference settings to find things out about the system, such as whether multiple document mode is enabled or the screen menu is turned on. Other information in the preferences section includes file search directories, locations for fonts and other support files, and display controls for the cursor and screen colors. Any changes made to the preferences by a program should be undone when the application finishes or is un-installed from the system.

The information in the Preference object can be saved to disk in the form of a profile file. Normally a profile is attached to a particular user's preference setting. Profile files are used when the same user is logged on to AutoCAD but a different setup is required due to the application or preferences of another operator. They are also a handy way to save the existing profile for restoration when an application is about to make changes to the settings.

The Preferences object is divided into multiple objects. When you run the Preferences command inside AutoCAD, a dialog box will appear. Each object inside the Preferences object corresponds to a tab in the Preferences dialog box inside AutoCAD.

Property	What it is
Drafting	All of the auto snap features and onscreen tracking tools.
Display	All data associated with the display system, colors, fonts, cursor, and so forth.
Files	All data associated with files and directory paths used by AutoCAD.
OpenSave	Add data associated with the Open and Save operations of drawing files.
Output	Plot control options including the default plotting device selection.
Profiles	Settings for save and load profiles to disk.
Selection	Settings related to object selection such as grip box size and so forth.
System	Systems-related settings, such as the single document mode indicator.
User	User configuration settings for keyboard style, units defaults, and content explorer settings.

In the majority of cases the preferences are accessed only to determine if a particular feature has been enabled in AutoCAD or not. Users of AutoCAD R14 VBA will find that the preferences object is very different from what is described above. AutoCAD 2000 organized the Preferences information in a better fashion than R14, which simply contained a large set of parameters, all of which were associated with the base.

Example Sequence

The tables presented in this chapter are extensive: there appears to be a lot to learn in order to become productive with the VBA interface. The reality is that programming in VBA is very simple and with a little practice, it is easy to recall the proper objects and associated methods and properties.

Let's turn to a couple of simple examples to illustrate how the object functions operate for AutoCAD. For those readers new to reading VBA code, a single quote mark (') is used to note that the remainder of the line is a comment. The pound sign (#) following a number signifies a real number or one that contains a decimal point. The pound is used for whole numbers only, such as 1#, 2#, and 3#.

```
'Draw a line from the point (2, 3, 0) to the point (5, 2, 1).

'Use BASIC Dim statement to declare variables.

Dim P1(0 to 2) as Double 'Define array of double precision.

Dim P2(0 to 2) as Double 'Array of numbers for point 2.

Dim Obj as AcadLine 'Define line object variable.

P1(0) = 2# : P1(1) = 3#: P1(2) = 0# 'Set the value of point 1.

P2(0) = 5#: P2(1) = 2#: P2(2) = 1# 'Set the value of point 2.


'The next statement creates the line object from P1 to P2

Set Obj = ThisDrawing.ModelSpace.AddLine(P1,P2) 'Create the new line
```

The line created in the code above was on the current layer and with the current linetypes assignments for style and scale. To change these values to something new, we need to use the line object reference. The next code example takes the existing line object reference in the variable Obj and changes the layer to "A2A". The layer name is a property that can be set directly with the name of the layer desired. The layer should already exist in the drawing for proper execution of this assignment.

```
Obj.Layer = "A2A"
```

As seen, object manipulation is pretty easy once you know the names associated with the methods and properties. One question that often comes up at this point in time is how to access a generic object. The problem arises when accessing objects for general edits such as changing the layer names for each one selected.

The following code example asks the user to select an object; when one is selected, the layer is reset to the value "NEWLAYER". The first step is to create the new layer name. In Chapter 5 we will see how to check if it exists and then add it.

```
ThisDrawing.Layers.Add "NEWLAYER"
```

The next few lines declare the variables used for the entity selection function.

```
Dim Uobj as Object

Dim Pnt as Variant
```

Whenever file or user input and output are involved, the error handling system of VBA should be enabled and given some consideration. In this case we are going to ask the user to select an object. If successful, the variable object Err will have a null or 0 value. If not successful, the variable object Err will have a non-zero value.

It is recommended to perform error trapping using the Resume Next option instead of the Goto option for the On Error statement. The reason is that your error recovery will be easier to program, and it will be easier to determine exactly where things are going wrong. When the Goto option is used, you will need to set an additional variable indicating where the jump originated.

```
On Error Resume Next
```

With the error handler ready, the program is now ready to ask the user for some input. The next statement accomplishes this using the utility object method called GetEntity. For AutoLISP programmers, this is the same as the (ENTSEL) function.

```
ThisDrawing.Utility.GetEntity Uobj, Pnt, "Pick an object: "
```

When the Resume Next option is used, program flow continues after the statement that caused the error. The next statement after a potentially offending command should deal with the basic error condition check.

```
If Err <> 0 then

    Err.Clear

    MsgBox "You didn't pick an object!"

  Else

   Uobj.Layer = "NEWLAYER"

End If
```

In the previous example we used the layer property since it is common to all entities. When you want to make changes to specific entity types only, you need to check the type of object to make sure it matches what you are changing. For example, the following code will continue working with the Uobj entity object. It will test to see if it is an arc and if so, the radius will be changed to a value of 1.5 units.

```
If (Uobj.EntityType = acArc) Then

        Uobj.Radius = 1.5

        Uobj.Update

End If
```

The nicest feature of the object-oriented approach to AutoCAD programming is that many of the tools used by Autodesk are available to the applications programmer. A good case of this exists with the IntersectWith method that allows our programs to compute object intersections with ease.

The coding example continues by asking the operator to select another object, then places a circle at the intersection points.

The first step is to set up the variables to be used when obtaining the entity object to intersect with. This code is identical, except for the variable names, to the code seen already.

```
Dim Vobj as Object

Dim Pnt2(0 to 2) as Double
```

Next we ask the operator to select another entity. Note that the error object must be reinstated since we have already passed one instance of using it for input. Each time a program is going to perform input from the user, it is a good idea to include an error trap.

```
On Error Resume Next

ThisDrawing.Utility.GetEntity Vobj, Pnt2, "Select another object: "

If Err <> 0 Then

    Err.Clear

    MsgBox "You didn't pick an object!"

Else
```

At this point in the program we have two valid AutoCAD entity objects. The intersection method can now be used to find any and all intersections between the two. IntersectWith returns a variant array of real numbers where every three numbers represent a point. The point information is in X, Y, Z order, however, there is no delineation between the points themselves. If two intersecting points were found, the array would return with them stored as (X1, Y1, Z1, X2, Y2, Z2). If there are no intersections found, the variant array is set to empty.

The program code first sets up a variant array, then calls the Intersection method. The return array is then tested to see what its value is. If it is not empty, the program proceeds to report the intersection points found.

```
Dim Pnts as Variant

Pnts = Vobj.IntersectWith(Uobj, acExtendNone)

If VarType(Pnts) <> vbEmpty then
```

The VBA LBound and UBound functions provide the required information as to how many values can be found in the array. These values are used to define the limits to be used in a For-Next loop that will go through each value in the list.

Note how the point values themselves are accessed from the array. The X value is found at position (I) while the Y value is found at (I+1) and Z at (I+2). In order to advance a whole point at a time in the For-Next loop, the loop counter variable (I) is incremented by two during each pass of the loop. It will automatically be incremented by a value of 1 because of the For-Next loop.

```
Dim I as Integer
For I = LBound(Pnts) to UBound(Pnts)
    S$ = Pnts(I) & ", " & Pnts(I+1) & ", " & Pnts(I+2)
    MsgBox "Found intersection at " & S$
    I = I + 2
Next I
```

If the resulting Pnts array was empty, the following code is executed. The user is told via a message box that there are no intersections between the two objects. The second End If statement closes the earlier test to see if the second object was selected properly.

```
Else
    MsgBox "No intersections found"
End If
End If
```

It does not take long to get used to working in the VBA environment. In fact, with the programming tools native in the VBA IDE, you will spend less time learning the objects than might be expected. This has to do with the automatic typing feature that accompanies all objects known to the system. With the easy access of the online help facility, you can quickly find the object details in question. Perhaps the only difficulty with the online help system is that the VBA files have some information,

and the AutoCAD help files have more. For example, if you are searching the AutoCAD help files for ActiveX, you will find no direct references to the Err object. That information is found in the VBA specific
help files.

CHAPTER FIVE

Working with Entity Collection Objects

A collection object is a set of things all collected into one object. A group of entity objects can be considered a collection as can a list of text styles. This chapter explores the basic concepts behind collections and how to work with them. We will give specific attention to entity collections.

The Collection Object

A collection object provides a mechanism by which several items, data or other objects, can be linked together and referenced as a singular item. The easiest way to view a collection is to think of a selection or pick set. A selection set results when you are picking entity objects such as in the COPY or MOVE commands. A selection set can have any number of entity objects in it, and these objects can be of any type—ranging from lines to block insertions—referencing even more objects. The collection of objects can then be referenced as a single item. Say the AutoCAD operator wants to both move and rotate a set of objects. For the first command, he or she needs to select the objects to be manipulated but in the second command, he or she can use the "previous" selection set. Obviously, this reduces the amount of work since the operator can reference the entire collection of objects as a single item.

In Visual BASIC, a collection object is like an array or a list. The main difference is that every element does not have to be of the same data type. In some applications that involve collections, the data type may be standardized for each object. This situation will occur when interfacing to programs such as AutoCAD because only through the standardization of the information is data transferred without any problems. An example of this in AutoCAD is the layer table that is treated as a collection of layer objects.

Generally, there are three methods associated with collections. The methods provide the basic functions needed to add new items, remove existing items, and access the items in the collection. AutoCAD collections are not general-purpose collections but are collection-like objects. You can think of them as being created from the collection object, but with their own special traits. As a result, special collections in AutoCAD such as selection sets tend to have more methods specific to the type of collection in question.

Selection Sets Collection

In the AutoCAD drawing object model there is a collection called the Selection Sets Collection. This collection is a storage place for all of the selection sets in the drawing. When you want to create or access a selection set, it will be from this collection. Selection sets are referenced by name inside the collection. The name can be anything that fits your application; we recommend that you use the same naming structure as applied to the variable names to avoid conflicts with existing collections. Selection sets collection member names are strings.

As a drawing edit session is started, the selection sets collection object is created and is ready for use. There can be any number of selection set objects within the selection sets collection. Each selection set object is a special type of collection in that it contains none or many entity object references. So the hierarchy starts from the current drawing object and then goes to the selection sets object (figure 5.1). There can be multiple

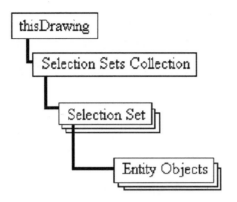

Figure 5.1: Selection Set Collection Hierarchy

selection sets defined as members of the selection sets object. Each selection set can then have multiple entity objects as members.

In order to use a selection set in a program, it must first be created. Adding a new member to the selection sets collection creates a new selection set as in the following code segment.

```
Dim S1 as AcadSelectionSet
Set S1 = thisDrawing.SelectionSets.Add("S1")
```

In the code just shown, the variable S1 is defined as being of the type AcadSelectionSet. Dimensioning it gives it a structure, while the Set statement gives it a value. In this case the new selection set added to the selection sets collection is named "S1". The name string does not have to match the name of the variable used, but it does help to keep things straight. Adding an existing selection set name to the collection will result in an error, meaning that you have to add the name only once. We will cover how to reuse the same selection set reference later in this chapter.

Building a Collection of Entity Objects

After the code to create the storage location of the selection is completed, an empty selection set exists by the name "S1". Because of the special nature of selection sets, there are several methods unique to the class for manipulating entity objects. Instead of just a single Add method to append new members, there are several methods available to add objects to the selection set. The one to use is based on the application at hand. There are options for user input as well as for programmatic creation of a selection set.

104

Entities can now be added to the selection using any of the following methods. They can be executed in any order; however, you should be cautious when merging automatic and user-driven selections.

Method	What it does
AddItems	Appends an entity object to the selection set.
Select	Adds entity objects using any of the valid selection mechanisms such as the previous selection set or all entity objects in the drawing, in a box, in a fence, and so forth.
SelectAtPoint	Adds any entity objects found at a given point to the selection set.
SelectByPolygon	Adds entity objects found inside a polygon area (fence).
SelectOnScreen	Operator selection of objects to add to the selection set.

The following example demonstrates how to have the operator select objects and add them to a new selection set named "S2". First the selection set object is created as a member of the selection sets collection. Then the SelectOnScreen method is run to allow the operator to pick the objects to place into the selection set. Between the two is the AppActivate statement. This function brings the AutoCAD window to the foreground so that the operator may select the objects. The only time this is an issue is when you are using a form for user input or are testing your macros from within the development environment.

```
Dim S2 as AcadSelectionSet

Set S2 = ThisDrawing.SelectionSets.Add("S2")

AppActivate ThisDrawing.Application.Caption

S2.SelectOnScreen
```

The following code expands on our example by creating a point object and adding it to the selection set S2. This example demonstrates the AddItems method. Since the program created the object, it knows the name of it and can add the new object directly. The entity object is stored as variable Apoint. It is first dimensioned as a point object and then set to the value returning from the AddPoint() method. Note that the point object is added to Model Space. Now we can add it to the selection set. The addItems() method requires that we supply an array of object references, and it will not accept just a single object. An array with one element is defined named varApoint and that element is assigned the value of the Apoint. The last statement in this block of code adds the new object to the select set object S2.

```
Dim Apoint as AcadPoint
Dim PNT(0 to 2) as Double
PNT(0) = 0# : PNT(1) = 0# : PNT(2) = 0#
Set Apoint = ThisDrawing.ModelSpace.AddPoint(PNT)
Dim varApoint(0) As AcadPoint
Set varApoint(0) = Apoint
S2.AddItems(varApoint)
```

Accessing Selection Set Members

Retrieving selection set members in a random access manner is done using an offset value into the selection set. The first member of the selection set is at an offset of 0, and the last member is at an offset that is computed as the number of objects in the set minus 1. In most cases the selection set was created in a random order and you will be accessing the set sequentially within a loop.

There is one method, item, which is used to retrieve the members of a selection set. The value returned is an object of a type unknown to your program until you interrogate the EntityType property. You can accomplish many object manipulations such as layer changes without knowing the exact type of entity.

Because a selection set is a collection, a For-Each-Next loop can also be used to iterate through the selection set and work with each entity one at a time. This is generally the preferred mechanism to use when working with the entity objects in a selection set one at a time. The loop will extract an entity object each time the loop iterates. That object is placed in a variable that is defined in the For-Each-Next sections of the loop as seen in the example below.

The next section of code demonstrates the item and the For-Next-Loop versions of working with entity objects in the example S2 selection set. The program will get the entity type and layer of the first object in the entity list. It will then change the layers of matching entity types in the remainder of the selection set.

```
Dim MatchIt as Object
Dim Ent as Object
Set MatchIt = S2.Item(0)
For each Ent in S2
   If ((MatchIt.EntityType = Ent.EntityType) And _
       (MatchIt.Layer <> Ent.Layer)) Then
         Ent.layer = MatchIt.Layer
         Ent.Update
   End If
Next Ent
```

When iterating through a selection set, the easiest programming strategy is to use the For-Each-Next loop structure. If you know exactly where in a selection set the object in question resides, the item() method is best. Between the two you have access to selection sets built by whatever mechanism.

More Selection Set Methods and Properties

In addition to the selection set building methods and the item() method for accessing the selection set contents, there are several maintenance methods that are also associated with the object definition. The following tables summarize the methods and properties for maintaining the selection set object.

Method	What it does
Clear	Clears the selection set. The result of running this method is that the selection set still exists but with no entity objects in it.
Delete	Deletes the selection set from the selection sets collection. The linkage to the selection set object is broken, and any references to the selection set will result in an error.
Erase	Deletes the items from the drawing. The selection will still exist but will no longer have any entity objects in it. The entity objects are removed from the drawing as in the AutoCAD ERASE command.
Highlight	Highlights the objects in the selection set. The method is used when your application has automatically started the creation of a selection set and you are now going to show the operator what has been selected. Transparent zoom and pan of the display will cause the highlighting to disappear. To prevent that, use the command reactors and highlight the objects again inside that call-back function. In order to do this, the selection set object will have to be defined in the global declarations.
RemoveItems	Removes one or more entity objects from the selection set. The objects will remain in the drawing; they just will no longer be a member of the selection set.
Update	Regenerates the entity objects on the screen.

Property	What it's for
Count	Number of entity objects in the selection set. To get the last object in the selection set using the Count, remember to subtract 1 from the value to compute the offset in the collection.
Name	Name of the selection set. When iterating through the selection sets collection the name property can be compared for whatever purposes your application requires.

Selection Set Collection Iterations

There are times when iterating through a selection set that the For-Each-Next loop structure may not be the best solution. A classic situation is when you're selectively removing objects from the selection set. Even though you can use filters to selectively build the set, there are times when additional programmatic filters may be required by an application. In those cases, we will need to remove objects from a selection set based on our own criteria. Because the For-Each-Next loops starts at the beginning of the list and works its way to the end of the list, the removal of an object from the list inside the loop will cause the loop to skip one.

There are two ways to solve this problem, as seen in the following two listings that contain complete subroutines. There are two parameters to each of the routines: a selection set and an entity. The routines test to see if the members of the selection set are of the same entity type as the entity. Those members that do not match are removed from the selection set.

In the first listing an array is built containing the object references to the items to be removed from the selection set. After the loop is finished, the items are all removed with the RemoveItems method. In the second version, the items are removed as found but this time it is within a While loop that is starting at the back of the collection and working forward. Both approaches are equally valid—it's just a matter of style.

```
' Version 1 of a selection set filter.
Sub My_Filter1(SS As AcadSelectionSet, ET As Object)
    Dim Ents() As Object
    Dim Ent As Object
    I = 0
    For Each Ent In SS
        If Ent.EntityType <> ET.EntityType Then
            ReDim Preserve Ents(0 To I)
            Set Ents(I) = Ent
            I = I + 1
        End If
    Next Ent
    If I > 0 Then
        SS.RemoveItems (Ents)
    End If
End Sub
```

```
' Version 2 of a selection set filter
Sub My_Filter2(SS As AcadSelectionSet, ET As Object)
    Dim Ent(0) As Object
    I = SS.Count
    While (I > 0)
        I = I - 1
        Set Ent(0) = SS.Item(I)
        If Ent(0).EntityType <> ET.EntityType Then
            SS.RemoveItems (Ents)
        End If
    Wend
End Sub
```

There are a couple of items of note for beginning VBA programmers in the listings above. Both of these subroutines work with selection set collections and entity objects, but you will notice that the variable references are to general-purpose objects. The reason is that in most cases, we do not know what we will be working with other than to say that it is an object.

Listing 1 contains an array named Ents that is initially defined as being empty. The ReDim statement in VBA allows our application to add more space to the array on the fly. But ReDim by itself will destroy the current contents of the array, which we certainly do not want to have happen. The keyword Preserve will maintain the values in the array as it is expanded. The reason we have to build the array in this manner is that we do not know how many elements we will be putting in it, if any. The RemoveItems method is finicky in regards to accepting arrays of objects. If you supply an array that has ten elements defined for it but place only five objects in the array; the function will not operate properly and will result in an error with the AutoCAD Release 14 implementation of VBA.

Listing 2 demonstrates a short way of coding for the same problem. In this case, a While loop is used to loop through the selection set. The variable I is set to the count of the number of items in the selection set, and so long as it is greater than 0, the While loop iterates.

ModelSpace and PaperSpace Collections

Entity objects in the drawing are stored in either Model Space or Paper Space. From the VBA perspective, these two spaces are collections of entity objects and are processed in the same manner as a selection set. That is why one or the other must be specified when adding new objects to the drawing. Adding entity objects to these spaces is how drawings are built.

Using collections for holding the Model and Paper Space objects provides an easy mechanism for accessing the entities in the drawing. You can employ the same techniques when working with selection sets as with the entity objects in the drawing. To get the last entity in the database, access the count property, then use it to compute the offset into the space collection desired. The first entity object would be at an offset of 0. The following code demonstrates how to access the first and last objects in the drawing.

```
Dim EntFirst, EntLast, MdlSpc as Object
Set MdlSpc = ThisDrawing.ModelSpace
Set EntFirst = MdlSpc.Item(0)
I = MdlSpc.Count - 1
Set EntLast = MdlSpc.Item(I)
```

Note the technique of setting a variable to the ModelSpace object. The variable MdlSpc is set to an instance of the ModelSpace object. This is done to save typing requirements, as the remainder of the routine accesses ModelSpace. In most cases, a reference to the Model (and/or Paper) Space object is established in the global memory of the VBA application so that all routines and modules can share it. As the application is loaded, the set statement can be executed to establish the link between the variable reference and the actual space of interest. As you create larger applications, the savings in time and typing resulting from the use of global references, as just described, can be considerable.

The Model and Paper Space collections are different from selection set collections. There are a larger number of methods supported by these collection objects for the purpose of creating new object instances. In other words, there are functions for adding new entity objects to the drawing. At the same time, there are no methods for removing objects from these collections. Instead, you'll use the erase method for the object.

Thus, even though both selection set and the space collections are indeed collections, they are different in how they work within the context of the drawing system. Selection set collections work with existing entity objects in the drawing. They are a duplicate reference mechanism for our own purpose. There can be any number of selection sets created and maintained within a drawing. When the drawing is saved and the edit session finished, the selection set collections are discarded, as they are no longer in use. The space collections, on the other hand, are the drawing database. As such there can be only one instance of the model space and paper space collections. Each time the drawing is loaded, the model and paper space collections are rebuilt given the information in the drawing data file. Even an empty drawing contains these collection references ready to receive new entity objects.

Even More Selection Set Methods

The following tables are the methods and properties associated with the model and paper space collection objects. All of these methods and properties are also applicable when building a block definition. Block collections are essentially the same as the paper and model space collections. That is, they have the same properties and methods. They are different in how they are created; we will discuss blocks in Chapter 6.

Method	What it does
Add3Dface	Adds a 3D face object given three or four 3D points.
Add3Dmesh	Adds a 3D mesh object given a matrix array of vertex points and the size of the rectangular region (number of rows and columns).
Add3Dpoly	Adds a 3D polyline object to the drawing given an array of variants. Every three values in the array are treated as a point, so the array length must be a multiple of 3.
AddArc	Adds arc objects to the drawing given the center, radius, starting angle, and ending angle.
AddAttribute	Adds an attribute definition to the drawing given the text height, display mode, insert point, prompt, tag name, and default value.
AddBox	Adds a 3D solid object in the shape of a box given the center, length, width, and height.
AddCircle	Adds circle objects to the drawing given the center and radius values.
AddCone	Adds a 3D solid object in the shape of a 3D cone object given the center point, height, and radius at the base.
AddCustomObject	Adds a custom object as defined in an ObjectARX program. This method will add the object to the database given the class name (rxClassName from the ObjectARX program).
AddCylinder	Adds a 3D solid object in the shape of a solid cylinder given the center point, height, and radius.
AddDimAligned	Adds an aligned dimension object to the drawing given the extension line points and text location point. Dimension objects are created using the current dimension style and settings. To change these values or any other property of the dimension object, reference the object values after it has been created.
AddDimAngular	Adds an angular dimension object to the drawing given the center, extension points, and text location. You can create dimension objects using the current dimension style and settings. To change these values or any other property of the dimension object, reference the object values after it has been created.
AddDimDiametric	Adds a diameter dimension object to the drawing given the chord points and extension line length. You can create dimension objects using the current dimension style and settings. To change these values or any other property of the dimension object, reference the object values after it has been created.

Method	What it does
AddDimOrdinate	Adds an ordinate dimension object to the drawing given the base point, leader end point, and whether this is an X or Y value being generated. You can create dimension objects using the current dimension style and settings. To change these values or any other property of the dimension object, reference the object values after it has been created.
AddDimRadial	Adds a radius dimension object to the drawing given the center point, leader start point, and length. You can create dimension objects using the current dimension style and settings. To change these values or any other property of the dimension object, reference the object values after it has been created.
AddDimRotated	Adds a rotated or skewed dimension object to the drawing given the extension points, text point, and rotation. You can create dimension objects using the current dimension style and settings. To change these values or any other property of the dimension object, reference the object values after it has been created.
AddEllipse	Adds an ellipse object to the drawing given the center point, major axis diameter, and ratio between the major and minor axes.
AddEllipticalCone	Adds a 3D solid object in the shape of an elliptical cone given the center point, height of the cone, and the length of both the major and minor axes.
AddEllipticalCylinder	Adds a 3D solid object in the shape of an elliptical cylinder given the center point, height of the cylinder, and the length of both the major and minor axes.
AddExtrudedSolid	Adds a 3D solid object that is created as an extrusion from an existing region object. The height and taper angle are supplied as parameters when using this function.
AddExtrudedSolid AlongPath	Adds a 3D solid object that is created as an extrusion of an existing region object along a profile path.
AddHatch	Adds a crosshatch pattern to the drawing. The crosshatch does not have any boundaries defined during the initial creation. There are two methods used to define the boundaries to the hatch object called AppendOuterLoop and AppendInnerLoop. Use these methods after the hatch object has been created using AddHatch with the pattern name.
AddLeader	Adds a leader object to the drawing given an array of points, a leader annotation object, and a flag indicating the leader style. The annotation object is any one of an Mtext, Tolerance, or BlockRef object.

Method	What it does
AddLightweight Polyline	Adds a lightweight polyline object to the drawing given an array of points. Bulge factors are added after the initial lightweight polyline object has been defined. Use the SetBulge method for the lightweight polyline object to add bulge factors for arcs at particular vertices. Note that all point values in the input array are considered 2D, so the array must contain an even number of elements.
AddLine	Adds a line object to the drawing given the start and end points.
AddMText	Adds an Mtext object to the drawing given the insertion point, width of the box area, and the text. The text information can contain format data specific to the Mtext object.
AddPoint	Adds a point object to the drawing given the point array.
AddPolyline	Adds a polyline object to the drawing given an array of 3D points. The array of variants must have a length that is a multiple of 3. Bulge factors are added after the initial polyline object has been created. The SetBulge method defined in the polyline object is used to set the bulge factor for individual vertices.
AddRaster	Inserts a raster image object from a raster image file. The parameters include the file name, insertion point, scaling factor, and rotational angle.
AddRay	Adds a ray object to the drawing given two 3D points.
AddRegion	Adds a region object to the drawing given a series of objects such as lines, arcs, and polylines that define a closed region.
AddRevolvedSolid	Adds a 3D solid object that is the result of revolving a profile about an axis. The parameters are the profile object, a base point, a directional point, and angle of rotation.
AddShape	Adds a shape object reference to the drawing given the insert point and shape name.
AddSolid	Adds a 3D solid polygon object to the drawing. The first two point array parameters define a base line, and the next two describe a diagonally opposite line to form the solid polygon.
AddSphere	Adds a 3D solid object that is in the shape of a sphere given the center point and radius.
AddSpline	Adds a spline object to the drawing given an array of points and the starting and ending tangents.
AddText	Adds a text object to the drawing given the text string, insert point, and text height. All other text parameters are adjusted after the text object has been initially created, or are established in the current style. Alignment points and rotations are applied after the initial text object has been defined.

115

Method	What it does
AddTolerance	Adds a tolerance object to the drawing given the text string, insertion point, and rotation. All the remaining tolerance parameters are set after the initial object has been created.
AddTorus	Adds a 3D solid object in the shape of a torus (doughnut) given the center point, radius, and radius of the tube.
AddTrace	Adds a trace object to the drawing given the four points in an array (total length of variant array should be sixteen elements).
AddWedge	Adds a 3D solid object that looks like a wedge to the drawing given the face center point, width, length, and height.
AddXLine	Adds an Xline object to the drawing given two 3D points.
InsertBlock	Adds an insertion (BlockRef) object to the drawing given the insertion point, name of the block, X scale, Y scale, and rotation factor.
Item	Retrieves the object at a given offset position. This is the only routine you'll use to get information from the collections directly into a program.

There are numerous methods in this set that create objects using only partial information. The object's specific methods and properties are then used to set any of the remaining data to the value needed by the application. The following code section demonstrates this simple principle at work when you're creating text objects. The program will create a new text object with a string value of "This is a test", height of 0.2 units, rotation of 90 degrees, an oblique angle of 22.5 degrees, and an insertion point at (5,10).

```
Dim MyObj as AcadText

Dim IP(0 to 2) as Double

IP(0) = 5#: IP(1) = 10#: IP(2) = 0.0

Set MyObj = ThisDrawing.ModelSpace.AddText("This is a test", IP, 0.2)

' Text object is created, and can now be updated to what we need

MyObj.Rotation = D2R(90#) 'D2R defined below..

MyObj.ObliqueAngle = D2R(22.5#)   'Angles must be in radians

' The text object now exists in the drawing as desired.
```

116

```
' The function D2R does not exist in the VBA library,
' you must create it as follows.
Function D2R (D as Double) as Double
    D2R = D * 3.141592653590 / 180#
End Function
```

For the more complex entities, your programs will have to update the properties after the initial object has been created. Further examples include bulge factors in polylines; Mtext, Text, and Attrib properties; and partial ellipses. Use the online help when programming these objects to find the name of the appropriate property or method.

Filtering the Selection Set

When selecting entity objects in an application, you may want to work with just a specific subset of the entity objects in the drawing. Selection sets are subsets of the entity objects in the drawing. When building a selection set, you may want to select only certain types of objects or objects that share specific property traits. An example would be a program that counts how many bolt holes are in a design. Such a program would search for just circles. You can use a filter when you're building a selection set based on such criteria.

A filter is a set of properties that the entity objects need to match in order to be included in the selection set. The properties can be specific object types as well as ranges of values—such as selecting all circles with radii between 1 and 2 drawing units.

In VBA, a filter is constructed as two arrays of variants. The two arrays contain related information that consists of group codes and data values. The first array contains group codes only. Group codes are integer values that indicate the type of data being referenced. The data itself resides in the other array. The index value links the two arrays. The first value in the group codes array corresponds with the first value in the data array.

Group codes that are used the most frequently in applications programming are listed in the following table. There are lots more. A complete list is documented in the DXF section of the AutoCAD reference information. The group codes listed here are those most frequently used in an application.

Group code	Contents
0	Object type string – such as LINE, ARC, or CIRCLE
1	String value in Text, Mtext
2	Object name string – needed only for Block names and, Table names
8	Layer name string
10	Primary point
11 …	Secondary points for text alignments, line endpoints, traces, and so forth
40	Arc and circle radius
62	Color number (integer)
67	Model/paper space integer flag. A value of 1 indicates the object is in paper space.
-4	Grouping operator string or relational test

The second array contains the data elements associated with the group codes. The data elements will be of different data types that correspond to the integer codes. A group code 40 will have an associated real number while a group code 2 will have a string.

These two arrays must then be assigned to variant variables that are passed to the selection set function. Beginning VBA programmers may find that the variant passing system is somewhat awkward; however, it is a common practice when sending information from BASIC to other programming environments. The reason is that the variant data type is a container holding a description of the data type and a pointer to where the data is stored. Instead of sending a complete array through the parameter list, a pointer is sent to its location in the computer. Another reason for using variants is that inside the computer, arrays are stored differently in the two languages. A variant data structure provides a linkage mechanism that tells the C++ component all about the array and helps to set up the conversions required.

An example of using a filtered selection, the following code segment builds a selection set from the entire drawing that will contain only CIRCLE entity objects with a radius of 5 drawing units.

```
Dim Ftyp(1) As Integer

Dim Fval(1) As Variant

Dim Filter1, Filter2 As Variant

Ftyp(0) = 0: Fval(0) = "CIRCLE"

Ftyp(1) = 40: Fval(1) = 5#

Dim S1 As AcadSelectionSet

Set S1 = ThisDrawing.SelectionSets.Add("S1")

Filter1 = Ftyp: Filter2 = Fval

S1.Select acSelectionSetAll, , , Filter1, Filter2
```

The arrays must be dimensioned to the proper size for the filters. If you are using only two filter items, the array length should be exactly 2, meaning that the dimension statement should call out a dimension size that is 1 less than the number of elements that will appear in the array. VBA arrays start indexing at a value of 0, hence the need to subtract 1 from the dimensioned size. There are two ways to dimension these arrays, and it is a matter of style as to which you will use in your programming. You can specify the lower and upper bounds of the array or simply specify the upper bound and let the 0 value default. Both approaches work fine, but we happen to find the version that declares the range to be more readable. Programmers who work in multiple languages where array declarations are not based on bound definitions will find the range more readable as the other looks like an array that is defined too small.

```
Dim AnArray(0 to 1) as Variant


Dim AnArray(1) as Variant
```

Whichever style you select, we strongly recommend that you remain consistent throughout the application. Future programmers may have to read your code!

Refining the Filters—Numeric Tests

There are times when an application may need to build a selection set based on specific criteria. Suppose you wanted a selection set that contained all circles with a radius value less than or equal to 5 drawing units. You can use filter in conjunction with a relation test to accomplish what is needed. It would not be necessary for the program to look at each and every circle entity in the drawing—the filter would accomplish this testing instead.

The following code example is a variation of the routine just presented. Instead of checking for an exact match of 5 drawing units, this version looks for circles that have a radius value of 5 units or less.

```
Dim Ftyp1(2) As Integer: Dim Fvar1(2) As Variant
Dim Filter1, Filter2 As Variant
Ftyp1(0) = 0: Fvar1(0) = "CIRCLE"
Ftyp1(1) = -4: Fvar1(1) = "<="
Ftyp1(2) = 40: Fvar1(2) = 5#
Filter1 = Ftyp1: Filter2 = Fvar1
Dim S1 As AcadSelectionSet
Set S1 = ThisDrawing.SelectionSets.Add("S1")
S1.Select acSelectionSetAll, , , Filter1, Filter2
```

The filter in the code above uses the (–4) group code. When a comparison test is used in the filter, it is applied to the values that follow. In this case, the radius value is used for the relational test.

Numeric relational tests are as follows. These tests are typically applied against real numbers found in the entity object properties. They can also be applied for points.

120

=	Equal to
<	Less than
>	Greater than
<=	Less than or equal to
>=	Greater than or equal to
!= or /=	Not equal to
*	Always-true returns true every time. Used when testing point values.

When your program is testing point values, the point value tests are combined with commas separating them. You can test the X, Y, Z components of the point independently of each other. That means that you can have the filter look for points that have an X component greater than a value and have a Y component that is less than another value. If the Z component is not supplied, it is assumed to contain an always-true test associated with it.

The following example program tests for objects that are located in the first quadrant (that is, they have X and Y values that are greater than or equal to 0). This version tests the primary point value of all objects in the drawing. The primary point value is group code 10. The test to be used is written as "$>=,>=,*$" which means that we want X and Y values that are greater than the test value and that we don't care what the Z value is.

```
Dim Pnt(0 To 2) As Double

Dim Ftyp(1) As Integer: Dim Fval(1) As Variant

Dim Filter1, Filter2 As Variant

Pnt(0) = 0#: Pnt(1) = 0#: Pnt(2) = 0#

Ftyp(0) = -4: Fval(0) = ">=,>=,*"

Ftyp(1) = 10: Fval(1) = Pnt

Filter1 = Ftyp: Filter2 = Fval

Dim S1 As AcadSelectionSet

Set S1 = ThisDrawing.SelectionSets.Add("S1")

S1.Select acSelectionSetAll, , , Filter1, Filter2
```

121

In the code segment above, a point (Pnt) is defined as an array of double precision numbers. Then that array is set into the variant array (Fval), which in turn is set into the variant variable (Filter2) for passing into the Select function that builds a new selection set. At first glance, this seems like a lot of extra work to have to do in order to get what you want. That is one of the trade-offs in object-oriented programming when you're working with more complex objects; you can either have a lot of methods or you can have a lot of options available in a smaller set of methods. The Select function is one of those that have a lot of options. The empty parameters in the examples presented thus far are there in case you want to send point constraints as required when using window-based selections.

The following example looks for small arc objects (radius less than 1.0) in the drawing. It uses a window-based selection method and supplies two points along with a filter. The window is from (0, 0, 0) to (15, 15, 0). The point arguments are supplied as arrays of numbers.

```
Dim Pnt1(0 To 2) As Double

Dim Pnt2(0 To 2) As Double

Dim Ftyp1(2) As Integer: Dim Fvar1(2) As Variant

Dim Filter1, Filter2 As Variant

Pnt1(0) = 0#: Pnt1(1) = 0#: Pnt1(2) = 0#

Pnt2(0) = 15#: Pnt2(1) = 15#: Pnt2(2) = 0#

Ftyp1(0) = 0: Fvar1(0) = "ARC"

Ftyp1(1) = -4: Fvar1(1) = "<"

Ftyp1(2) = 40: Fvar1(2) = 1#

Filter1 = Ftyp1: Filter2 = Fvar1

Dim S1 As AcadSelectionSet

Set S1 = ThisDrawing.SelectionSets.Add("S1")

S1.Select acSelectionSetWindow, Pnt1, Pnt2, Filter1, Filter2
```

The value you're testing must be of a data type that makes sense for the test. Numbers can be tested greater or less than relationships, but strings cannot. After all, one string cannot be greater than another string in a form that makes sense for such a test. Wild cards can be used for string testing in a filter instead.

String Tests in Filters

Wild cards are characters that symbolize a test. The most common wild card used is the asterisk (*). We use an asterisk when we mean "anything." The other wild card characters used in testing strings are defined in the table that follows.

*	Anything
?	Any single character
#	Any single digit
@	Any single character
.	Any non-alphanumeric character (such as a dash)
`	Escape character, use the next character as is (as in `*to look for asterisk)
[ ]	Match any of the characters inside the brackets
[~]	Match when the characters inside are not found
~	First character in search pattern means "NOT". This causes a match when the pattern is not matched.
,	Separate more than pattern such as in LYR*,LAYER* to look for a match starting with either LYR or LAYER.

You do not need a relational test group code (-4) when you're doing string pattern matches. As an example, the following code builds a selection set of objects that are on any layer starting with the characters AA or AB. In this example, the variables Filter1, Filter2, and S1 are already dimensioned to the proper data types. They should match the previous examples in this chapter for the same variable names.

```
Dim Ft(0) As Integer: Dim Fv(0) As Variant
Ft(0) = 8: Fv(0) = "AA*,AB*"
Filter1 = Ft: Filter2 = Fv
Dim S1 As AcadSelectionSet
Set S1 = ThisDrawing.SelectionSets.Add("S1")
S1.Select acSelectionSetAll, , , Filter1, Filter2
```

The example just shown tests the entity objects for two different layer name groups, those that start with AA and those that start with AB. The two tests are combined into a single test separated by the comma character. This forms an implicit OR test, which means that a true result will come back if either or both of the tests turn out true. When you consider an entire filter, each of the individual matches are combined together in the form of an AND test. An AND test is true only when all of the sub-tests are true. In some of the previous examples we tested for multiple items such as circles with a specific radius value. Because the AND test combines all the parts of the filter, we do not get objects that match only one or two of the tests. That means we cannot build a filter that would look for both circle and arc objects since one or the other would cause the selection to skip an entity. For example, if the object is an arc then the circle test will fail.

Combining Multiple Tests

To combine tests that would otherwise cancel each other out, such as looking for two types of entities, use the logical combination tests. There is an implied AND condition for all elements in a filter, but a set of -4 group code options can be used to establish a different testing logic. Tests can be constructed using more advanced logic—such as looking for arcs and circles or looking for radius values within a particular range to assemble the selection set desired. The table entries that follow contain the combination tests available when building a filter. When the test result indicated is true, then the entity being questioned will be added to the selection set (provided any other tests also prove to be true).

AND	Will return true if all grouped tests are true.
OR	Will return true if any of the grouped tests are true.
XOR	Will return true if any one of the grouped tests are true.
NOT	Will return true if the next test is false.

The combinations are defined by using a group code (-4) followed by one of the options above. When the option is typed, place a less-than sign (<) in front of it. At the end of the group of tests the combination is used again with a (-4) group code and a greater than sign at the end. If you wanted to perform an OR combination test, the first (-4) group code would be "<OR"; after giving the individual tests, another (-4) group code is used with "OR>". By using the less-than and greater-than signs in this manner, tests can be nested within each other.

In the following example, an OR combination test is used to obtain entity objects that are of different types. The OR combination test in the filter causes the selection set building routine in which it is employed to return objects that are of the type CIRCLE, ARC, or ELLIPSE.

```
Dim Ftyp4(4) As Integer: Dim Fvar4(4) As Variant
Ftyp4(0) = -4: Fvar4(0) = "<OR"
Ftyp4(1) = 0: Fvar4(1) = "CIRCLE"
Ftyp4(2) = 0: Fvar4(2) = "ARC"
Ftyp4(3) = 0: Fvar4(3) = "ELLIPSE"
Ftyp4(4) = -4: Fvar4(4) = "OR>"
```

You can accomplish testing by just laying out the testing sequence in a logical manner. The first step is to attempt to state the test in the terms supplied. Suppose our application was looking for either CIRCLE entities with a radius greater than 0.25 but less than 0.75 as well as ARC entities on layer "PART" with a radius less than 1. In this case, we would set up the filter list to contain an OR test looking for either entity type; within each OR test there are additional tests. For the circle, the radius must be between the values specified, and for the arc it must be on a specific layer and with a radius less than 1. The diagram that follows shows the tests combined by boxes. There are two AND boxes and one OR box.

Now let's look at the code required to create this filter. The

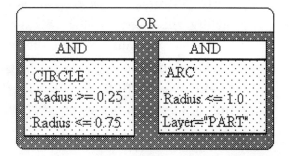

Figure 5.2: Combined Logic in a Filter

arrays are much longer than the ones shown thus far. When your program is using filters containing logical combination tests, the number of elements in the array will increase due to the (-4) group code additions.

```
Dim Ftyp14(14) As Integer

Dim Fvar14(14) As Variant

Ftyp14(0) = -4: Fvar14(0) = "<OR" 'Start the overall OR test

Ftyp14(1) = -4: Fvar14(1) = "<AND" 'Start the AND test for ARC

Ftyp14(2) = 0: Fvar14(2) = "ARC"

Ftyp14(3) = 8: Fvar14(3) = "PART"

Ftyp14(4) = -4: Fvar14(4) = "<="

Ftyp14(5) = 40: Fvar14(5) = 1#

Ftyp14(6) = -4: Fvar14(6) = "AND>"   'End the AND test for ARC

Ftyp14(7) = -4: Fvar14(7) = "<AND"   'Start the AND test for CIRCLE

Ftyp14(8) = 0: Fvar14(8) = "CIRCLE"

Ftyp14(9) = -4: Fvar14(9) = ">="

Ftyp14(10) = 40: Fvar14(10) = 0.25

Ftyp14(11) = -4: Fvar14(11) = "<="

Ftyp14(12) = 40: Fvar14(12) = 0.75

Ftyp14(13) = -4: Fvar14(13) = "AND>" 'End the AND test for CIRCLE

Ftyp14(14) = -4: Fvar14(14) = "OR>" 'End the overall OR test
```

Virtually any selection criteria can be defined using the combination tests. Here are some more examples presented in a tabular form for readability. The values would be assigned as presented to the two arrays.

The first example shows a filter to test for objects that are not circles and arcs and that are on layer "ABC". This filter uses the fact that there is an implicit AND by starting with the layer test. The next part then informs the filter processing system that we are NOT interested in circles OR arcs.

Group code	Value
8	"ABC"
-4	"<NOT"
-4	"<OR"
0	"CIRCLE"
0	"ARC"
-4	"OR>"
-4	"NOT>"

As another example, here is a filter to test for text objects that are not on either layer TITLE or BORDER. Text objects include the Text, Attrib, and Mtext entity objects. An OR test is required to test for each possible entity object. The portion of the filter that tests whether or not the objects are not on a layer is accomplished with a pair of (8) group codes containing the layer names preceded by the tilde (~) character. When that character is present, the test is reversed. Instead of being an equal test, it is a not-equal test. The two individual tests are required and cannot be combined into a single test with the command as in ~BORDER, ~TITLE since the comma acts an OR combination which would always return true in this case. After all, if an object is on layer BORDER, it is not on layer TITLE, and the OR combination would result in a true result. An AND combination is required, and that is why two separate (8) group codes are involved.

Group code	Value
-4	"<OR"
0	"TEXT"
0	"ATTRIB"
0	"MTEXT"
-4	"OR>"
8	~TITLE
8	~BORDER

Selection Set Maintenance Issues

Once a selection set has been created via the ADD method in the SelectionSets collection, it is up to the application to keep track of the selection set object. It is not a good idea to simply create selection sets on the fly, then leave them behind. When you create one, you should delete when you are finished. That is why it is a good idea to use your own naming strategy for selection sets. When your application is finished, you can clean out the selection sets. The following code snippet demonstrates a clean way to get your own selection sets for the drawing. The function below shows a new selection set object created in the SelectionSets collection.

```
Function SS_Create() As AcadSelectionSet

  Dim SS1 As Double

  Do

    SS1 = ThisDrawing.GetVariable("DATE")

    S$ = "SS" & Str$(Fix(1000000# * (SS1 - Fix(SS1))))

    Err.Clear

    On Error Resume Next

    Set SS_Create = ThisDrawing.SelectionSets.Item(S$)

  Loop Until (Err.Number <> 0)

  Set SS_Create = ThisDrawing.SelectionSets.Add(S$)

End Function
```

SS_Create uses the system date and time information in AutoCAD to create a unique integer value. Since selection sets are transient—that is, they are not intended to survive more than a single edit session—the names will repeat on a daily basis. The key is that they don't collide too often, and you will always get a unique selection set object when asking for one.

This function works by taking the system date value and subtracting the day portion. What is left is a fraction of a day. Multiplying that number by 1,000,000 provides unique (but incrementing) numbers every tenth of a second. That number is concatenated onto the string "SS" to form a new string. The string is in turn used by the selection sets collection Item() function to see if it already exists. If the selection set is already in the collection, the error number will be 0. The loop tests to see if the error number is non-zero, meaning that the name was not in the collection and that we are free to add it. When the loop finishes, the Add() method is used to add the new name found to the selection sets collection.

The error handler is required because we are accessing a collection to look for something. Using the "On Error Resume Next" structure will allow an error to take place, but then it is our responsibility as application programmers to test it in our programs.

When you are done with a selection set but are planning to use the name again later in the application, you should clear it. To clear the selection set, you'll have to remove the entity object names from the set; they are not removed from the drawing. The Clear() method is used with the selection set object.

You can purge the selection sets collection using the Delete() method, which is associated with the selection set objects. The Delete() method will remove the selection set name from the sets collection and free up the name for others to use. If you are planning to use a selection set frequently, as most AutoCAD applications programmers tend to, you should set up standard selection set names for your applications. You can assign these names in a global module and access them in each routine as needed. It is more efficient to do this than to create new selection sets all the time, even if you remember to delete them when done. You should clear the selection sets before each use. Either establish the practice of clearing the set immediately after it is used or before you make any new attempts at it.

When selecting objects for a selection set using one of the select methods, the new entities selected will be appended to the selection set. Entities that were already in the set will remain in the set, and the new ones selected will be added at the end of the set.

```
Set S1 = ThisDrawing.SelectionSets.Add("NewOne")
Dim Filter1, Filter2 as Variant
Dim Gcodes(1) as Integer: Dim Dvals(1) As Variant
Gcodes(0) = 0: Dvals(0) = "CIRCLE"
Gcodes(1) = 8: Dvals(1) = "0"
Filter1 = Gcodes: Filter2 = Dvals
S1.Select AcSelectionSetAll, , , Filter1, Filter2
' Selection set contains all the circles in the drawing
Dvals(0) = "LINE"
Filter2 = Dvals 'variant MUST be reassigned after change.
S1.Select AcSelectionSetAll, , , Filter1, Filter2
' Now S1 has all the lines added after the circles.
```

Working with Collections

Collections of objects are an important part of Visual Basic programming, and except for the specialized nature of the AutoCAD user interface, they are not too difficult to use in AutoCAD VBA development. The selection set collection is the most interesting, not only because of its potential power but also in the way it is manipulated. Because selection sets contain variable entity objects, they are treated differently, as seen in this chapter. The key item to keep in mind when working with selection sets is that a named selection set needs to be added to the collection of sets only once. Once that name is on the set, you must use the item() method to reuse it.

CHAPTER SIX

Drawing Tables

This chapter explores the tables in AutoCAD. AutoCAD tables include layers, linetypes, blocks, dictionaries, views, view ports, dimension styles, text styles, groups, registered applications, layouts, and plot configurations. Tables are stored as collections of specific objects and follow most of the standard methods of collections with some notable exceptions. In this chapter we will discuss how to manipulate tables in general, then we'll focus on some of the specific table details. We finish the chapter with an in-depth study of the blocks table and an explanation of how to manipulate blocks in VBA.

AutoCAD Drawing Tables

AutoCAD drawing tables consist of information referenced by multiple objects. They exist primarily to conserve space in the entity objects by providing a common area where information may be accessed. Consider layers as an example. Every entity object in AutoCAD has a layer, and it would greatly inflate the database to have the layer information (such as color and linetype selections) attached to each and every entity. Although you can assign specific linetype and color selections to individual entity objects, most production-oriented CAD operators are advised to use layers.

Tables also allow you to directly manipulate multiple objects as a common group. Changing the color property of a layer will cause entity objects on that layer to change to that color (unless they have specific entity color overrides in effect). This is why operators are advised to use the tables. A single change in a table can result in many entity objects being updated.

Tables Are Collections

AutoCAD tables are stored as collections referenced from the Document object. Once you have a drawing selected (such as ThisDrawing), you can access the tables for that drawing. For each collection there is a property in the document object that is used to access the table.

Each table collection is made up of the same object type. The Layers collection contains Layer objects, the DimStyles collection contains Dim-Style objects, and so forth. Each of the objects in the collection will have its own associated properties and methods.

Table collections are different from normal collections in VBA. A normal collection can have any type of data associated with it. Additionally, every collection in VBA supports the methods Add(), Item(), and Remove(). Because of the special nature of the collections that are used as tables in AutoCAD, only the Add() and Item() methods are supported.

Add() is used to append a new member to the collection (table).

Item() is used to retrieve a specific member of the collection given either the index number in the collection or the name of the specific object being sought after.

The Remove() method does not exist for table collections inside Auto-CAD. Instead, the individual objects contain a method to remove the object from the collection. The reason behind this is that removing table object entries can sometimes involve more than simply taking it out of the collection. Before being removed, the drawing is checked to make sure there are no more references to the table object. If there were still references to the object (such as a layer name) and the object did not exist in the layer table, then the drawing is corrupted. Thus the table objects contain specific removal functions, all named Delete(). This ensures that the proper checks can be done inside the drawing. It would be very difficult to implement a Remove() function for all drawing table collections that worked at the table level.

The properties that are found in an AutoCAD table collections include a count of the number of objects in the table. The count property is accessed to determine how many objects are in the collection.

The individual objects inside the tables contain more properties and methods that allow you to manipulate specific objects. These are described in the following sections.

The Dictionary Collection

A dictionary is a housing place for custom objects and non-graphical collections. Although it is easy to think that this is where the special additions to the spelling dictionary are placed, that is not the case. (If you are looking for the linkage to the spelling dictionary, see the Preferences object in the online help.)

In the AutoCAD dictionaries are collections of anything you want them to be. A dictionary can contain any type of object, including entity object references and other dictionary object references. Most often, dictionaries are used to house collections of data objects specific to a custom object or application. As such, they are wide open for access and manipulation and perform no data type checks to speak of when you use them.

A blank drawing contains two dictionaries automatically. They are ACAD_GROUP and ACAD_MLINESTYLE. The ACAD_GROUP dictionary contains the group collection data. Groups in AutoCAD are actually dictionary object entries, but it's better to access them through the GROUP collection. The ACAD_MLINESTYLE dictionary is used to define the multiline objects used in the drawing. Even if none are used, there are several predefined for immediate use.

Your own application uses dictionaries, most frequently when working with Xrecords and custom objects created by ObjectARX.

The following table contains the methods available with the dictionary object. Most involve accessing specific object references in the dictionary or manipulating the key value.

Method	What it does
AddObject	Adds a new member to the dictionary.
Delete	Deletes the dictionary entry from the dictionaries collection.
GetName	Returns the key name of an object that is an entry in the dictionary.
GetObject	Returns the object given the key name from the dictionary.
GetXData	Retrieves extended data if it's attached to the dictionary object.
Remove	Removes a named entry from the dictionary. This method removes individual members of a dictionary, not the entire dictionary.
Rename	Renames a named entry in the dictionary. Allows keys to be changed.
Replace	Replaces the object for a named entry in the dictionary.
SetXdata	Sets the extended data for a dictionary object.

The DimStyles Collection

Control over the dimensioning of AutoCAD is controlled by system variable settings. The system has the ability to store multiple instances of the dimension variable set using a named approach for later retrieval. This allows an operator or a programmer to reset the entire dimensioning variable collection by selecting a dimension style name instead of changing each property one at a time.

The DimStyles collection contains the names of the dimensioning styles known to the system. An application can query the dimension style table (collection) and learn if a particular name has been used in the drawing. If not, a new name can be added using the dimension style properties of the currently active dimension style. To make modifications to the dimension style settings, set the active dimension style to the style to be changed, then modify the AutoCAD system variables associated with dimensioning. Changes from the standard will be automatically stored with the currently active dimension style only. Unfortunately, this is the most that the ActiveX interface for AutoCAD currently allows as far as changing dimensioning styles. You can edit the system variables only for the current dimensioning style. In order to have your changes saved, the user must run the DDIM command and save the new, modified style. This means that you can change only one dimension style in a VBA macro. Do not switch to another dimensioning style in the middle of a macro, as the changes will not be saved with the dimensioning style just edited.

The following program section will define a new dimensioning style if one does not exist with the name "MY_STYLE1". This new style will then have the units changed. Remember that these changes will not be saved until the operator runs the DDIM command and saves the style changes.

```
Dim STD_Style, New_Style As AcadDimStyle

Err.Clear

On Error Resume Next

Set New_Style = ThisDrawing.DimStyles.Item("MY_STYLE1")

If Err.Number <> 0 Then

   Err.Clear

   Set New_Style = ThisDrawing.DimStyles.Add("MY_STYLE1")

End If

ThisDrawing.ActiveDimStyle = New_Style

ThisDrawing.SetVariable "DIMTOL", 1

ThisDrawing.SetVariable "DIMUNIT", 1
```

There are no special properties or methods for the DimStyles collection other than the Add() and Item() methods as found in all the tables. To remove a dimensioning style, first get the object reference, then use the Delete method found in the dimension style object. Note that this will work only if the style being referenced is not the current dimension style. Otherwise an error will result, stating that the object cannot be deleted because it is referenced by another object, the drawing.

```
Set New_Style = ThisDrawing.DimStyles.Item("MY_STYLE1")

New_Style.Delete
```

The Groups Collection

A group is a collection of AutoCAD entity objects combined together. A group is not a block; it is a grouping of independent entities as defined by some application or user. Grouping entities allows you to address them as a singular item when you're performing commands that move or change the objects. Groups are permanent selection sets from a programming point of view. They are saved in the dictionary information of a drawing and are carried from one edit session to the next.

Group objects are referenced in the groups collection. Given the name of a group, you start at the groups collection and use item() to locate the group object. The following methods and properties are associated with group objects.

Method	What it does
AppendItems	Adds objects to the group.
Delete	Deletes the group from the collection. Removes the name of the group.
GetXData	Retrieves extended data attached to the group.
Highlight	Highlights all of the objects in the group.
Item	Retrieves a member of the group using an index ranging from 0 to count minus 1.
RemoveItems	Removes entity objects from the group.
SetXData	Stores extended data in the group.
Update	Regenerates the members of the group on the display.

Properties	What it is
Count	Number of entity objects in the group.

There are more properties for the group object, but they are not of any real use to most applications. The primary operations are adding and removing objects from the group. The following code example creates a new group from a selection set of objects. The selection set and group name are supplied as parameters to the function. The value returned from the function is the new group object with the entities from the selection set as members. If the group already exists, the selection set objects are added to any other entity objects that are already in the group. If the group does not exist, it is created.

```
Function SS_2_Group(SS As AcadSelectionSet, Nm As String) As AcadGroup
    Err.Clear
    On Error Resume Next
    Set SS_2_Group = ThisDrawing.Groups.Item(Nm)
    If Err.Number <> 0 Then
        Err.Clear
        Set SS_2_Group = ThisDrawing.Groups.Add(Nm)
    End If
    Dim I, J As Integer
    J = SS.Count - 1
    ReDim Items(0 To J) As Object
    For I = 0 To SS.Count - 1
        Set Items(I) = SS.Item(I)
    Next I
    SS_2_Group.AppendItems (Items)
End Function
```

Note that the items are defined as generic objects, then assigned to the individual entity objects in the selection set. The array is then passed to the AppendItems() method to add these objects to the group.

137

Note also the use of the Err object when you're accessing the group collection. If the group name is not a member of the groups collection, an error will result when attempting to locate it via the Item() method. An error code that is non-zero means there was a problem accessing the name in the collection, thus the program proceeds into adding a new member to the collection. The result of creating a new member is the same as accessing an existing member with Item(): an object reference is created to the group.

Perhaps the most confusing aspect of using groups is that the Item() method is used in two different places. It is used when accessing the groups collection to obtain a group, and it is used again inside the group to access the individual entity objects that are members of the group.

Groups versus Dictionaries

At first it may appear that dictionaries and groups are the same. They are stored in the same manner but treated differently by the system. There are differences both in the way the operator perceives them and in the way the programmer can work with them.

The operators can manipulate a group. They can change the name and modify the members. When an operator selects an object that is a member of a group, the remainder of the group is also selected. Dictionaries are not like that. Instead, when an operator selects a member of a dictionary, the remainder of the dictionary remains unchanged. If the operator deletes a selected member from the drawing, the dictionary is updated to reflect the change, but that is all. Unless the members of a group are selectable, the operator cannot individually delete or change them.

For the programmers, dictionaries are protected from user interference as well as other meddling programmers. A dictionary requires you to know the key name of the object in order to get at it. It also requires you to know a programming language to access it. The latter requirement keeps most users at bay, while the naming requirement slows most programmers.

The group mechanism is preferred for most applications in which you want to save a selection set from one edit session to the next or need to provide a singular selection method for a group of independent objects. Dictionaries work best when using ObjectARX and the C++ programming interfaces.

The Layer Collection

The layers of a drawing are where most color and linetype settings are located for the entity objects. Although each entity object can have its own color and linetype setting, most simply use the layer name to reference the layer table. In VBA, the layers are stored as a collection that is accessed from the document object. Each member of the collection is a layer object that contains the details about the layer itself.

The following tables are the methods and properties of the layer object. New layers are added using the Add() method associated with the Layers collection. To obtain an individual layer object, the Item() method is used, as will be seen in the examples that follow.

Method	What it does
Delete	Removes the object from the Layers collection.
GetXData	Retrieves extended data that has been attached to the object.
SetXData	Saves extended data with the object.

Property	What it is for
Color	Color number for entities drawn on this layer.
Freeze	True if the layer is frozen, false if the layer is thawed. The default state is false.
LayerOn	True is the layer is on, false if the layer is off. The default state is true.
Linetype	Name of the linetype for entities drawn on this layer.
Lock	True if the layer is locked, false if the layer is unlocked. The default state is false.
Name	The name of the layer.

The following is a quick example showing how to manipulate the layer collection. The layer table is read sequentially, and any layers discovered to have a color assignment that is not white (7) will have their color property value changed to white.

```
Dim L1 As AcadLayer
For Each L1 In ThisDrawing.Layers
    If L1.Color <> acWhite Then
        L1.Color = acWhite
    End If
Next L1
```

The next example code sequence shows how easy it is to access a layer given the name. The Item() method of the layers collection is used to search for the layer object. Remember to include the On Error test for cases in which the layer might not exist.

```
Dim LYR As AcadLayer
Dim ABC As String
' ABC contains a layer name of interest
Err.Clear: On Error Resume Next
Set LYR = ThisDrawing.Layers.Item(ABC)
If Err.Number <> 0 Then
    ' Layer did not exist
    Err.Clear
Else
    ' Layer found okay
End If
```

The following code shows how to create a new layer. Before creating a new layer, you should check to see if it already exists. One way is to use the error handler as in the example above. If we wanted to add the ABC layer to the drawing when not found, the Add() method is inserted into the clause after the If test when an error is found. Another

140

way is to loop through the collection looking for a match, and that is shown next.

```
Sub MakeLayer(NewLayer As String, Clr As Integer, LT As String)
Dim L1 As AcadLayer: Dim I As Integer
I = ThisDrawing.Layers.Count - 1
While (I >= 0)
    Set L1 = ThisDrawing.Layers.Item(I)
    If L1.Name = NewLayer Then
        I = -1
    End If
    I = I - 1
Wend
If I <> -2 Then 'Was not found.
    Set L1 = ThisDrawing.Layers.Add(NewLayer)
    Err.Clear: On Error Resume Next
    L1.Color = Clr
    If Err.Number <> 0 Then
        MsgBox "Color number is invalid in MakeLayer function."
    End If
    Err.Clear: On Error Resume Next
    L1.Linetype = LT
    If Err.Number <> 0 Then
        MsgBox "Line type name invalid in MakeLayer function."
    End If
End If
End Sub
```

The color number and linetype name must also be valid, or an error will result. In the previous example the error system is used to trap this situation. Alternatives would be to test the range or see if the linetype specified is in the linetype table before making the assignment.

Regardless, it should be obvious to the new VBA programmer by now that the error handling system in VBA can be extremely useful when manipulating AutoCAD objects. This can be crucial when you're building a library of functions that you intend to use over and over again in future projects.

The Linetypes Collection

The Linetypes collection houses all the linetypes known to an AutoCAD drawing. All drawings recognize the continuous linetype by default. Other linetype definitions must be loaded or defined before being used. There are three methods associated with the linetypes collection: Add(), Item(), and Load(). The Add() and Item() methods behave in the same manner as already seen in all collections. Item() can be used to access linetype objects by name or by index into the table. Add() allows a new name to be added to the table. VBA does not allow you to define or access the generation properties of the linetype objects. That means that you cannot create a new linetype of your own design and simply add it as a new member to the collection. Instead, you will need to define the linetype in a linetype file (.LIN) and load it into the editor.

The Load() method is used to load linetype definitions from a file. Typically, linetypes are stored in an ASCII text file that contains multiple linetype definitions. For example, all the standard linetypes can be found in the ACAD.LIN file. If you are using one of the existing linetypes or a linetype that is defined in an LIN file, you can employ the Load() method to bring that linetype into the collection. Note that you do not have to use the Add() method to add the name first: Load() will add it automatically.

You can access the description of a linetype and change it, but you cannot access the definition of the linetype directly. Thus, the only way to define your own is to create a linetype definition file, then load it. Once loaded, your program has no way of knowing what the linetype actually looks like.

The following code demonstrates how a custom linetype can be created and loaded into the current drawing. Once loaded, it is a member of the linetypes collection and can be referenced in layer and entity objects.

```
Open "MY_LIN.LIN" For Output As #1

Print #1, "*MY_LIN,My line-type experiment"

Print #1, "A,0.5,-0.25,0.25,-0.25"

Close #1

Dim LTs As AcadLineTypes

Set LTs = ThisDrawing.Linetypes

LTs.Load "MY_LIN", "MY_LIN.LIN"
```

The Registered Apps Collection

Registered application names are the names associated with extended data that can be attached to the drawing objects. Registered application names are defined by the applications that use them; once defined, they can be used over and over again in the application. Extended data cannot be saved with drawing objects until the application name is registered.

To register an application name, you add a new name to the collection, as demonstrated in the following code segment. You do not have to include the error object checks for registered applications unless you're checking to see if one already exists using the methods demonstrated for other collections. When adding a new application name the request is simply ignored if the name is already on the list.

```
ThisDrawing.RegisteredApplications.Add "MYAPP"
```

The Text Styles Collection

Text style collections house the information pertaining to fonts and text generation defaults. Stored as objects, text styles influence the generation of Text, Mtext, and attribute text objects. You'll create new text style objects by first adding them to the collection, then setting the prop-

143

erties. You must declare the new text style as the active text style by setting the document's ActiveTextStyle property to the name of the text style. All new text objects created will have the properties of the active text style.

A text style can be applied to a text object by setting the style name property for the object. When used in this manner, the text object will be generated with the text style defined. The active text style setting is used when no specific style name property has been assigned during the new text object creation.

If you change the properties of a text style object, the drawing will not immediately reflect the modifications. You'll need to regenerate the current document object after completing all text style object changes. Using the Regen() method with the current document will force all of the graphics to be redrawn on the screen, which will incorporate all of the text style object changes.

As in all other collections, you'll use the Add() method to add a new text style. To access a text style, use the Item() method with either the name of the style you are after or the index into the collection where it is stored. To remove a text style object from the collection use the Delete() method associated with the object. You can delete text styles only if there are no other references to them in the drawing. If a text object is using the style, even in a block definition that is not inserted but present in the drawing, the text style cannot be purged from the list.

The following tables are for the text style object properties.

Property	What it contains
BigFontFile	The name of the big font file to be used when generating the text. Big fonts are used for Asian language fonts that contain a significantly greater number of characters than other language styles. Big font files are always of the type SHX.
FontFile	The name of the font file. Font files supported in AutoCAD can come from a variety of sources. File formats supported include AutoCAD Shape (SHX), Windows True type fonts (TTF), and Adobe Postscript (PFA, PFB).

Property	What it contains
Height	The fixed height of new text objects. When the height is specified, the operator will not be asked for a text height.
LastHeight	The last height used when creating text in this style. This value is the default setting for future text objects created while the text style is active.
Name	Name of the text style.
ObliqueAngle	Default setting of the oblique angle for the text. New text objects will use this oblique angle when generating the characters. The oblique angle is stored with the text objects; you can change it to a different value if needed by modifying the properties of the text objects.
TextGenerationFlag	The text style generation flag controls whether the text is drawn backward or upside down. There are two constants, acTextFlagBackward and acTextFlagUpsideDown, that you can use to control this property. Add the two together if the application requires both features or set the flag to 0 to disable both.
Width	The text width factor for character generation. The width controls the spacing between the characters. This value is a factor, and a setting of 1.0 will use the text as defined. Make it smaller to condense the text spacing and larger to spread it out.

The UCS Collection

User coordinate systems (UCS) are stored as objects in a collection. The UCS collection is the list of named coordinate systems known to the drawing. UCS objects are used to define the relationship of coordinates entered (or shown) and 3D space. Using a properly defined coordinate system, you can render 2D objects such as arcs and circles in a plane other than normal. When working with complex 3D drawings it is not uncommon to encounter many named UCS objects in the collection.

UCS objects are accessed by name or index number in the collection via the Item() method. A new UCS object can be added to the collection using the Add() method. To remove a named UCS object, first access the object, then use the Delete() method associated with it. Since entity objects are created using what is called an Object Coordinate System

(OCS) derived from the input data and current UCS, the UCS objects can be removed from the collection at any time.

The following tables are some of the methods and properties associated with the UCS object.

Method	What it does
Delete	Removes the UCS object from the UCS collection.
GetUCSMatrix	Returns a variant that is a 4-by-4 transformation matrix to be applied to the coordinates of entity objects. When the transformation is applied, the object is rotated and repositioned relative to the UCS.
GetXData	Returns extended data that is attached to the UCS object.
SetXData	Attaches extended data to the UCS object.

Property	What it is
Name	UCS object name for referencing purposes. This is the same name used by the Item() method in the collection to get to the UCS object.
Origin	An array with three elements representing the origin of the UCS object in the WCS. When obtained from the object, it is returned as a variant.
Xvector	An array with three elements representing the direction in the WCS of the UCS object's X-axis. Returned as a variant when accessed.
Yvector	An array with three elements representing the direction in the WCS of the UCS object's Y-axis. Returned as a variant when accessed.

UCS objects can be very useful when creating objects in 3D space. The reason is that new objects are always drawn in the UCS and have an OCS applied to them. When you're creating an object in the World Coordinate System (WCS) that is to be placed relative to a UCS, you can use the TransformBy() method to correct the entity object by applying an OCS. The transformation method uses a transformation matrix which you can create by defining a 4-by-4 array of double precision numbers or by obtaining one from the GetUCSMatrix() method of the UCS object to be used.

The following code example shows how to apply the transformation matrix from a UCS object. The example uses a coordinate system previously created and saved with the name "MY_UCS". A circle is defined in the WCS, then rotated relative to the stored UCS. The center point of the circle is reset after the transformation so that the selected point remains the center point of the object. The transformation will most likely change the circle object center point value thus making this operation a requirement.

```
' Current UCS is expected to the World Coordinate System (WCS)

Dim UCS_Mine As AcadUCS 'get UCS info from table

Set UCS_Mine = ThisDrawing.UserCoordinateSystems.Item("MY_UCS")

Dim p1 As Variant 'user input of a point

p1 = ThisDrawing.Utility.GetPoint(, "Center point")

Dim Obj As AcadCircle 'draw the circle, radius is one

Set Obj = ThisDrawing.ModelSpace.AddCircle(p1, 1#)

Dim TrnsMtx As Variant 'get the transformation matrix

TrnsMtx = UCS_Mine.GetUCSMatrix

Obj.TransformBy (TrnsMtx) 'apply transformation

Obj.Center = p1 'reset center point to original

Obj.Update 'regenerate the object on the screen
```

If you modify an existing UCS, you must update the document object after all modifications are completed. To update the current UCS, simply set the active UCS to be the UCS name once again. Any changes made to the UCS object will now be applied.

The Views Collection

The various 3D views that have been saved with names using the VIEW command in a drawing are stored in the views collection. This collection consists only of view objects, the properties that define the view. To create a new view, use the Add() method in the Views collection. The views collection is also where views are referenced by name or index. To remove a named view from the collection, the Delete() method is used. Like most other AutoCAD special object collections, the Delete() method is found in the view object and not in the collection.

The following table lists the primary properties used to manipulate view objects.

Property	What it is
Center	Where the view originates. This can be thought of as the location of the observer.
Direction	Vector describing the direction of the view.
Height	Height (Y) of the view in the drawing.
Name	Name of the view.
Target	Target point. This can be thought of as the location the observer is looking toward.
Width	Width (X) of the view in the drawing.

The View Ports Collection

The view ports collection is where named view ports are stored for the drawing. The user creates a named view port with the VPORTS command while in model space. Programmers can create named view ports by adding new names to the view ports collection with the Add() method. It is important to note at this time that view ports, as used in this context, are not the same as paper space view ports, and they are not the same as named views.

A view port is a rectangular area that defines a region of the display where a portion or all of the drawing can be shown. View ports are not the same as views. A view simply describes how the observer is oriented relative to the objects in either model or paper space. A view port not only describes that orientation; it also describes the area or region where the view is displayed relative to the display device. Paper space view ports, which we will explore in the next section, define a rectangular display area that is relative to paper space.

New view ports that have been added to the Viewports collection can be retrieved using the Item() method. Item() will accept either a view name or a number. Please note that multiple views can share the same name, so accessing the collection with the name value may not always return what you expect. For example, suppose you create a display containing three view ports in model space, then save that view port using the name "FUN". When looking at the view ports collection, you will find three view ports that share the name "FUN", but each will have different property values.

There can be multiple tiles (view ports) visible in a drawing at the same time (the maximum is based on the display system and can be found in the AutoCAD system variable MAXACTVP). An important thing to realize when working with view ports is that there can be only one active view port at any one time. The active view port is where the operator conducts all edit work. Switching the active view port as a user is simply a matter of picking the view port with the pointing device. In programming, the ActiveViewport property of the document object is set to the view port object you want to work within. This sort of control is used in model space (when the view ports are visible) to enable your program to adjust the zoom and rotation of each view port area.

To add a new view port to the view port collection, the collection is first accessed so that the Add() method may be used. In this case, a Viewport object is created. You can gain access to existing view ports by name or index using Item(), and you can use the Delete() method to remove view ports from the collection. (Note: it's a rare case in AutoCAD VBA when a specialized collection supports the Delete() method at the collection level.)

View Port Object

Method	What it does
GetGridSpacing	Gets the X and Y grid spacing values.
GetSnapSpacing	Gets the X and Y snap spacing values.
SetGridSpacing	Sets the X and Y grid spacing values.
SetSnapSpacing	Sets the X and Y snap spacing values.
SetView	Sets the view port to matching properties given the name of a saved view.
Split	An integer code: signifies how to split up the graphic display. There are a series of constants defined that can be used such as acViewport3Right.
ZoomAll	Performs a ZOOM to the limits of the model in the view port.
ZoomCenter	Performs a ZOOM with a center point and a magnification factor.
ZoomExtents	Performs a ZOOM to the limits of the model in the view port.
ZoomPickWindow	Performs a ZOOM based on two input points supplied by the operator when the method is run.
ZoomScaled	Performs a ZOOM based on a scaling factor that is relative to the current window, current drawing extents, or the paper space units.
ZoomWindow	Performs a ZOOM based on two points supplied as parameters.

Properties	What it is
Center	The location of the viewer's eye relative to the view port.
Direction	A vector describing the direction from the center point to the observer. The vector is a line from which the observer is looking back toward the origin (0,0,0) of the view port.
GridOn	Boolean indicating whether or not the grid is being displayed.
Height	The height of the view port along the Y-axis.
LowerLeftCorner	The coordinates of the lower left corner of the view port.
Name	Name of the view port.

Properties	What it is
OrthoOn	Boolean indicating whether or not the orthographic drawing mode is on.
SnapBasePoint	Base point for the snap grid.
SnapOn	Boolean indicating whether or not the snap grid is enabled.
SnapRotationAngle	Rotation angle for the snap grid.
StatusID	Boolean that is true if this view port is the current view port.
Target	Point that is the target location for the observer. The observer is at the center point looking towards the target point. The relationship between the target and observer point provides perspective views of 3D models.
UCSIconAtOrigin	Boolean indicating if the UCS icon is to be displayed at the origin point.
UCSIconOn	Boolean indicating if the UCS icon is to be displayed at all.
UpperRightCorner	The coordinates of the upper right corner of the view port.
Width	Size of the view port along the X-axis.

The upper and lower corners of a view port are expressed in ratios. A value of 1 indicates that it is at the maximum upper level, while a 0 value is used to indicate the lowest possible level. Thus a corner at (0.5,1.0) is halfway across the view port in the X-axis and at the top in the Y-axis. You'll use these values to determine which window to use when you have saved the view port using the VPORTS command in AutoCAD.

Only one view port is considered the active view port, and that one is defined in the drawing property ActiveViewport. The active view port is where drawing edits take place from the operator's perspective. Programmers use the ActiveViewport property to cause changes made to the view port properties to be reflected in the display. When you are changing view port properties, nothing will change on the display until the view port is established as the active view port. Even if the view port is already the active view port in the drawing, it must be re-established as such before any of the changes made will be visible.

The Paper Space View Port Object

When the paper space system was developed at Autodesk, the view port object concept was expanded from providing just a split screen in the traditional display system to what are called Paper Space view port objects. A paper space view port (PViewport) object is a rectangular area that is defined relative to the base point of paper space as opposed to the display screen. Most applications that deal with view ports deal with paper space view ports by providing automated routines to set up the drawing environment. An example would be a utility that takes a completed 3D model and generates the four standard views for front, side, top, and isometric.

PViewport objects are stored in paper space as entity objects and are not part of a collection (unless you construct a selection set of the objects). Most of the methods and properties associated with the Viewport object are also found in the PViewport object. But because this object is part of the entity objects, it also contains methods associated with the editing of the object such as Copy() and Move().

The following tables list some of the methods and properties that are associated with the paper space view port object (PViewport).

Method	What it does
Display	Causes the view port to be displayed in paper space. A single Boolean parameter indicates if the view port is to be displayed or not. After creating a new view port object, this method must be run to see it, as the default property is off.
Erase	Removes the view port from paper space so you can no longer see or access it.
Zoom...	Performs a zoom operation of choice within the view port. This function will work only when the current mode is for model space editing.

Property	What it is
Center	The center of the view port in paper space coordinates.
Direction	The viewing vector from the origin toward the observer.
Height	The Y-axis size of the view port in paper space units.
TwistAngle	The view is rotated by the amount in this property that is always measured counterclockwise and in radians. The display contents are rotated, not the view port rectangle.
Width	The X-axis size of the view port in paper space units.

Using paper space view ports is not difficult. You create a new paper space view port object through the AddPViewport() method found in the paper space object. A new view port requires three parameters: the center point and the size of the view port along both the X-axis and Y-axis. The following code creates a new paper space view port centered at (7,9) that is 12 units wide and 16 units high.

```
'switch to paper space
ThisDrawing.ActiveSpace = acPaperSpace
Dim PT(0 To 2) As Double
PT(0) = 7#: PT(1) = 9#: PT(2) = 0#
Dim NVP As AcadPViewport 'create new paper space view port object
Set NVP = ThisDrawing.PaperSpace.AddPViewport(PT, 6#, 8#)
PT(0) = 1#: PT(1) = 1#: PT(2) = 1#
NVP.Direction = PT 'point is (1,1,1) for isometric view
NVP.Display True 'force display update
ThisDrawing.MSpace = True ' switch to model space
ThisDrawing.ActivePViewport = NVP 'set the active paper space port
ZoomAll
ThisDrawing.MSpace = False ' switch back to paper space
ZoomAll
```

Most applications that use paper space also make use of view ports. A couple of basic rules that must be followed when programming view ports in paper space:

- Changes can be applied to only view ports when they are not the active paper space view port and have been turned off. What this means is that you can make adjustments to the view port properties only when first creating it or by setting another view port as active while the changes are applied. The Display() method must be used to turn the view port off if it is currently on.

- The view port must be turned on via the Display() method before it can be named as the active paper space view port for the drawing.

- The model space edit features cannot be activated for a view port unless the display mode has been turned on via the Display() method for that view port.

The Blocks Collection

The block table for a drawing is stored in the blocks collection. Each member of the blocks collection is a block object. Block objects are collections of entity objects just like paper space and model space. Block objects contain the same methods as found in the model and paper space objects for adding new objects to the block definition. The previous chapter lists the methods and properties that exist for entity collections such as blocks, model space, and paper space. A block is used in a drawing when referenced by a BlockRef object.

Blocks save storage in a drawing and represent the easiest form of programming available to the AutoCAD operator. Blocks are sequences of entity objects that can be used over and over again. Simple transformations can be applied to blocks such as scaling and rotation, making them valuable tools for experienced AutoCAD operators.

From a programmer's perspective, blocks are complex objects, but that's only because there are multiple, variable steps involved in the creation of the blocks. They are really quite simple to create and manipulate in a programming environment such as VBA.

Creating a New Block Definition

Creating a new block definition starts in the same manner as creating a new entry for the layer or style tables: you must add a name to the collection. The blocks collection object is first obtained from the drawing object. The collection is then queried to see if the block already exists. If it does, then the program must decide what to do next. The choices are to make up a new name, ask the operator for a new name, or give up the creation process as the block in question is ready for use. The result of successfully adding a new name to the blocks collection is a block object. The block object can be thought of as the same as model or paper space. New entity objects are added to the drawing database, but instead of attaching them to one of the space options, the block object reference is used instead.

```
Dim B1 As AcadBlock

Dim PT(0 To 2) As Double

PT(0) = 0#: PT(1) = 0#: PT(2) = 0#

Set B1 = ThisDrawing.Blocks.Add(PT, "MYBLOCK")

'Block object is B1, we can now add entity objects to it.

'This example draws a 1x1 square with a cross

'connecting opposite corners

  Dim P1(0 To 2) As Double

  Dim P2(0 To 2) As Double

  Dim P3(0 To 2) As Double

  Dim P4(0 To 2) As Double

  P1(0) = 0#: P1(1) = 0#: P1(2) = 0#

  P2(0) = 1#: P2(1) = 0#: P2(2) = 0#

  P3(0) = 1#: P3(1) = 1#: P3(2) = 0#

  P4(0) = 0#: P4(1) = 1#: P4(2) = 0#
```

```
'Draw the 1x1 square as four lines

B1.AddLine P1, P2

B1.AddLine P2, P3

B1.AddLine P3, P4

B1.AddLine P4, P1

'Draw the crossing lines from corner to corner

B1.AddLine P1, P3

B1.AddLine P2, P4
```

Any number of entity objects can be added to a block definition. You can also add to a block definition well after it has been defined. In fact, you can edit the block programmatically to alter the contents at any time. All you have to do is open the existing block object using the Item() method of the blocks collection.

The following example opens an existing block for access by VBA. The block object (stored in variable B1) is set with the result of the Item() access. Note the use of the Error object to trap the potential situation that the block does not exist.

```
Dim B1 As AcadBlock

On Error Resume Next

Set B1 = ThisDrawing.Blocks.Item("MYBLOCK")

If Err.Number <> 0 Then

   'The block does not exist in the drawing

  Else

   'The block exists, B1 is a collection of entity objects

End If
```

Reading a Block Definition

The fact that blocks are collections allows programs to sequentially access the entity objects contained inside the block. To read through a block definition you'll use the Item() method again, only this time with the block object. The Item() method for block collections uses the index number only as there are no names to search for specifically. Although it may seem confusing to have Item() used over and over again, it really isn't. It actually makes the coding easier because you know that every collection uses Item() to iterate through it or to provide access by name.

Figure 6.1 shows the relationship of the block object within the scope of the drawing object. The entities of a block definition are attached to a block object, which is in turn attached to the blocks collection. The blocks collection is a property of the drawing object. In the case of the block objects, the programmer can either access them by name or an index number. Most of the time a name will be used; however, there are applications that need to sequentially search the blocks table. In those cases, the index value can be used to step through each block member.

Access to the entity objects within the block objects is by index number (zero-based) only. Entity object IDs and handles cannot be used as keys into the block collections.

To help illustrate the methods involved in block manipulations, the following subroutine shows how to iterate through a block definition. The block object is obtained from the blocks collection using the Item()

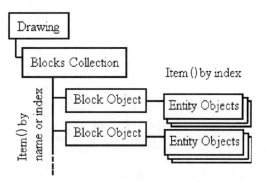

Figure 6.1: Relationship of the block object within the scope of the drawing object

method with the block name as a string. The block object returned from the Item() method is then used to iterate through the block definition. Using the Count property of the block object we get a loop counter to use so that each object can be accessed directly.

Inside the loop, the GetBoundingBox() method returns a pair of points indicating the minimum and maximum points surrounding the object. Since our function seeks to find out what the bounding size of all the objects are in the block definition, we need to iterate through the entire collection and look at each object. The result of the bounding box

157

is a pair of variants that can be accessed directly to see if they are greater or less than the maximum and minimum stored values. At the end of the loop, the values saved for the minimum and maximum are saved into the variant parameters MinPnt and MaxPnt. Note how variants are assigned point values. First build an array of doubles, then simply assign that array to the variant variable.

```
Sub Block_Extreme(Nam As String, MinPnt As Variant, MaxPnt As Variant)
    Dim B1 As AcadBlock
    Set B1 = ThisDrawing.Blocks.Item(Nam)
    Dim XMin, YMin, XMax, YMax As Double
    XMin = 999999.9: YMin = 999999.9
    XMax = -99999.9: YMax = -99999.9
    Dim E1 As Object
    Dim P1, P2 As Variant
    J = B1.Count - 1
    For I = 0 To J
        Set E1 = B1.Item(I)
        E1.GetBoundingBox P1, P2
        If P2(0) > XMax Then XMax = P2(0)
        If P2(1) > YMax Then YMax = P2(1)
        If P1(0) < XMin Then XMin = P1(0)
        If P1(1) < YMin Then YMin = P1(1)
    Next I
    P1(0) = XMin: P1(1) = YMin: MinPnt = P1
    P1(0) = XMax: P1(1) = YMax: MaxPnt = P1
End Sub
```

In most applications involving blocks, the programs work with block references or insertions into the drawing. The Name properties of the BlockRef objects (block reference) will return the name of a particular instance of the block object. The name can then be used to get the block definition from the blocks collection, and from there the block can be accessed directly.

The following code example demonstrates how to access a block from a selection on the screen. The operator is asked to pick an object using the GetPoint() utility function. This function returns a variant that can be used to define a selection set built using the SelectAtPoint() method. One item of note in the code is that after declaring our selection set, we clear it just to make sure no one else has used the same name. That includes us testing the code.

```
Dim PP1, PP2 As Variant
Dim PP0 As Variant
PP0 = ThisDrawing.Utility.GetPoint(, "Pick an object: ")
Dim S1 As AcadSelectionSet
   On Error Resume Next
   Set S1 = ThisDrawing.SelectionSets.Add("SS1")
   If Err.Number <> 0 Then
      Set S1 = ThisDrawing.SelectionSets.Item("SS1")
   End If
   S1.Clear
   S1.SelectAtPoint (PP0)
   Dim E1 As Object
   Set E1 = S1.Item(0)
   If E1.EntityType = acBlockReference Then
      MsgBox "Found a block reference! - " & E1.Name
      Call Block_Extreme(E1.Name, PP1, PP2)
   ' ...
```

The primitive example just shown tests the entity type property to see if it matches a particular entities number. Specifically, the AutoCAD constant acBlockReference was used to test for a block insert. This constant, along with others, can be used when accessing entities under operator control to test exactly what was selected. It is up to your program to perform adequate error checking when operator input is involved, as the operator will not always input or select something you want.

AutoLISP programmers who are learning VBA must learn to think in terms of what the objects can do for the application. There are different tools available for solving some problems that in the past have taken a great deal of time.

The next example code section expands on the previous example by using the selected entity object to build a selection set of objects that potentially intersect with the block. Using the IntersectWith() method from the entity objects, the application looks for intersection points, and when they are found, they are noted as point objects. The PDMODE system variable can be changed to see the points created with this example after it is run.

```
Dim PP0, IPs, PP1, PP2 As Variant

Dim S1 As AcadSelectionSet

Dim E1, E2, E1S(0) As Object

Dim IP(2) As Double

Dim I, J, K As Integer

'

PP0 = ThisDrawing.Utility.GetPoint(, "Pick a block insert: ")

On Error Resume Next

Set S1 = ThisDrawing.SelectionSets.Add("SS1")

If Error.Number <> 0 Then

    Set S1 = ThisDrawing.SelectionSets.Item("SS1")

End If

S1.Clear

S1.SelectAtPoint (PP0)

Set E1 = S1.Item(0)

'only work with block reference (insert) objects

If E1.EntityType = acBlockReference Then
```

160

```
'Get limits of inserted block
E1.GetBoundingBox PP1, PP2
'Build selection set of objects crossing the bounding box
S1.Clear
S1.Select acSelectionSetCrossing, PP1, PP2
'Remove block reference from selection set
Set E1S(0) = E1
S1.RemoveItems E1S
'Loop through selection set
J = S1.Count - 1
For I = 0 To J
    'Compute the intersection points
    Set E2 = S1.Item(I)
    IPs = E1.IntersectWith(E2, acExtendNone)
    'Go through the intersections found
    For K = LBound(IPs) To UBound(IPs)
        IP(0) = IPs(K): IP(1) = IPs(K + 1): IP(2) = IPs(K + 2)
        K = K + 2
        'draw a point at the intersection location.
        ThisDrawing.ModelSpace.AddPoint IP
    Next K
Next I
Else
MsgBox "You selected the wrong type of entity!"
End If
```

A block can contain any type of entity, including other block refer-ences. The only thing a block definition cannot contain is a block reference back to itself, which will cause a problem, as the block can never finish drawing itself. Most entity objects behave as normal when inside a block, but there is one important exception: attribute objects.

Working with Attribute Objects in a Block

When an attribute definition object is part of a block definition it will modify itself when the block is inserted and will create an attribute object. The attribute objects normally follow the block reference in the drawing database (as you see when you run the DBLIST command inside AutoCAD). Things are different when working in the ActiveX/VBA interface. The attribute objects do not appear in the model and paper space collections when iterating through them using the Item() method. Instead, you use a specialized method of the BlockRef object to retrieve the attribute objects for that particular block reference.

Attribute definition objects will appear when iterating through a collection such as a block, model, or paper space. But these are definition objects and not data-carrying attributes. You use the GetAttributes() method of the block reference object to access attributes that have data assigned.

When the GetAttributes() method is run, a variant is returned. This variant contains an array of object references in which each reference is to an attribute object. To find out how many attributes a particular block reference has attached to it, use the Ubound()function of VBA. Ubound() will tell you how many members the variant array has, and you can use it as a loop counter to iterate through each of the attributes.

The following code is a quick example of how to access attributes that have been inserted with a block. In this case, we are going to assume that the variable E1 points to an already opened block reference object. The GetAttributes() method is used to return a variant (ATS) containing the attributes that are attached to the block reference object (E1). Since there can be any number of attributes, most applications loop through them using the upper bound of the variant array (ATS).

```
' E1 is either type Object or AcadBlockReference and has a value.
Dim ATS As Variant
ATS = E1.GetAttributes
Dim EA As AcadAttributeReference
```

```
For I = 0 To UBound(ATS)

    Set EA = ATS(I)

    ' Variable (EA) now contains the attribute reference object

Next I
```

The object(s) that are returned when you use the GetAttributes() method are attribute references. Attribute references are different from attribute definitions. An attribute definition contains the default value, prompt string, tag name, and all the default generation parameters of the attribute text. An attribute reference, on the other hand, contains an instance of the attribute with the text value, location, sizing, and tag.

For the most part they are easy to keep straight. You will encounter attribute definitions while sequentially scanning the drawing or a block. Attribute references, on the other hand, are found associated only with a block reference.

If you make a request to get the attributes for a block that does not have any attributes, the resulting value in the variant will be an array of length 0. Thus the Ubound() function will return minus 1 (-1) when the array is empty, meaning that there are no attributes to be found for that block reference.

The following subroutine demonstrates the basics of accessing attributes by reading through model space and looking for any entity objects that are blocks. When a block is found the GetAttributes() method is called to build the variant array (ATS). The upper bound (Ubound) value is incremented to form a count of the number of attributes (variable K). When a block is found that contains attribute references, it is reported to the operator using a message box. The output string (S$) for the message box is built from the various properties of the block reference and attribute references. Specifically, it contains the block name followed by the count of the number of attributes found. Also included in the output string are the tag names and values of the attribute references associated with the block. This function will report on each individual block it locates in model space.

```
Sub ViewAttribs()
  Dim E1 As Object
  Dim ATS As Variant
  Dim EA As AcadAttributeReference
  Dim MS As AcadModelSpace
  Set MS = ThisDrawing.ModelSpace
  I = MS.Count - 1
  For J = 0 To I
    Set E1 = MS.Item(J)
    If E1.EntityType = acBlockReference Then
      ATS = E1.GetAttributes
      K = UBound(ATS) + 1
      If K > 0 Then
        S$ = "Found block - " & E1.Name & _
           " - with " & Str$(K) & " attributes { "
        For L = 0 To K - 1
          Set EA = ATS(L)
          S$ = S$ + EA.TagString & "/" & EA.TextString & " "
        Next L
        S$ = S$ & "}"
        MsgBox S$
      End If
    End If
  Next J
End Sub
```

You create attribute definitions with the AddAttribute() method just like adding other entities into the drawing database. You can use AddAttribute()with model space, paper space, or with a block definition object. Adding attributes to model and paper space is not as common when working in VBA. When creating new attribute definitions it will most likely be in a block reference.

The parameters to the AddAttribute() method are the text height, attribute generation mode, prompt string, insert point, tag string, and default value string. The insert point is supplied as an array of three double precision real numbers. The attribute generation mode is an integer code number from the following table.

Mode	What it means
AcAttributeModeInvisible	Attribute is invisible and cannot be seen by operator.
AcAttributeModeConstant	Attribute value is constant and cannot be changed.
AcAttributeModeVerify	Operator will be requested to verify entry of attribute data.
AcAttributeModePreset	Sets the value of the attribute to the default value automatically on insert.

If the application requires that the attribute take on more than one mode, simply add these constants together. Mixing some of the codes will not make much sense (such as verify and constant modes); however, there are many cases in which constant or preset attributes are expected to be invisible, requiring a combination of mode settings.

Attribute definition and references contain many of the same properties. The most important ones are listed in the table below; most of the others match the basic text object in their usage and names. Like other entities, there are methods for computing intersections and other edit manipulations; however, you will not use them when manipulating attribute references as often as the ones listed below.

Property	What it is
Height	Text height of the attribute.
InsertionPoint	The point where the text starts.
Mode	This is the integer mode value as described in the previous table. Use these constants to preserve your code from one release of AutoCAD to the next. This value is only in the attribute definition and does not appear in the reference.

Property	What it is
PromptString	This is the prompt string the user sees when the attribute is being referenced inside AutoCAD. This string is only in the attribute definition and does not appear in the attribute reference.
TagString	The tag for the attribute. The tag is used when referencing the attribute in the attribute extract.
TextString	In an attribute reference, this value is the text entered by the user (or application). For an attribute definition, this string is the default value of the attribute.

Working with attributes is quite easy inside of VBA. You can add and manipulate them within block object definitions, and when you use them in a drawing, you'll find them only when you're accessing the block reference objects specifically. Compared with the techniques you use to get at attributes inside of the AutoLISP environment, this is a vast improvement.

CHAPTER SEVEN

Working with Other Applications

The primary feature of VB is that it is capable of working with other programs that support automation inside of Windows. Some of the programs that support automation include the Microsoft Office 97 programs Word, Excel, and Access. This chapter demonstrates the basic strategies of interfacing AutoCAD VBA with these tools. In particular, we will pay attention to interfacing AutoCAD VBA with Microsoft Excel. This chapter is merely an introduction to using automation tools with these other packages. There are other books available that deal with the interfaces into the packages in much more detail. This chapter continues with an exploration of the techniques involved in building links between AutoCAD and external data systems using extended data (Xdata). We also cover the Dictionary and Xrecord objects in how they can be used in relation with external interfaces.

Object Models

Every program that supports ActiveX automation has an object tree that is similar to the AutoCAD object tree. The difference is that the tree for the other application will be specific to that application just as the Auto-CAD object library is dedicated to AutoCAD.

The object model in the other applications will follow the basic strategy (figure 7.1) of having the application at the root. There will be various properties, methods, and events associated with the application that may interest you, but normally your first step is into the documents. Inside the collection of documents will be the one document the application wants to access.

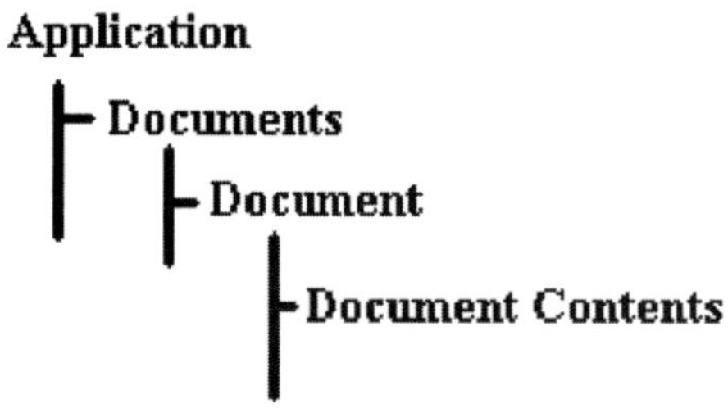

Each of the applications in Office 97 has specific names for each of the levels just described. In Microsoft Excel, a single spreadsheet document is a work sheet. Work sheets are contained inside of workbooks. Thus, workbooks are at the documents object level, and work sheets are at the document level. Inside the work sheets are cells that are the individual data items.

Application

├ **Documents**

│ ├ **Document**

│ │ ├ **Document Contents**

Figure 7.1: Generic object tree

When you're talking to a spreadsheet or some other automation interface system you will have to navigate through the object tree to get at what you want. This is not as difficult as it may sound: it is just a matter of learning the various branches and what they can do for you. The online help and object browser can be very helpful in locating these items.

Before you can use the online browser to locate the items of interest, you must first attach the object models you want to use. You link to an object library through the references setting located in the Tools pull-down menu of VBAIDE. Selecting the References option in the Tools menu brings up a menu of the available object references. You might be surprised at the selection available. It's generally pretty obvious which reference library to use when it comes to specific applications. For example, if you want to link in with Microsoft Excel, page through the list to the Microsoft Excel option, then pick it. The selected object library will now become available to your application. If more than one option is available, pick the most recent edition (highest release number).

To manipulate the objects from the other environments, you should have a good idea of what you want to do and how. That is, if you don't know how to use the Excel spreadsheet system, you will have difficulty understanding all that you can do with the objects that are available. It will be worth your while to spend time learning how to manipulate the system in its native mode in order to gain an appreciation of what the tool can do for an application. The objects and manipulation tools available to ActiveX are generally quite extensive, and your application programs can take advantage of virtually every feature of the other software system.

For you to have access to these tools they must be installed on the computer you are using. That is, you cannot possibly access the object model of Excel without Excel first being installed. For object models to work, the parent task or host must be available to service the requests. The same is true of AutoCAD and any other program of such sophistication. The term automation means just that — automation of the tasks on your computer so it does them more quickly and efficiently.

Interface to Microsoft Excel

This section will show you how to interface to the Microsoft Excel spreadsheet system of Office 97. Excel is a spreadsheet system, so it is exceptional at manipulating tabular data. AutoCAD-based applications can take advantage of Excel to build reports based on information found in the drawing. At first it may seem like magic to run a program from another program, but once you get used to object-oriented programming of this nature it seems primitive to do it any other way.

The Excel object tree starts at the Excel application (figure 7.2). Given an object pointer to the application, you access the workbook object to get to the worksheets level. From there you select

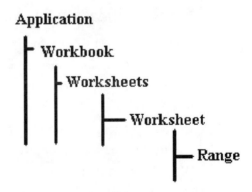

Figure 7.2: Excel object tree

an individual worksheet and a range manipulated inside of that sheet. A range can be a single cell or multiple cells inside the sheet. There are numerous methods, events, and properties associated with each of these levels in the system that you can explore using the online help and object browser systems. We will now turn our attention to the details involved when interfacing Excel and AutoCAD using VBA.

Interfacing Excel to AutoCAD can result in elegant solutions to common problems found in the design and drafting field. Using the strengths of each system you could construct a bill of materials system that counts blocks or other tagged objects in a drawing by building a spreadsheet detailing what was found. The spreadsheet can then be further instructed to calculate the costs associated with the values found. The next step would be to read the spreadsheet contents back into the drawing to create a bill of material table inside the drawing. A variation of the same idea would be the construction of hole charts in a spreadsheet based on the locations of circles found in the drawing. Once in the spreadsheet, locations can be sorted and other data appended to the report to finish it quickly. Even if you're not an advanced systems programmer, you can enhance productivity by merging the power of a graphics system such as AutoCAD and a data table manipulation tool such as Excel.

Excel Application 1 – Simple Database

Let's start with a simple application example. Excel serves excellently as a simple database for information based on tables of properties. That is, you use Excel to keep track of various constants indexed by a key name. This is a simple spreadsheet of the most basic nature, in which each row in the spreadsheet represents a record associated with the key name stored in one of the columns (typically the first column, but it doesn't have to be). We will use a simple spreadsheet of this style to demonstrate how to obtain information from Excel via a VBA program running inside AutoCAD. Obviously, the main advantage of doing this is that the end user can maintain the table of data using a table-editing tool (Excel) and does not have to work in a text editor or in the source code of an AutoLISP routine.

The following is an example spreadsheet that has the first column as a key name and the next two entries as scalar values. These scalars could represent dimensions, tolerances, physical properties, or some other data of interest to our application. The goal of this example is to access them by name and retrieve the values from the spreadsheet, thereby demonstrating the basic strategies of opening a spreadsheet and obtaining information from one via VBA.

In the following spreadsheet (figure 7.3), columns are labeled with letters (A,B,C) and rows are numbered (1,2,3,4,5) just as found in Excel.

EXAMPLE1.XLS – spreadsheet contents

	A	B	C
1	Name	Dim1	Dim2
2	AA-1	1.5	1.5
3	AA-2	2.5	1.75
4	AA-3	3.5	1.85
5	AA-4	4.0	2.0

Figure 7.3: Example 1XLS—spread sheet contents

You will create the XLS file ahead of time using normal Excel operations. The file name to use for our example is "EXAMPLE1.XLS" and the sheet name will be "Sheet 1", the default. You can use normal Excel operations to define this table in the system if you want to try it yourself.

Link to Excel

The remainder of the programming takes place inside VBA in AutoCAD. When you're starting a new project, the first step is to link the Excel object library using the Tools-Resources menu selection with the project. The specific library to select will vary depending on what version of Excel you have installed. For example, the name may appear as Microsoft Excel

8.0 Object Library if you have Office 97 installed. Now our VBA program will know how to talk with Excel. (Remember that you must have Excel installed on your computer to access the library.)

Variable Declarations

After adding the linkage references for Excel, the next step is to start coding the interface. After inserting a new module into the project, we type in the following declarations.

```
Dim ExL As Object

Dim XLWorkBook as Object

Dim excelSheet As Object
```

We use generic object containers for these values when interfacing to Microsoft Excel. You can use the object types from the Excel library as well (when available). When used as shown, the objects are bound to the Excel objects at run time. This is called *late binding* in programming. If you use the definitions of specific objects from the Excel class, the object types are considered *early bound*. Early binding helps applications run faster, as the system does not do the binding work when the user is at the helm. Instead, in early binding the linkage is done when the application is built, hence the system knows how to manipulate the references right away. The problem with early binding is that the variables defined in this manner cannot be used to hold any other types of objects if that was desired later in the program. Since this application does not vary the types of objects held in the object references, we could also have coded the declarations as follows.

```
Dim ExL As Excel.Application

Dim XlWorkBook As Excel.Workbook

Dim excelSheet As Excel.Worksheet
```

The primary advantage of using early binding is that the system can assist you in typing in object references. As you type the variable name used, a list box of available selections will appear. When the generic object definition (late binding) is used, the system doesn't know what kind of object you are referencing during the coding and cannot possibly assist in the typing.

These definitions are global to our module, and you can access them by any of the subroutines or functions we include in that module. If we wanted to make these variables available to other modules, we would change the Private statement to Public. This allows the variables to be addressed as part of our module (named Module1 by default) by other source code modules. The visibility, or scope, of variables from one module to another is covered in more detail in a later chapter.

If speed of execution is an issue, and it normally is, be aware that running Excel from inside AutoCAD will not be as fast as if the same VBA module were running inside Excel. Within larger applications, you may want to have the VBA in Excel handle the Excel side of the problem and have the VBA in AutoCAD simply launch the macro in Excel. The reason is that the VBA code inside Excel is tightly coupled to Excel while the VBA code running inside AutoCAD is bound at runtime with Excel. That means that every transaction that takes place between AutoCAD and Excel must go through a series of interfaces before getting to the other application. For simple manipulations this will not be an issue, but when working with more advanced applications the time savings could be significant.

Excel Linkage Function

Now we need a function that will start Excel and assign the object to the variables dimensioned above. Staying in the code window for the module just started, we type the following line of code.

```
Sub Set_Up_Excel
```

VBA fills in the rest for us, adding in a new subroutine definition to the module. The parentheses are added, as is the End Sub statement. All we have to do is fill in the middle part. When you type in the Sub statement with the name of a new function, the code editor will contain the following after you press the Enter key.

```
Sub Set_Up_Excel ()

End Sub
```

The following is what we filled in for the function. This function will start Microsoft Excel with the "EXAMPLE1.XLS" workbook (must be located in the default Excel document directory) and "Sheet1" worksheet loaded and ready to go. Each line of the code is explained in the text that follows. All the code is presented together for those just scanning for examples.

```
Sub Set_Up_Excel()

   On Error Resume Next

   Set ExL = GetObject("", "Excel.Application")

   ExL.Visible = True

   If (Err.Number <> 0) Then

      Err.Clear

      MsgBox "You must have Excel loaded on your computer!"

      Exit Sub

   End If

   Set XLWorkBook = Workbooks.Open("EXAMPLE1.XLS")

   Sheets("Sheet1").Select

   Set excelSheet = ExL.ActiveWorkbook.Sheets("Sheet1")

End Sub
```

The first part of the program will attach the Excel application object. GetObject() is a VBA function that retrieves an application object given the executable file name or the class name of the application. If Excel is running, the class name "Excel.Application" will find a link and return the application object for our program to use. If Excel is not running, the GetObject() function will start Excel. If Excel is not available on the computer, the program will fail. That's why the error handler is turned on before the call to GetObject(). If the error handler was not enabled and Excel was not available, the program would crash in an ugly manner.

This way we can control the exit situation and issue a proper error message that makes sense to the user.

By including the empty string as the first parameter to the getObject() function, we are instructing VBA to run Excel if it is not already running in the computer. Leaving the first parameter blank will cause an error if an instance of Excel does not already exist in the machine.

Another way to access the workbook object is through the createObject() function. This function behaves just like getObject() except that it will start the application. If your application knows it will be starting Excel when it is going to run, then the createObject() function is a better choice.

The next step is to open the workbook using the Open method of the Workbooks object in Excel. You'll supply the complete file name, with extension, to the Open function. No directory was specified in the example routine. The file is assumed to be in the Excel or system search path. If it's not in the search path, you'll need to provide a complete path name. The extension XLS will not be appended automatically, which means that your application can use alternative extensions as a minimal form of data security. The result of a successful open call is a workbook object.

Workbooks contain worksheets, so the next level into the object tree takes our application to the specific sheet we wish to have available. The example program selects "Sheet1", the default sheet name in a new workbook. The worksheet object is then assigned to the variable excelSheet.

The result of running this function is that the workbook and worksheet are opened and their respective object references are stored in the variables defined in the declaration section.

Closing the Workbook

Something to remember for later coding is that after you have opened and manipulated a workbook, you should close it using the Close method. The workbook object close method releases the workbook for other applications (including Excel) to access. The following subroutine shows how to close a workbook.

```
Sub Close_book ()

    XlWorkBook.Close

End Sub
```

Searching the Worksheet

The function we need now is one that searches the worksheet to find a match. Specifically, we are interested in searching for something in one of the columns. In this application we want to search the spreadsheet for a match with a key name in column one. That means that the application will look for matches with values like "AA-1", "AA-2", and so forth. When a match is found, we want the values from the next two columns.

To locate a particular cell in a spreadsheet we can use the Find() method that is associated with a range object in Excel. A range object defines a section of the worksheet. Worksheet ranges are defined by row and column location such as A1, which represents that single cell located at column A, row 1. A range can specify more than one cell, such as a column of cells in the spreadsheet designated as A1:A10 for column A, rows 1 through 10. Ranges are typically rectangular and can span multiple rows and columns as in A1:B3, which represents the cells found within columns A and B from row 1 through 3.

Given a range of cells, you can apply the Find() method to look for a matching value. The find method will return a range of cells that match the find requirements. The resulting range can be a single cell or a group of cells. When an application is dealing with a list of unique key names, there should be only one match. If there is a situation in which Find() could locate more than one, then a range is returned that you can traverse using subsequent calls to the FindNext() method. Each call to FindNext() will return the next cell found to match the search criteria. When there are no more selections, FindNext() is null. Our application example expects the key names to be unique, meaning that no key is repeated, so the FindNext() loop is not required.

The value returned from the find method is a Range object. The address method of the Range object is used to obtain the location of the cell that was located and is returned as a string. When the address method is used, a dollar sign will proceed each part of the address so that if a match was made with column A and row 3, the result would be A3. You can change the response of the address method by using the variable parameters; however, the default approach is good enough for our purposes.

When you are searching a table using a specific column, you know the column value and can remove it from the result string to extract just the row number where the match was made. In our example, we are searching the A column for a key name match and can thus remove the first three characters of the resulting address (the "A" part) to obtain only the row number (3). Now if our application wants to obtain the value of a particular column member of that row, it can access the Cells().Value directly.

The following code segment searches the open worksheet saved in the object variable excelSheet. It searches column A between rows 1 and 10 to find a match with the value "AA-3". When the match is found, the data value found in column B is accessed and placed in the variable Resulting_Value.

```
Dim Fnd As Excel.Range

Set Fnd = excelSheet.Range("A1:A10").Find("AA-3")

R$ = Fnd.Address

Rw = Val(Mid$(R$, 4))

Resulting_Value = excelSheet.Cells(Rw, 2).Value
```

To search the entire column labeled as A, you can specify the range as ("A:A") instead of limiting the range search to rows 1 through 10 as in the code above. In Excel, this format is considered "A1" notation. Most spreadsheet users are used to denoting areas or ranges in the document with "A1" notation. "A1" notation uses letters to represent the columns and numbers to represent the rows. In this notation the value B5 would refer to the fifth entry in the second column.

When using the "A1" notation, you can shortcut the code entry by just specifying the desired range inside of square brackets as in [A1:A10] instead of Range("A1:A10"). Note that the quotation marks are not needed when defining the range using the shortcut approach.

There are other ways to denote ranges of cells inside Excel from VBA. An easy alternative is to use the Rows and Columns properties of a worksheet. You can use these properties to define a range based on an entire row or column. Using the column property, you would rewrite the code as follows.

```
Set Fnd = excelSheet.Columns(1).Find("AA-3")
```

The entire first column of the spreadsheet is searched to locate the desired match. The Columns() property of the worksheet returns a range and that satisfies the Find method.

There is another way to search a spreadsheet for some information: you can use the Cells() property with index values of the row and column. You could change the example search to read as follows.

```
R$ = ""
For I = 1 To 10
    If excelSheet.Cells(I,1).Value = "AA-3" Then
    R$ = excelSheet.Cells(I,2).Value
    I = 11 'break out of the loop
    End If
Next I
```

At the end of the loop, the variable R$ would either hold the value from the second column of the row in which the "AA-3" match was made or it will be an empty string.

So which style should your application use? Use whatever makes sense for the application at hand. The Find() method will locate a match inside of a range faster than a direct iteration loop; however, it is limited to finding exact matches. If you need to test values to see if they fit a particular range for a selection to be made, then the direct iteration approach will probably work better for the application. An example is a program that searches a database of available sizes and selects the one nearest in size (but larger than) a theoretically calculated size. In this case, there may not be an exact match, and some logic must be applied to the spreadsheet data in order to make a selection.

For most applications, you apply a specified range and an exact value (often called a key) for the search. In those cases, the "A1" notation style will work nicely in conjunction with a Find(). The range to search could be hard coded as in these examples, or it could be supplied in the form of a range variable. And because strings can also be stored inside a spreadsheet, there is nothing that would stop an application from obtaining the range value to use from some other cell in the spreadsheet.

When you're searching through a spreadsheet, the best solution for any given application to use is the one that reads in a logical manner. For example, if someone said to search the first column, then the Columns() property seems to make the most sense. On the other hand, if someone specified that the application should search through a specific set of rows and columns, then the "A1" notation works best. And if there is a need to perform calculations or comparisons with the values, a direct iteration is the only way to get the job done.

Another Example Interface to Microsoft Excel

Simple examples demonstrate how easily you can use Excel to create reports from AutoCAD drawing information. This function will create a hole chart from all the circles found in the drawing. A hole chart is a table that lists holes found in the drawing along with their X-Y location. The hole chart is typically used for drill programming or for locating bolted attachments in an assembly.

This simple function set will create a chart with sequential hole number, X, Y location of center point, and the radius of the hole. The hole number will then be written back into the drawing at the center point of the circle using the current default text height. This example demonstrates just how simple it is to build a powerful reporting tool for Auto-CAD with Excel.

The application is broken down into small modules to make the code easier to read. The first listing contains the global variable declarations for the module. There are two variables that we will declare as global (available to all functions and subroutines in the module), and they are a link to the active Excel spreadsheet and an AutoCAD selection set collection.

```
Dim excelSheet As Object

Dim SS As AcadSelectionSet
```

The main program macro is called Holes and it is defined in the following listing. The Holes function calls other functions that perform the detail operations. First the Excel object is found and linked. (Note that we have removed the normal error checking from this example to keep the code simple and brief.) Once the link has been established with Excel, the function Get_Circles is called to obtain a selection set collection of all the circles found in the drawing. The collection is then used by the subroutine Send_Holes_To_Excel that reads each object and places the coordinates and radius in a spreadsheet.

We sort the spreadsheet using the Sort() method of Excel. The Sort() method implements the standard sorting available in the Excel system. In this application we will sort by the X, Y, and Radius values in ascending order. After the sort, the spreadsheet data is read back into the program in sorted order. A text note is then placed at each hole indicating its position in the sorted list, and the handle is replaced with the hole number in the spreadsheet. When this function is completed, the holes will be labeled in AutoCAD and a supporting report is ready to be finished in Excel.

```
Sub holes()

   Dim Excell As Object

   Set Excell = GetObject(, "Excel.Application")

   Set excelSheet = Excell.ActiveWorkbook.Sheets.Add

   Set SS = Get_Circles

   Send_Holes_To_Excel
```

```
excelSheet.Range("A1").Sort _

  key1:=excelSheet.Range("B1"), _

  key2:=excelSheet.Range("C1"), _

  key3:=excelSheet.Range("D1")

Set_Hole_Numbers

End Sub
```

The Sort() method can be a tad confusing at a quick glance. From the example above, it appears as though the sort would do only a single cell—certainly not the desired operation. Actually, the value supplied is either a range or the first cell of a region. In this case, we are sorting a region that is designated as starting at "A1". The sort fields are defined by assigning the parameter variables Key1, Key2, and so forth to the first sort fields in the spreadsheet. For our example we are sorting by the X, then Y, then the radius values. You can sort the fields in ascending (the default) order or in descending order. To have a field, such as the Y values, sort in descending order, use the Order2 parameter variable and set it to a value of xlDescending. Order1 will change the sort order of the first key field, and Order3 will change the order of the third set. There are up to three sort fields that can be defined in the Sort() method.

Let's turn our attention to the first of the subroutines called from the main function. The Get_Circles function will build a selection set collection of circles found in the drawing.

```
Function Get_Circles() As AcadSelectionSet

  Dim Cir1, Cir2 As Variant

  Dim CirA(0 To 0) As Integer

  Dim CirB(0 To 0) As Variant

  CirA(0) = 0

  CirB(0) = "CIRCLE"

  Cir1 = CirA: Cir2 = CirB

  On Error Resume Next

  Set Get_Circles = ThisDrawing.SelectionSets.Add("HOLES")
```

```
      If Err.Number <> 0 Then
        Err.Clear
        Set Get_Circles = ThisDrawing.SelectionSets.Item("HOLES")
      End If
      Get_Circles.Clear
      Get_Circles.Select acSelectionSetAll, , , Cir1, Cir2
    End Function
```

The value that will be returned from the Get_Circles function is a
selection set collection. The function is defined as being of the type selection set, and we can use the name in our program as a variable to house
the selection set collection while it is being constructed. Get_Circles uses a
filter to construct the selection set collection. The filter is to look for
circles only and can be expanded to include layer names and other criteria as well.

Given the selection set collection, the next step is to write the values
out to Excel in the worksheet already started. At the beginning of this
subroutine, the worksheet is expected to be empty.

```
    Sub Send_Holes_To_Excel()
      Dim Ent As AcadCircle
      CN = 1: CX = 2: CY = 3: CR = 4
      R = 1
      Dim PTV As Variant
      For Each Ent In SS
        excelSheet.Cells(R, CN).Value = Ent.Handle
        PTV = Ent.Center
        excelSheet.Cells(R, CX).Value = PTV(0)
        excelSheet.Cells(R, CY).Value = PTV(1)
        excelSheet.Cells(R, CR).Value = Ent.Radius
        R = R + 1
      Next Ent
    End Sub
```

This function loops through the selection set collection (stored in global variable SS, which was set in the main program as the result of calling Get_Circles). Each entity is assumed to be a circle object, meaning that certain values are known to be available such as the center point and radius. As this subroutine reads through the selection set collection each entity is placed in the variable Ent for processing. The first column of the spreadsheet is set to the entity handle. Handles are the best way to link entity objects with external data structures; we will be discussing them in more detail later in this chapter. The second and third columns of the spreadsheet are then set to the X and Y values of the circle center point. The fourth column is set to the radius value found in the circle object.

The variable R holds the row number as the program adds each hole location to the spreadsheet. After the user writes the hole location and size information to the spreadsheet, the subroutine ends and control is returned back to the main program.

The main program then sorts the spreadsheet as already discussed. The sorted spreadsheet contains the data sequenced by X, Y, and Radius values. The next subroutine will read the spreadsheet and place hole numbers at each circle location. There are two operations that will take place as this function iterates through the spreadsheet. The first is to place the hole number in the drawing. The second is to replace the handle entry in the spreadsheet with the sequential hole number.

```
Sub Set_Hole_Numbers()

   Dim PTV As Variant

   Dim PTC(0 To 2) As Double

   I = 1

   TH = ThisDrawing.GetVariable("TEXTSIZE")

   While excelSheet.Cells(I, 1).Value <> ""

      PTC(0) = excelSheet.Cells(I, 2).Value

      PTC(1) = excelSheet.Cells(I, 3).Value

      PTC(2) = 0#

      ThisDrawing.ModelSpace.AddText Str$(I), PTC, TH
```

```
        I = I + 1

    Wend

End Sub
```

The function begins by obtaining the current default text size for the drawing. This value will be used when adding the text objects for the hole number. A While loop is started that will iterate so long as the cell in the first column of the current row number (in variable I) has a non-blank entry. Handles are never blank, thus when the program encounters a blank cell, it has hit the end of the list. This version of the function doesn't do anything with the handle other than test to see if one is there.

The X and Y values for the center of the circle are retrieved from the spreadsheet and placed into an array of doubles. This array is set into the variant variable PTV which is needed by the addCircle() function. You must use variants when sending and getting points from objects. The reason has to do with the way the BASIC language (as implemented in VBA) passes parameters internally and the fact that array references are handled better using a variant pointer.

The row number is incremented, and the loop continues until the last hole has been read and the text placed in the drawing, at which point the subroutine finishes.

This function set demonstrates the basics and performs a very useful operation as well (should you need hole charts and a numbering system for holes). VBA provides a powerful way to tie various tools together so that each can be used in its own way to make the application dream a reality.

Using Handles

The last example used handles but didn't really do anything with them other than look for a blank handle indicating the end of the list in the spreadsheet. Handles are strings that uniquely identify each object in a drawing. AutoCAD assigns handles as the objects are created and never reuses the same handle in the drawing. There are tools in AutoCAD's programming systems for converting handles to entity objects. As such, handles present a way that entity object references can be moved to an external system such as a spreadsheet for later reference.

In VBA, a handle is converted to an entity object through the Handle-ToObject() method. This method is associated with the document object and can return values only when that document is the current document. That is, you can get handles converted into objects only in the currently opened drawing.

Using this conversion utility you can update the drawing based on the values in the spreadsheet as in the following example, which looks at the same spreadsheet. In this subroutine, the values in the spreadsheet are read one at a time and the radius values checked against the original drawing objects. If changed, the drawing object is updated and the layer changed to layer "CHANGED". The layer is assumed to exist before the macro is run.

```
Sub update_radii()

  Dim Excell As Object

  Set Excell = GetObject(, "Excel.Application")

  Set excelSheet = Excell.ActiveWorkbook.Sheets("Sheet32")

  Dim Ent As AcadCircle

  I = 1

  While excelSheet.Cells(I, 1).Value <> ""

    HN$ = excelSheet.Cells(I, 1).Value

    Set Ent = ThisDrawing.HandleToObject(HN$)

    If Ent.Radius <> excelSheet.Cells(I, 4) Then

      Ent.Radius = excelSheet.Cells(I, 4)

      Ent.Layer = "CHANGED"

    End If

    I = I + 1

  Wend

End Sub
```

Object ID versus Handle

An alternative to handles are Object ID values. Object ID values use less storage space compared with handles (in medium and larger drawings). An Object ID is a long integer value instead of a string. Thus, once the entity handle names exceed four characters in length, the length of a handle is longer than the object ID storage space. Another attractive feature of Object ID values is that they are integers and can be compared more quickly than character strings.

Object ID values are mostly used in ObjectARX applications and are available to VBA programmers for that purpose. ObjectARX applications use the object ID values when connecting with the various objects in the drawing database. Some of the VBA utilities and event handling functions supply or require object ID values as well.

To get an object ID value from an existing object, use the ObjectID property of the object. If we have an entity object stored in the object variable Ent, then the expression Ent.ObjectID will return the object ID value. Object ID values are read-only and cannot be set by an application.

You can convert object ID values to objects via the utility method ObjectIDtoObject() available in the current drawing database. This method is used in a manner just like the handle conversion utility to obtain the object. Also, like the handle conversion utility, the object ID conversion utility can be used only in the current drawing to obtain an entity object. That is, if you have another drawing open (from the documents collection) you cannot access the objects inside with just an object ID value.

The problem with object ID values is that they will change as the drawing is saved and reloaded. That is, they are not persistent inside the drawing file. Handles never change in a drawing file; once used, a handle is never repeated. This makes handles the ideal tool for linking AutoCAD drawing objects with outside applications. Object IDs are not well suited for that sort of interface unless the application will not exit the drawing during the life span of the external data.

Linking with Other Applications

Linking graphic data in AutoCAD with parameters and associated databases requires you to think carefully about the tools involved and which one does which job best. AutoCAD is obviously superior in graphics manipulations when compared with applications such as Word or Excel. On the other hand, these other applications manipulate words and data charts much better than AutoCAD.

At first it would appear that the delineation between the different applications is pretty cut and dried. This is not the case. Excel is very good at making charts as well as manipulating tables. At the same time, AutoCAD includes custom dictionary objects for storing tables of data internal to the drawing. And Word provides table-generating features that make for very good charts and material lists.

So how do you know what way to turn when looking at integrated applications of this nature? Generally, the best answer is to consider what needs manipulating and what tool is best at that manipulation. Consider an application in which a data table containing a set of standard sizes is referenced. Storing that table inside each and every AutoCAD drawing may seem ludicrous at first glance. If someone needs to change the standard values, he or she might have to change them in every drawing. It would be much easier to change them in a spreadsheet or database, then have the newer values available for all drawings. However, suppose that the standards are changed every so often but that an associated application must work with the standards that applied when the drawing was created. Under those circumstances, it might be better to store the data table inside the drawing or at least in a database closely associated with just that drawing.

The circumstances of the application and how the data will be needed will greatly influence what tool is used to accomplish the job. For most applications, the clear delineation between AutoCAD as the graphics engine, Excel as the table engine, and Word as the reporting engine is enough to get started. In general, the more you know about a particular application, the more you will be able to exploit its abilities when inter-facing AutoCAD with it. The reason is that the same software that services the operator commands processes the automation tools you can use. Objects are a powerful way for one application to link up with another.

Storing Data in AutoCAD

So far we've looked at handles as a way to store a reference to an Auto-CAD entity object in another database. But what about linking some other database's key in an AutoCAD drawing? Since a key is typically text, it could be stored as a very small text object in the drawing. But keys are not graphic objects, and it is not desirable to have text objects cluttering up the drawing. To aid applications facing this dilemma, Auto-CAD has some other mechanisms for storing non-graphical information in a drawing.

There are two tools that can be used to store non-graphical informa-tion inside a drawing. The first is a dictionary, which can house lists of objects. The second is extended data. The primary difference is that extended data is attached to existing objects in a drawing, so it is limited in the amount of data that can be added. Dictionaries can contain inde-pendent objects, and these objects can be of any size.

Dictionary Object

A dictionary is a collection of objects; it can contain any objects the application requires. Dictionary objects are members of the dictionaries collection, as we discussed in Chapter 6. The objects that make up a dic-tionary can be of our own custom design (you must use ObjectARX to create a truly custom object). Dictionary objects can also be other Auto-CAD drawing objects such as lines, arcs, and circles. In this manner, a dictionary can be used to store a selection set between edit sessions, much like a group but without any operator control options. Lastly, there is an object available in AutoCAD that is found only in dictionaries called an Xrecord. Dictionaries can be made up of Xrecords or any combination of entity objects.

Xrecord Objects

When interfacing with external systems or using custom design software, Xrecords present an interesting method of storing data inside a drawing that is not directly attached to an entity object. An Xrecord is a non-graphical object that can contain any number of parameters, just like a graphic object. That means you can store points, strings, integers, real numbers, and so forth. Xrecords are located using a dictionary and a key name. The key name is a string that is stored with the Xrecord inside the dictionary. Since your application stores the key name, it should also know how to retrieve it for later use.

Xrecords provide a way to store the values of various variables that might be used in an application. A program can write Xrecords containing the values of key variables in response to a save-event taking place. That way, when the program is started again in the same drawing at a later time, the variable values can be retrieved.

Accessing a Dictionary

Creating a dictionary object in VBA is simply a matter of adding a new member to the dictionary collection of the drawing. When the drawing is saved, the dictionary is saved with it. The following code segment will create a new dictionary object in the current drawing.

```
Dim Dict As AcadDictionary
Set Dict = ThisDrawing.Dictionaries.Add( "My Dictionary")
```

You need to create a dictionary object only once; doing so a second time will result in an error trigger. If a particular dictionary object already exists in the drawing, you'll access it using the Item() method. The following code will access the dictionary object named "My Dictionary" and if it is not found, will create it.

```
' Dictionary objects should be global

Dim Dict As AcadDictionary

'

On Error Resume Next

Set Dict = ThisDrawing.Dictionaries.Item ( "My Dictionary")

If Err.Number <> 0 Then

   Err.Clear

   Set Dict = ThisDrawing.Dictionaries.Add("My Dictionary")

End If
```

The dictionary object can be used to reference the objects within the dictionary. What you will find in a dictionary is entirely up to the application that maintains the dictionary. In most cases, the dictionary will contain object references. The objects in the dictionary are accessed just like a collection in that you use names or the index number to obtain the reference.

For most applications the dictionary serves as a wonderful place to store variable values and parametric data. A dictionary can also be used to store tables of data reflecting standards in effect when the drawing was created. As a result, the most common member of a custom dictionary is the Xrecord. Because Xrecords can contain any data and make use of the same numbering system as AutoCAD objects, they are very easy for most AutoCAD programmers to use.

Xrecord Contents

An Xrecord contains variable data: one Xrecord does not have to look like the next in the dictionary collection. The data for an Xrecord is supplied in two arrays. The first array contains integer group codes that specify the kind of data that will be found at the same offset in the second array. The second array is of type variant, meaning that it can contain anything. When accessing or writing an Xrecord, these two arrays are used. They must be the same size, and the data contents are entirely up to the application. The only integer codes not permitted are 5 and 105, as these are reserved for AutoCAD handles. New Xrecords will have handles added automatically when they are first created. All of the remaining group codes are at the disposal of the application. That is, you can use group code 40 over and over again for a sequence of real numbers, or you can use 40, 41, and so forth. Whatever works best for the application.

To add an Xrecord object to a dictionary, first open the dictionary. We recommend that you dimension objects such as dictionaries in global memory so that they may be accessed by all modules in the application that need to get at them. With the dictionary already open, the next step is to add the Xrecord object to it with the AddXRecord() method. The AddXrecord() method creates an Xrecord object that is attached to the dictionary collection. The Xrecord data is then written to the object using the SetXRecordData method.

To learn how an Xrecord object is created, consider the following code. A new Xrecord object is attached to an already open dictionary object referenced by the variable Dict as in the previous code segment. The subroutine will store a real number, an integer, and a string, which are all provided as parameters to the function. The key parameter is the key name that will be used for accessing the Xrecord in the dictionary at some time in the future.

```
Sub WriteXrecord(Key As String, R As Double, I As Integer, S As String)
    Dim Xtyp(2) As Integer
    Dim Xvar(2) As Variant
    Xtyp(0) = 40: Xvar(0) = R
    Xtyp(1) = 60: Xvar(1) = I
    Xtyp(2) = 1: Xvar(2) = S
    Dim Xrec As AcadXRecord
    Set Xrec = Dict.AddXRecord(Key)
    Xrec.SetXRecordData Xtyp, Xvar
End Sub
```

The function just provided might be used by an application that has three variables to be stored for future referencing. This function could be part of a module that reacts to the begin-save event. The first step would be to open the dictionary object by accessing an existing one or creating a new one. Next you'll write the variables. That would end the begin-save event reactor. You'll need to do additional programming for the drawing-open reactor, in which a module would open the dictionary and read the three variables back into the application.

Reading Xrecords

To read an Xrecord you must first know the key name it was stored under. The only alternative is to loop through the dictionary one item at a time and examine the contents of each. In either case, the Item() method is used with the dictionary object to obtain the Xrecord object. From there, you'll use the GetXRecordData() method to get at the group codes and data stored inside.

<XrecordObject>.GetXRecordData() uses two variant parameters. When the function returns, these two will reference arrays of data. The first will contain an array of integer values, and the second will be an array of variants.

The next code example will read the Xrecord created in the previous example given the key name as a parameter. The values read from the Xrecord are put back into the parameter variables to be used by the calling program. You'll use the function GetXRecordData() method to return the Xrecord contents given the Xrecord object reference. To obtain the Xrecord object reference, the Item() method is applied against the already open dictionary object Dict.

```
Sub ReadMyXrecord(Key As String, R As Double, I As Integer, S As String)
    Dim Xtyp, XVar As Variant
    Dim XR As AcadXRecord
    Set XR = Dict.Item(Key)
    XR.GetXRecordData Xtyp, XVar
```

```
For J = LBound(Xtyp) To UBound(Xtyp)

   If Xtyp(J) = 1 Then S = XVar(J)

   If Xtyp(J) = 40 Then R = XVar(J)

   If Xtyp(J) = 70 Then I = XVar(J)

 Next J

End Sub
```

In this function, the values returned from the Xrecord read are processed into variables that are passed back to the calling function. They could just as easily been placed into global variable locations for the application or returned as a result of a function instead. The key item to remember is that Xrecords are under the control of the application program manipulating them. They can contain any type of data desired and can be of any length. Note that they are not protected from other programmers who understand how to navigate the object system of AutoCAD, but they are well protected from the normal AutoCAD user.

Group Codes in Xrecords

Using group codes in an application is entirely up to the applications developer who is working with Xrecord objects. However, we strongly recommend that the following standards be followed in order to remain consistent with the AutoCAD drawing database. There are other group codes that can be used: these are merely suggestions.

Codes	What they are
1-9	Strings. Do not use code 5, it is for the entity handles!
10-29	Point lists.
30-39	Z values. Sometimes these are also used for point lists.
40-49	Real number scalar values. Typically used for sizes and scale factors.
50-59	Real number angular values. Typically used for angles.
60-69	Integer numbers, counters, and values for numeric coded items.
70-79	Integer numbers, bit coded flags combined into single integers.

In the previous examples, the group codes used were 1 for the string, 40 for the real number, and 60 for the integer. They could just as well have been 1, 2, 3 if the application creating them wanted the codes in that order.

Xrecords may use group code numbers 1 through 369. You should not use group codes 5 and 105, as they are for AutoCAD. AutoCAD will add the entity handle information required to these codes. You may use all other codes in any manner you desire.

Extended Data

The other way to attach data that is non-graphical to a drawing is to use extended data. You attach extended data directly to objects in the drawing database; these can contain numbers, points, and strings. The only real limit to keep in mind with extended data is that an object can have only about 16 kilobytes of data attached to it. Now, that is a lot of data to attach to an object in a drawing, and it would not be good to attach even half that amount to objects throughout the database. Operators will most definitely complain about the excessive disk space being consumed.

When setting up extended data, you'll use a group code system much like the Xrecord objects with the exception that extended data group codes are all numbered in the 1000 series. Extended data attachments must use these group codes when attaching data to an entity object.

Code	Extended data type
1000	String.
1001	Application name.
1002	Control string for nested information. Open bracket for start of the nest, close bracket for the end of it.
1003	Layer name. If the layer name is changed in the drawing, this field will be updated to reflect that change.
1004	Binary data storage. Data cannot be accessed by AutoLISP and is used primarily by ObjectARX applications.

Code	Extended data type
1005	Handle to another object. Can be used to link one object to another.
1010	Point.
1040	Real number.
1041	Distance — will be scaled with the parent object.
1042	Scale factor — will be scaled with the parent object.
1070	Integer.
1071	Long integer.

Every object in the AutoCAD drawing database can have extended data attached to it. But before you can use extended data, the application ID must first be added to the registered applications collection. The Add() method is used to add the name of your application to the registered applications collection object in the current drawing, as in the following line of code.

```
ThisDrawing.RegisteredApplications.Add "MyApplication"
```

An application name needs to be added only once to a document. Once it has been added, it will be saved with the drawing and can be used when addressing extended data for objects.

There are two methods associated with all AutoCAD objects that you use to access the extended data. They are SetXdata() and GetXdata(). The SetXdata() method is used to add extended data to an object. The registered application name must be supplied with the data provided to SetXdata(). If there is already data attached to the entity with the same name, it is overwritten. When writing extended data to an object, you must update all the information associated with the application, or some data may be lost. If the application name is not supplied or has not been registered with the drawing, the extended data will not be attached to the object.

The extended data itself is supplied in two variables. The first variable is an array of integer group codes. The second is a variant array of whatever data is needed and matches the group codes. You must use the

195

group code with the data type that matches the data being supplied—otherwise, the extended data will not be written properly.

When retrieving extended data from an object, you'll use two variant objects. These objects are actually arrays containing the extended data in the same fashion as it was supplied to the object in the first place. Applications can rely on the order of group codes being preserved in extended data, unless some other application changes them because it used the same name.

Simple Xdata Example

The example presented will create a line, then add extended data indicating the date and time the object was added to the drawing. The AutoCAD system variable "CDATE" is used for this purpose. "CDATE" contains the current date and time stored as a real number that can be preserved with the entity object. The format of the "CDATE" variable is thus: the year, month, and day value are concatenated into the front part of the number (before the decimal point), and the time of day values make up the part that appears to the right of the decimal point.

The first step is to create the line object. You'll create a new line from (1,1) to (2,1). It is left on the current layer and no other changes are made to it. The line is then added to the model space of the current drawing and the line object variable saved in variable Lin.

```
Dim Lin As AcadLine
Dim PV1 As Variant, PV2 As Variant
Dim PT1(0 To 2) As Double
Dim PT2(0 To 2) As Double
PT1(0) = 1#: PT1(1) = 1#: PT1(2) = 0#
PT2(0) = 2#: PT2(1) = 1#: PT1(2) = 0#
PV1 = PT1: PV2 = PT2
Set Lin = ThisDrawing.ModelSpace.AddLine(PV1, PV2)
```

As in Xrecords, extended data records use two arrays that contain the integer group codes and variant data values that comprise the extended data. The next section of code initializes the arrays, retrieves the "CDATE" value, adds the registered application name to the drawing, and places the extended data onto the line object.

```
Dim PT(1) As Integer
Dim PV(1) As Variant
Dim RR As Double
RR = ThisDrawing.GetVariable("CDATE")
PT(0) = 1001: PV(0) = "CREATED"
PT(1) = 1040: PV(1) = RR
ThisDrawing.RegisteredApplications.Add "CREATED"
Lin.SetXData PT, PV
```

The SetXData method is used with the line object to add the extended data arrays to the object. Group codes 1001 and 1040 were used to hold the registered application name and the real number value for the CDATE system variable. If you need to store an additional real number, the group code 1040 is used again. One problem that can come up is if multiple applications are working with the same extended data. In those cases, it is possible that the order of the data elements could get confused. We highly recommend that you keep extended data grouped in small data packs if there is a requirement for multiple applications to be messing with the data. Each of the data packs is assigned a registered application name, making it easy to retrieve just the data sought after.

This next section of code will locate the line with the "CREATED" extended data and read the saved value for the CDATE system variable. In order to accomplish the task, the function must first locate the line. This is done with the selection set utility function. The function Getdate() is presented in pieces, followed by a description of each section of code.

```
Function Getdate()As Double
    Dim SS As AcadSelectionSet
```

197

```
On Error Resume Next

Set SS = ThisDrawing.SelectionSets.Add("TEMP")

If Err.Number <> 0 Then

   Set SS = ThisDrawing.SelectionSets.Item("TEMP")

   Err.Clear

   SS.Clear

End If

'function continues
```

The function starts by defining a selection set object named SS. When you add the selection set "TEMP" to the selection set collection of the drawing, an error will result if it is already in there. Thus we enable the On Error trap to force VBA to continue in the event an error is reported.

If the error number is not 0, then VBA had a problem adding the name "TEMP" to the selection set collection. That means it is already in there, and we must use the Item() method to get it. Because selection set is already defined, it may also contain objects. The Clear method is employed to clear out any objects that may be in the selection set named "TEMP".

At this point in the code, the variable SS is a selection set object with nothing in it. The next step is to locate the "LINE" object that contains the extended data.

```
'function continues

Dim FT(1) As Integer, FV(1) As Variant

Dim vFT As Variant, vFV As Variant

FT(0) = 0: FV(0) = "LINE"

FT(1) = 1001: FV(1) = "CREATED"

vFT = FT: vFV = FV

SS.Select acSelectionSetAll, , , vFT, vFV

'function continues
```

You'll use the Select method from the selection set object to locate the desired graphics. We are interested in finding a "LINE" object that has extended data attached to it. The technique involved in building the filter for extended data is somewhat different in VBA compared with Auto-LISP/Visual LISP. Instead of searching for a −3 group code, it searches for the 1001 group code. The 1001 group code contains the application name that will be exactly the same as the application name supplied in the function that wrote the extended data in the first place. For our application, that name is "CREATED".

The filter list is built by first defining two arrays. The first array contains the integer group codes for the data we are filtering. In this example we are looking for a "LINE", thus group code 0 is used. Entity names are always associated with group code 0. The extended data application name is represented by the 1001 value. In the second array, the values for these variables are set. The second array is of the type Variant so that it can hold any type of data: string, double, or integer.

Due to the way variants are stored in the VBA system, a second assignment is made for the arrays to another pair of Variant variables (vFT, vFV). All the input elements for the selection set building function are ready, and Select() is called on to put entities into the selection set SS. The acSelectSetAll is an AutoCAD constant that tells the select method to search the entire drawing database.

At the end of this section of code, the selection set variable SS now contains a "LINE" object that has the extended data attached to it. If the "LINE" object is not found in the drawing, the selection set will be empty.

```
'function continues
If SS.Count > 0 Then
    Dim Ent As AcadLine
    Set Ent = SS.Item(0)
    Ent.GetXData "CREATED", vFT, vFV
    GetSavedDate = vFV(1)
  Else
    GetSavedDate = 0#
  End If
End Function
```

The selection set Count property tells us how many objects were found matching the filter description we just used. If the Count is greater than 0, then the Select() method was successful in locating objects that fit our criteria.

We know that the object we want is a line, so we define an AcadLine object. If the extended data had been attached to any AutoCAD object, a better choice would have been to use the AcadObject definition instead. However, due to the way VBA works with libraries and objects, the general rule of thumb is that when you know exactly what object type will be encountered, use that definition. This will improve the performance of the applications.

The application looks at the first line in the selection set with Item(0). The GetXData() method is used with that entity object to retrieve two variants that are arrays containing the extended data. Since our application wrote only two pieces of data to the extended data, the name of the application and the data value, we know for certain that the value saved can be found in the second element. Thus, use vFV(1) to get the saved value and place it in the return value of the function.

If the selection set count was 0, the function didn't find any "LINE" objects with the extended data attached. At this point, the return result of the function is set to 0.

A more advanced look at extended data manipulations is presented in a later chapter. Extended data provides a powerful way to associate non-graphical data to existing graphical objects. There are other techniques that can be used as well, including Xrecords with hard ownership relationships. However, these are more difficult to manage under VBA, and most applications will find extended data to suffice.

CHAPTER EIGHT

Managing Multiple Projects

The macro system in VBA is excellent for creating small applications that solve specific problems in AutoCAD. Using VBA macros, you can greatly enhance the way AutoCAD works for a particular discipline. In this chapter we are going to explore how to keep track of the VBA macros and how to integrate them into normal AutoCAD operations. We are also going to be looking at the different ways to store VBA macros in AutoCAD drawings or as projects.

Putting Complete Applications Together

Building a complete application in VBA requires bringing together different pieces of code and dialog boxes into something the operator can initiate. It is not reasonable, or in most cases desirable, to have operators enter the VBA development system in order to start the application. Not only does this expose the application to possible changes by unqualified individuals, it also is a cumbersome way for CAD operators to interface with the system. The goal when developing an application for AutoCAD is to make the new tool integrate seamlessly into the environment. That means having the application start when someone makes a menu selection or types a command at the keyboard.

As we will see in this chapter, it's best to start an application based on VBA through the AutoCAD menu system. VBA is not well suited for the AutoCAD command line and does not provide a facility for defining new command names as in AutoLISP or ObjectARX/ADS. Only veteran Auto-CAD users who learned how to draw by using the keyboard will find this aspect of VBA to be difficult, and for them there is a solution that involves using AutoLISP to load and start the program. Thus you can write VBA applications that behave like AutoCAD commands, are started like normal AutoCAD commands, and can significantly impact the productivity of AutoCAD operators.

Figure 8.1: Project Window

Complete applications in VBA are called projects. In VBA, a project is what we call the collection of modules that make up a program. Inside a project you'll find code modules, dialog boxes, references to other objects, and specific object definitions. In all VBA projects running inside AutoCAD you will find the ThisDrawing object. The remaining contents of a project are entirely up to you, the applications developer. The contents of a project are viewed with the Project window of the VBAIDE (figure 8.1).

If a project has a dialog box–based interface, there will be at least one form connected to the project. Add a dialog box to the interface by selecting the Insert - Form option from the pull-down menu or by picking the Insert Form icon. Forms are the combined definition of a dialog box and all of the callback functions associated with the dialog box. In other words, there are always two parts to a form. The first is the dialog box definition that is shown graphically to the programmer when the user form is visible. The other is a code window that contains all of the callback functions and associated code components for the dialog box contents. To switch between the code and dialog box views, use the window pull-down menu or the icons at the top of the Project window. When starting a form, both the form window and code window will be blank and ready to accept your definitions.

Forms are optional; if a project does not contain any dialog box interfaces, they will not be found in the project tree. Sometimes a complete application can be written with a single form. In that case, only one dialog box appears associated with the application. When a project needs more than one dialog box, there will be a form entry for each of the dialog boxes. And each form entry will have code associated with it. Applications that involve multiple forms are not difficult to manage with the tools provided in VBA.

There will generally be at least one module inside any project that can be started outside of the VBAIDE. A module is a connected group of subroutines and functions. Inside the module, there should be at least one subroutine that is public. That public subroutine will be used to start the application; it is often called a macro. It is important that you declare the macro as public so it is visible outside of the module and project. As functions and subroutines are defined, you can declare them as public or private. If you make no declaration, the definition is considered public. Private functions and subroutines cannot be seen or initiated outside of the project module.

To add a code module to the project, select the Insert—Module option from the pull-down menu or use the icon option from the toolbar. The code module will be initially blank and waiting for your input. To help keep things under control, there should be only one public subroutine definition for an application. That way, your program is always started at the same place. Your program can then call other private functions inside the same module and control the various forms attached to the project.

An operator can start any public subroutine defined in a code module. These macros are considered exposed to the operator. Operators can start a macro by using the Tools—Macros pull-down menu option. Once they load the project, the exposed macros are listed in the Macros dialog box. This is one way in which users can start an application. He or she selects one of the exposed macros from the Macros dialog box to run.

Loading Projects to Run

If the project is not loaded, the Macros dialog box has a button that takes the operator to the VBA Manager dialog box. The VBA Manager dialog box is where you can load projects stored on disk, thereby making the exposed macros visible for selection back in the Macros dialog box.

You can store projects either on disk or inside the drawing. When a project is stored inside a drawing it is considered embedded in the drawing. This makes the project immediately available whenever the drawing is open. Perhaps the most intriguing feature of an embedded project comes through the use of VBA reactors that are associated with the ThisDrawing object. Suppose you want a program that will request a user ID whenever the drawing is opened. You can provide the event routine AcadDocument_Activate with the code required to start a form that in turn requests the user ID. Only an embedded project can make use of such an event trigger with any degree of reliability. You must load and initiate externally stored projects first before event triggers can be enabled.

A project that uses event triggers only may not have any code modules or any forms attached to it. The code for such a project would all be found under the AutoCAD Objects member ThisDrawing. There are numerous event functions that can be programmed at the Objects level in the drawing and many applications that can be built around these triggers. For the most part, event triggers provide an excellent method of monitoring what is going on in the AutoCAD system.

We should mention to programmers who are considering the use of VBA for such applications work that ObjectARX provides a much greater level of control over the systems operations of AutoCAD compared with VBA. Not only is the ObjectARX runtime code more efficient, but the ObjectARX system provides greater flexibility when you're monitoring or controlling AutoCAD at that level. VBA can be used to test out ideas in regards to event-triggered applications, but we don't recommend using this tool as the foundation for any significant applications along these lines.

Embedded Projects

An embedded project is one that is stored inside the AutoCAD drawing. When the drawing is loaded, the operator will be given the opportunity to enable the embedded project. A stern warning about viruses is issued as the default in AutoCAD, so users may be a bit shy about allowing the macros to be loaded. You can disable the virus warning for future loads at the particular workstation, but this will let any drawing that has attached macros enter the system as well. The choice of using embedded projects is up to the environment. It does increase the drawing size, but depending on the application, that may not be by very much.

To embed a project in a drawing, load the drawing, then either define or load the project. In the VBA Project Manager program dialog, select the project, then select the Embed button. The project is now embedded into the drawing and will be saved with the drawing.

The next time the drawing is loaded, the project is immediately available. The AcadDocument_Activate function will then be run. You can use this function to load a dialog box (form.show) immediately to ask the user a question or two. You can create a time management system for each drawing using this simple approach.

There can be only one project embedded in the drawing at a time, however. That project can reference other projects stored on disk. To have an embedded project reference a stored project, load both into the VBAIDE. With the embedded project as the active project, select the Tools—References pull-down menu option. Find the object name of the other project in the list and select it. Save the project and drawing. The next time the drawing is loaded, the embedded project will be loaded automatically and the referenced project will be loaded at the same time.

Projects on Disk

Projects that are not embedded are stored on disk as DVB files. A DVB project file can be locked, thereby protecting it from changes by the user. A project is stored on disk when the Save project is used and the project is not considered embedded. A project contains all the modules, forms, and object reference information needed to run the project the next time it is loaded. If the project has public subroutines defined, they are listed in the macros list.

To load a project, you can use the VBALOAD command. You can also load VBA projects by entering the VBA Manager dialog box (command VBAMAN). The VBARUN command will display a dialog box for running the macros that are exposed in any of the projects loaded.

In AutoCAD 2000 you can have more than one project loaded and available at once. In AutoCAD Release 14's version of VBA, only one project can be open and available at a time. Thus the entire idea of referencing other projects is not something that can be explored with AutoCAD Release 14: it requires AutoCAD 2000.

You can load the project manager without the dialog box. This is how you place project load and start-up sequences into AutoCAD menus and AutoLISP macros. When you put a dash character (-) in front of the command, AutoCAD does not display the dialog box but instead prompts for the parameters required.

To illustrate, the following code segment is from a menu macro that will load the VBA project stored as MYPROJ.DVB, then start a macro named MYMACRO that is a public subroutine in the project. This menu macro can be added as a new toolbar entry or can be part of a larger menu source file.

```
[Run my macro]^C^C^C^P-VBALOAD MYPROJ.DVB VBARUN MYMACRO
```

When the DVB file does not exist in the search path for AutoCAD, the entire path name must be provided to properly load it. If the project is already loaded, the VBALOAD command will just exit, and the VBARUN command can then run the macro.

You can supply this same sequence in an AutoLISP program module to start a VBA macro. And you can employ the COMMAND subr to send the command stream to AutoCAD to launch the program.

```
(command "-VBALOAD" "MYPROJ.DVB" "-VBARUN" "MYMACRO")
```

Using the AutoLISP launch version, you can set up the ACAD.LSP files to contain a function that will load and start the VBA application. Note that in AutoCAD 2000 the usage of the ACAD.LSP file has changed, and it may not load for every drawing according to the AutoCAD system variable setting ACADLSPASDOC. When this variable is true, the default, ACAD.LSP, is loaded for each new drawing. When false, ACAD.LSP will be loaded once at the beginning of the AutoCAD session.

Both VBA program launch mechanisms can result in dialog box interruptions. The first is the Macro Virus warning. A stern warning is displayed in a dialog box stating that macros may contain viruses and that the user can disable the macros to make sure no viruses infect the system. Of course, this could result in the VBA macro not running at all. When running from a menu or from AutoLISP, that is not the desired result. Macro Virus warnings can be turned off by toggling the "Always ask before opening projects with macros" to the off position (not checked). Future warnings will not be issued until the feature is turned back on. Another dialog error that will result from using the load and launch will result when you're attempting to perform the same function a second time in the same drawing. Since the macro set is already loaded, an error message will result stating that the file is already loaded. There is no way presently to test if a VBA project is loaded from inside an AutoLISP routine or from a menu macro.

Thus the best way to load and launch VBA programs is using the menu system of AutoCAD. Inside the menu you can explicitly request the VBA application by name or force the load of the supporting AutoLISP code that runs the project. Once the menu macro has run the first time, it can be replaced with a simple macro that just reruns the VBA program. The user makes a single pick of the menu item and the program starts running. What could be simpler?

Re-using Code

As you develop applications with VBA, you will begin to build a toolbox of useful utilities. We are getting you started with a host of functions that will be introduced in Chapter 10. These utilities can be imported into your current projects by saving the individual modules as they are developed. Modules are saved as BAS files. To build a BAS file from inside the VBAIDE, select the Files—Export pull-down menu option. Modules are exported as ASCII text files with a default extension of BAS.

The same is true with forms. They can be exported to FRM and FRX files that contain the essential information related to the dialog box and associated code. The FRM file is an ASCII header file that points to the FRX file. The FRX file is a binary file that contains the actual dialog box definition and its associated code segments.

In a future project where the same program code or input form may be used again, you can import the saved components using the Files—Import pull-down menu option. Once you have imported the entire module or form, you can keep those sections that are of interest while you remove the remainder using the editors in VBAIDE.

Sometimes it is better to have a copy of another text editor (such as Notepad) running to load code modules (BAS files). You can copy the needed code to the clipboard, then paste it back into the VBAIDE in the module where the code will be used. This approach works great when you are working with a large library (like that provided with this book) and want to pull in fragments of the code to save yourself the typing.

Running a Macro from Another Project

Another choice available to the VBA developer for re-using code already developed is to load the project that contains the module desired and run it. AutoCAD VBA provides the tools needed to accomplish this task in AutoCAD 2000. There are three methods associated with the application object that can be used to load, run, and unload projects.

The LoadDVB method will load a project file (extension DVB). If the project is already open, an error will result, so it is best to invoke the error handler when using this method unless you know for sure that the project is not loaded and that you will be unloading it when you are done with it. LoadDVB has one parameter: the name of the project file as a string. You should provide the complete path name and extension DVB if the file is not in the current search directory. When the load operation is completed, the project is now available to the user as well as to your application.

After loading a project into the current application environment, you can use the RunMacro method to run a public subroutine from the project. You must define the subroutine as public since your application will enjoy only the same rights into the project as a user does. If the macro is not available for whatever reason, an error will result.

The only parameter to the RunMacro method is the name of the macro to run. When supplying a name for this function, the complete macro location must be specified. That is, you need to supply the module name plus the name of the subroutine.

RunMacro is associated with the application object that has just opened the project file. If you have a macro and module of the same name in your program set, they will not be run. The difference is the way you call on a macro in your own program versus in an external one, as we are discussing. When you call a macro in your own program you supply the name directly, and VBA finds the links right away. When you call a macro in a loaded DVB project file, you supply the macro name as a string parameter. The string is then used in a search of the project to locate the macro intended. At that time the macro executes.

If you want to run macros from multiple DVB files, it is best to close each one as soon as you are done with it. To close the project, use the UnloadDVB method. Once again, you must supply the name of the DVB project in order to ensure that the correct project is closed.

The following simple example will load a DVB project called CoolStuf that is saved in the \MyCoolStuff directory. Once the project is loaded, the macro VeryNeat is run from the module named Module1. Then the project is unloaded.

```
Dim ACADApp As AcadApplication
Set ACADApp = GetObject(, "AutoCAD.Application")
```

```
ACADApp.LoadDVB "C:\MyCoolStuff\CoolStuf.DVB"

ACADApp.RunMacro "Module1.VeryNeat"

ACADApp.UnloadDVB "C:\MyCoolStuff\CoolStuf.DVB"
```

This approach to running other projects should be used only if another programming group has denied you access into the internal routines or if the project is rarely used. When working with other projects on a more frequent basis, you should directly reference the project into the current project so it is readily available.

Sharing Data between Projects

Sharing data between VBA projects is a matter of using public, global variables that you can address directly in the same manner as used to address modules in another project. You must reference the variables using the complete project and module location as well as the variable name when you're putting values in or getting them out.

Another way to perform this activity is to make an import method (function) available for the project module. This function would have multiple parameters required and would be public. The parameters would be the values to change or obtain, and the function could then interface with the local variables directly, as it is part of the same project. Of course, this approach exposes the function to the user; however, because of the required variable parameters, it will be all but useless from the Macro start dialog box.

A third alternative is to store the data to be passed between applications in the drawing, on the disk, or in another ActiveX application such as Excel. The use of this style of data transfer will depend on the applications that are interfacing with each other. For example, the Excel option would be somewhat odd as a choice when the applications do not use Excel for any reason themselves. And a file transfer system may be excessive when all that needs to be shared is a string or two. The applications, as well as the tools used to create them, will dictate which solution is the best one to pursue.

210

The file or drawing option is also the only one available for sharing AutoLISP or ObjectARX variable data with VBA applications. You cannot pass variables to and from these other environments with VBA. If your application in VBA needs to obtain information from an AutoLISP program, that program must either save the data in the drawing at some known location (such as a User system variable) or write it to a file. The file name will have to be agreed on in advance by both the AutoLISP and VBA modules to effect the data transfer. These situations are rare and generally involve applications migrating from one environment to the other. In those cases, you can port and test modules using minimal project-to-project communications until the entire system is running in one programming environment.

If you want to interface from VBA with an application written in the AutoLISP or ARX environments, you must contact the vendor of the other products to see what options may exist. You can run commands created by these tools, but you cannot run functions or individual utilities unless they support a command line–based start option.

As mentioned earlier, you can use AutoLISP to start a VBA project. When you use the VBARUN command in this manner, the AutoLISP system is suspended until the VBA application is finished. Thus, if you need to send information from AutoLISP to the VBA program, you need to set up the transfer before starting the macro via VBARUN. Also, returning data from the VBA macro will be available immediately after the macro has finished and control has been returned to AutoLISP. Your host AutoLISP program will have no direct way of knowing if the VBA run was a success. That's why the VBARUN launch method is recommended only for menu usage or to allow a veteran AutoCAD user the luxury of starting your VBA macro from the command line.

Late and Early Binding in VBA

One factor that can greatly increase the speed of execution of a VBA project that uses multiple projects or involves objects from other ActiveX applications is when you make the binding between the various objects. *Binding* is the computer term that means the objects are connecting with each other. When a VBA program loads another project, it is binding with the project. When a VBA program attaches to the Excel spreadsheet system, it is binding with Excel. An object reference in your program will not know anything about what it is referencing until that binding is made. And that can take a while in some environments. For example, if Excel is used and is not loaded, it must be loaded first before your program can continue.

In early binding, the program knows about the objects it will be working with in the course of the application. When a library is referenced into a project, the early binding is available for use as you write the program code. In other words, your application can be made ready to work with the objects and know quite a bit about them even though the complete linkage is not fully enabled. To illustrate, you can define an object variable using the general-purpose type object, or you can define it as the exact type of data you will be manipulating. When your program is run, the object will have to be evaluated and set up to work with the object assignment. If the object type is already known, then the object is ready to go as soon as the linkage is available and no further processing is required by VBA at run time in regards to the type of object being manipulated.

For most ActiveX application interfaces, and when you're dealing with other projects with custom object definitions, using early binding in your coding will impact the run time. You can test this by trying to do everything with general object definitions and time the difference when the same objects are defined as being the target object type right away.

Multiple Projects in Release 14

It's easy to manage multiple projects in VBA through the use of the project manager utility provided in AutoCAD 2000. In AutoCAD Release 14, VBA is not able to manipulate multiple projects at the same time, and borrowing code between them requires that you make modules (BAS files) that can be attached to each of the projects. You should implement tighter programming controls at sites that use this approach, as a change to a BAS module may cause problems with other projects already built and working fine.

Data sharing is not relevant in Release 14, either, as two projects cannot coexist in the system at the same time. If your application requires that sort of power, it is time to upgrade the platform on which it is to run.

The differences between AutoCAD Release 14 and AutoCAD 2000 in terms of VBA are tremendous. VBA is much more powerful in AutoCAD 2000 than in AutoCAD Release 14. That's why most of the applications and examples in this book have dealt with AutoCAD 2000 specifically and not with both releases.

CHAPTER NINE

API Calls from VBA

A lthough VBA programs run inside of AutoCAD, they also run inside of Windows, and there are times when an application needs to perform tasks related to the operating system. This is where VBA greatly exceeds the abilities of AutoLISP. You can talk to Windows by calling functions that are available as objects and utilities to your program.

What's an API?

API is an acronym for Application Programmer's Interface. The Windows Application Programmer's Interface is a set of functions built into Windows that allow you to access the system's registry and INI files. Microsoft has included a robust set of information about the system in the registry, and you can write more exotic applications using this information. You can write sound generator programs or programs that animate the desktop or draw on it. Windows API is a whole world unto itself, and many a career has been made learning and using it.

AutoLISP programmers have not been able to access the Windows registry and therefore have limited or no experience with this rich environment. You can access any information stored in the registry through the API calls. This includes ActiveX information about other applications or even information about your printer or plotter. It all depends on the vendor setting up the information in the registry.

An example is AutoCAD and AutoCAD LT. AutoCAD is an ActiveX client and server. It can make calls to other applications, or it can receive calls from other applications. It has a switch that can be used to tell it that it is being used as a server (/Automation). When you use an API in a language such as VB to GetObject and tell it you want the AutoCAD.application, the function searches the Windows registry to see if AutoCAD is registered as an ActiveX application and uses the information, when found, to find AutoCAD and attach it to the object. An application like AutoCAD LT (the AutoCAD engine stripped down) is not directly programmable from VB because the hook inside the registry is missing and the switch has been turned off inside the application. By now, you're probably saying to yourself, "Great, but what's that got to do with VBA?" Simple: VBA supports the API calls necessary to access the system registry. You won't want to use it for attaching and manipulating AutoCAD because you're already inside AutoCAD, but you can still use it to access other applications that are ActiveX compliant. You can also use it to access INI files, directory information, file information, and printer information. It's great for querying the system to find out how much space you have left on a drive or how much memory is available. The list goes on and on. This chapter looks at only a few of the more common API calls you might regularly use. For more extensive reading on Windows APIs, we suggest that you pick up one of the many books on the subject. We recommend PC Magazine's Visual Basic Programmer's Guide to the Win32 API by Daniel Appleman (published by Ziff-Davis Press) for its coverage of topics such as directory and file APIs and system information.

The API Viewer

The API viewer is a handy little tool. Unfortunately, the program does not ship with AutoCAD VBA. You must purchase a separate language package such as VB or C++ to get it. We cover it here for those who might want to explore this tool further. If you are going to use API calls, then you must either buy a book that covers them in depth or get access to this program and its support data. We suggest doing both. For those of you who need to do it on the cheap, get your hands on just the Win32api.txt file and use any ASCII text editor as your search engine.

The viewer is a program that allows access to a text file or database containing all of the Declares, Constants, and Types for the Windows API calls. You can search either a text API file or a Jet database for a call and find its declaration. When you select a list of items you are going to use, it copies them into the Windows clipboard, allowing you to then paste them into your application's declaration section. This is certainly much easier than purchasing a book, then typing in each declare, constant, or type.

Once you declare an API declaration in your program, it is available in the program's procedures (depending on the scope of the declaration). Some API calls return strings, integers, or longs. Others might or might not return information, but they place the data in a buffer that is defined in the calling parameters. The latter is a little tricky to work with since you must then strip off the end of the line character and trim the string to get just the information you want.

Using the viewer program is very simple. When you launch the program, a dialog interface is shown as in Figure 9.1.

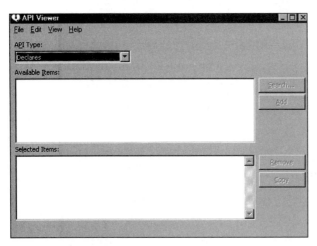

Figure 9.1: API Viewer interface

Load a text or database file into the program by using the File/Load Text File menu item. Several are shipped with the program but the one you will use most is the Win32api.txt file (or its database equivalent should you use the Convert text to database menu item to convert it into a Jet database). Once the file is loaded into the program a list appears in the Available Items list box. You can change from a list of Declarations to a list of Types or Constants by using the pull-down list labeled API Type, as shown in Figure 9.2.

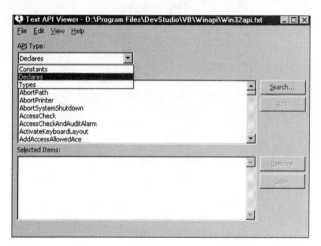

Figure 9.2: API Types pull-down menu

The Search button allows you to search for a specific item while the Add button allows you to add the item to the Selected Items list box. The Remove button allows you to remove an item from the Selected Items list box, and the Copy button allows you to place the items in the Selected Items list box into the clipboard for pasting into your program's declaration area.

The problem with this program is that it expects you to already know the declaration you are looking for. The search engine is keyed on the declaration names. You can use the slide bar on the list box window to scan all of the items, but that is very time consuming, and not all declaration names are intuitive. That's why we suggest that you purchase a book that explains what each declaration can do, then use the program to go find them instead of having to type them in by hand.

INI File Calls

INI files are simply ASCII text files in a set format that allows the programmer access to information to be used by the program. Opening, closing, reading, and writing in VBA is straightforward even though the reading and writing functions have many options. Simple ASCII text file manipulation does not require API calls. To experiment with examples of this type of file manipulation, load the project called FileIO.dvb provided on the accompanying CD and run the macro IOEXAMPLE from the immediate window. Simple input and output operations are provided as an example of ASCII file manipulation without API calls.

Many AutoLISP programmers have had to create their own routines for accessing INI files because the AutoLISP language does not have access to the API calls. Routines that segregate the sections, keys, and items into lists that allow the programmer to process the item data are not part of that language. You can build the same routines in VB and VBA, but you don't need to because those languages have access to the API calls for accessing INI files. There are two API calls that are used to retrieve and write item data in an INI file. They are

- GetPrivateProfileString; and

- WritePrivateProfileString.

Both of these API calls return a long telling you how many characters were placed in their string buffers. You can use this information to authenticate that you have written the number of characters back to the file when using the WritePrivateProfileString API call and you must use it to trim unwanted and unused space in the string buffer returned from the GetPrivateProfileString API call.

How the PrivateProfileString APIs Work

It is important to understand how API calls work in general. Both of these calls return information in the traditional way (passing back a long data type that tells you how many characters were in the buffer), but they also use the string buffer in their argument list to hold returned information. In fact, it is the string buffer argument that has the information you really want to process! The returned long is just the character count of the actual data in the buffer. This is typical of many

API calls, so a more detailed analysis of the API declaration will help in understanding API calls in general.

API Declaration breakdown

Let's start with the GetPrivateProfileString API call declaration and break down what it is doing. This is the function declaration that is placed in your declaration section. It is as follows on one line of code:

> **Declare Function GetPrivateProfileString Lib "kernel32" Alias "GetPrivateProfileStringA" (ByVal lpApplicationName As String, ByVal lpKeyName As Any, ByVal lpDefault As String, ByVal lpReturnedString As String, ByVal nSize As Long, ByVal lpFileName As String) As Long**

This is lengthy and worthy of understanding. Here is each piece broken down as to what it does:

- **Declare** tells VBA that you are starting the declaration (works like Dim, Public, or Private).

- **Function** is the type of procedure. A function returns a value while a subroutine would simply perform an action.

- **GetPrivateProfileString** is the name of the function.

- **Lib "kernel32"** is the name of the Windows library containing the function.

- **Alias "GetPrivateProfileStringA"** defines which internal function name in the library you want assigned to your function name. This is necessary because many API functions have different internal definitions for 16- or 32-bit functions, and many times a version works with only ASCII or Unicode. The A at the end of this alias means that it works on ASCII code.

- **ByVal lpApplicationName As String** is the section header name as the data type string.

- **ByVal lpKeyName As Any** is the key name as either a string or a Null value. The **Any** data type means that you are deferring the data type to when you use the call. Then the VBA interpreter will determine the data type of the data you pass in and act accordingly.

- **ByVal lpDefault As String** is a default return value placed in the result string buffer should the call fail to find any data.

- **ByVal lpReturnedString As String** is the string buffer that is filled with the data you are requesting.

- **ByVal nSize As Long** is the specified length of the string buffer that is returned.

- **ByVal lpFileName As String** is the name of the INI file you wish to access. Full path and extension are necessary.

- **As Long** is the returned number of characters in the string buffer.

There are a few items here that are very important to consider when you are declaring your API call:

1. It really doesn't matter what you name the arguments in the declaration. Even Microsoft changes them in the examples from version to version. Since you are using them in your program, you can call them what you want. Only the alias name must remain the same to ensure that you are getting the correct function from the library.

2. The alias function name for the library specifies which library function to use. If you forget the **A** at the end of the alias function name, your function will not work properly with ASCII text files.

3. A data type of Any (used for the lpKeyName argument) allows you to pass either a string to search for or a string having a value of 0 (vbNullString). A vbNullString being passed in tells the function to return a list of all keys in the INI file, separated by a Null character, in the string buffer. Just the keys are returned in this situation, not their items. You can then spin through the string buffer with your handy dandy parser function (see Chapter 10) and check out each key in the

file. This option is often used to gather a list of all keys in a file for examination. It should be noted that some programmers prefer to use two declarations, with different names, when they are dealing with an argument that has the **Any** data type. The thought process behind this is that it is clearer to have two slightly different declarations to keep track of, each one declaring specifically the data type to be used for the argument. Then they just use the proper one for the job rather than trust to memory that the one argument can be either data type.

4. The default string can be a zero-length string.

5. The returned string is a fixed-length string buffer that you must set up before the call. The returned value always ends in a Null string character [chr$(0)]. You must remove the Null string and any trailing characters before processing the string, or functions such as Len will report back erroneous information. For functions such as the PrivateProfileString function that returns a long telling you how many characters were put into the string buffer, the matter is simple. Use the Left function to parse out your data from the buffer. Other API functions don't report back how many characters are in the buffer, and that can be a small problem. For those situations you must find the length of the data, then parse it out. This is not all that difficult; the function you need to do it is supplied in Chapter 10: it is called StripTerminator.

6. The size argument must be large enough to hold all of the data. If it is not, the data is truncated.

7. If no filename is supplied, the default value is returned in the string buffer.

There are a few words of caution that we must share regarding the use of these API calls. To show them we need to use a code example as follows. This code shows a typical use of the API function. The string variables strSection, strKey, strDefault, and strIniFile and the global constant gintMAX_SIZE are assumed to have been already defined.

```
Dim strBuffer As String
Dim strResult As String
Dim lngPos As Long
strBuffer = Space$(gintMAX_SIZE)
lngPos = GetPrivateProfileString (strSection, strKey, strDefault, _
strBuffer, gintMAX_SIZE, strIniFile)
```

There are some subtle nuisances to the code shown in the above figure. First is the use of separate declarations for the strBuffer and strResult strings.

Many experienced VBA programmers prefer to use the handy shortcut of declaring like variables on the same line. A single-line declaration for the two variables follows.

```
Dim strBuffer, strResult As String
```

The code looks good and does not cause a compile (to pcode) or run-time error. But it does not work! The reason is that the strBuffer variable must be a string, and the declaration is actually setting it to a Variant type. This is because VBA assigns a default data type of Variant when no data type is specified, and the shortcut shown in the above code only assigns the string data type to the second (strResult) variable, not the first variable listed. In most situations the shortcut works because VBA is very forgiving but in this situation it does not work. To make sure that the data type you want for each variable is assigned to each variable listed in a shortcut, you must declare the data type for each variable as shown in the code below.

```
Dim strBuffer as String, strResult As String
```

Once the strBuffer variable is properly declared the string must be initialized to spaces. The line of code strBuffer = Space$(gintMAX_SIZE) places the specified amount of spaces defined in the global integer gintMAX_SIZE into the string. For clarity, gintMAX_SIZE is defined elsewhere in our program module and has an integer value specifying the size of the strings to be used.

If the size is too small for the returning data, the API truncates the returned data. We must also point out that you must initiate the buffer before giving it to the API as an argument. Should you not do so, the program will fail. When calling the API functions, VBA is really calling into a library of modules that have different specific requirements. In addition, they were written in different computer languages that have alternative ways of representing string variable data. The problem is that the API function called has no way of knowing how long a string you declared for the argument. You must define the length of the string so as not to overwrite any other variables in your memory pool. Finding this sort of error tracing and debugging can consume a lot of time.

Another important thing to remember about the resulting string data is that it is terminated with the Null string character chr$(0). The null string terminator is typically used in C/C++ programming, which should give you some idea as to what languages are used to create the API functions in the first place.

There is another technique for dealing with the string buffer's return argument size:

1. Initialize the string buffer to just one character and call the API function.

2. Examine the returned counter of the characters that should be in the buffer.

3. Use the returned number to reinitialize the string buffer and call the API again.

This involves some extra coding but it ensures that the returned buffer is exactly the length you need, so you don't need to strip it of trailing characters. The following code demonstrates the alternative way of getting the data.

```
Dim strBuffer As String
Dim strResult As String
Dim intPos As Integer
strBuffer = Space$(1)
```

```
intPos = GetPrivateProfileString(strSection, strKey, "default",
strBuffer, gintMAX_SIZE, strIniFile)

If intPos > 1 then

    strBuffer = Space$(intPos)

intPos = GetPrivateProfileString(strSection, strKey, "default",
strBuffer, gintMAX_SIZE, strIniFile)

End If
```

WritePrivateProfileString API Call

The WritePrivateProfileString API call declaration behaves much the same as its opposite, Get API call. The only difference is that there is no default argument. The returned long is a counter of how many characters were written to the file. The function always checks to see if the key you wish to write to is present in the section you requested. When the key is found, the function replaces the item information that is there with what you supply. When it is not found it writes the new key and item information at the end of the section. This is the function declaration on one line of code that is placed in your declaration section for the writing of INI file information:

Declare Function WritePrivateProfileString Lib "kernel32" Alias "WritePrivateProfileStringA" (ByVal lpApplicationName As String, ByVal lpKeyName As Any, ByVal lpString As Any, ByVal lpFileName As String) As Long

For a detailed breakdown of the arguments and their behavior, refer to the section on the GetPrivateProfileString function covered earlier in this chapter.

This section was designed to give you a better feel for API calls and the one used most commonly for INI files. There are several other API functions for dealing with INI files in general, including:

- GetPrivateProfileSection

- GetPrivateProfileInt

There are others that are specifically built for working with the Win.ini file. For more information on these and many other INI file API calls see the API viewer program or a good book on APIs.

Experiment with INI file manipulation by loading the project called INIFileIO.dvb supplied on the CD with this book and run the macro INIEXAMPLE from the immediate window from inside AutoCAD.

Registry Calls

Microsoft introduced the registry in Windows 95 and NT. It essentially replaced INI files (although you can still find many system INI files hanging around the Windows system directory for backward compatibility issues). The registry is made up of three binary files that you access through API calls. It is important to know how it works: It is set up along the lines of the INI file. You can have an Application name (which corresponds to the INI file name), a Section header (the same as in the INI file), and a key and item (again the same as in an INI file). A program for navigating the registry is supplied by Microsoft and called Regedit.exe. It represents the registry as a hierarchy of folders stemming from 'My Computer'. All application names, section headers, keys, and items are located under the 'folder' VB and VBA Program Settings. The location of the VB and VBA Program Settings folder differs depending upon the operating system of the computer. They are as follows:

Windows 95

```
HKEY_CURRENT_USER\Software\VB and VBA Program Settings
HKEY_USERS\.Default\Software\VB and VBA Program Settings
```

Windows NT

```
HKEY_CURRENT_USER\Software\VB and VBA Program Settings
```

An NT box will also mirror the settings in your personal profile area of the registry. Notice that the one common location on both systems is the HKEY_CURRENT_USER area. You can use the Regedit program to view your program's results when saving to the registry. Figure 9.3 shows the

Figure 9.3: Windows 95 Program Settings location

register editor open to the VBA Book's General key.

The sample project (RegistryIO) supplied with this book creates, reads, and removes the VBA Book registry entry shown above to show you how the VBA registry functions work. We will cover more on how it does that later in this chapter.

The Registry Editor

The program name for both Windows platforms is Regedit.exe, and it is found in your Windows folder. Windows NT has a 32-bit version (called Regedt32.exe) that separates each section into its own window. This is located in the Windows System32 directory. They both allow access to the registry for creating, editing, and removing registry items. They just organize the viewing of the registry differently.

You can start the program by double clicking on it in Explorer or by using the Run program menu item on the Start menu of Windows. Figure 9.4 shows how the registry looks when first opened using the Regedit program.

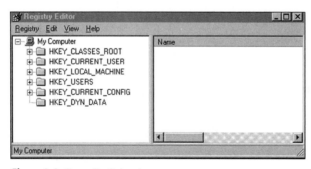

Figure 9.4: Regedit dialog box

Each key of the registry is used for organizing the system. Most of your work will be with the HKEY_CURRENT_USER root key as stated earlier in this chapter. All registry root keys are described in Table 9.1.

Table 9.1: Registry root keys

Root Key	Description
HKEY_CLASSES_ROOT	Stores information about classes of files and objects, associations between document types and applications, and class identifiers used by OLE objects.
HKEY_CURRENT_USER	Contains current configuration information for the current user.
HKEY_LOCAL_MACHINE	Contains in-depth information about hardware and software configuration on the system.
HKEY_USERS	Contains software and system configuration information that is unique to a particular user.
HKEY_CURRENT_CONFIG	Used to store general system configuration information. Used by Windows 95.
HKEY_DYN_DATA	Used to hold temporary data about current session. Windows 95 only.

The program has an import and export feature. The export feature takes whatever key you're on and stores it, along with its whole hierarchy all of the way up to the root key, into an ASCII file with a .REG extension that the import feature can use to recreate the registry on your system or any other. Another feature is the edit menu. With it, you can add a new key or section header and edit any existing keys.

While checking and working with the registry, you can refresh the view at any time with the function key F5. This is handy for verifying when your program deletes or adds items to the registry.

A final warning: Be careful in the registry. You can delete or change information about your computer that will totally cripple it! You should be safe if you stay in the VB and VBA Program Settings area under the root key HKEY_CURRENT_USER.

The VBA Registry Functions

There are more than twenty API calls built for dealing with various aspects of the registry. They include functions for retrieving values from keys, saving to the registry, dealing with registry information saved to a file, loading registry information, and dealing with a remote system's registry. The most commonly used functions for accessing the registry are not even API calls but are included with VBA. They are methods of the Interaction module in VBA. They are as follows:

- GetSetting

- SaveSetting

- DeleteSetting

The setting modules are used to get key information from a registry, save information to a key in the registry, and delete registry items. They are able to access only the special location in the registry under VBA and VBA Program Settings. Figure 9.5 shows the results of writing to the registry using the sample project supplied with the book.

Notice that the VBA Book is hanging directly off the VB and VBA Program Settings folder. This is a matter of programming style because there are no formal conventions for the VBA section of the registry. Some programmers will place a folder called Software under the VB and VBA Program Settings folder, then place all of their registry settings under that folder (you can see in Figure 9.5 that it has been done on our system in the past). This is done by placing a multiple folder name in the application name of the SaveSetting function. This is something we could not do with INI files. We have only the one

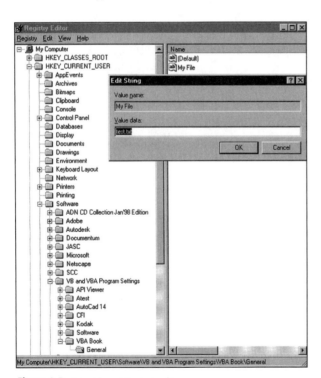

Figure 9.5: Sample project results

name we can use with INI files. Here you can specify as many levels deep as you like for the application name (very much like a directory structure). The original function call to create the registry entry seen in Figure 9.5 was

```
Call SaveSetting("VBA Book", "General", "My File", "test")
```

You could move the whole thing under the Software folder by changing the line to:

```
Call SaveSetting("Software\VBA Book", "General", "My File", "test")
```

This is a very straightforward method and simple to use. You can have as many levels deep as you like in the first argument. They will all hang under the VB and VBA Program Settings folder in the registry, and section, key, and item will hang under them.

Reading the information is the reverse of saving it. You use the GetSetting function and give it the exact same parameters, except it does not need the item argument. It returns the item information in string format.

Removing the registry entry is just as simple with the DeleteSetting function. You can remove data at any level just by supplying the name in the correct position of the function call's argument list.

To remove a key:

```
DeleteSetting "VBA Book", "General", "My File"
```

To remove a section header:

```
DeleteSetting "VBA Book", "General"
```

To remove the application name:

```
DeleteSetting "VBA Book"
```

The setting functions are all you really need to do most of the registry work you might want. You can store a dialog box's position on screen for later use or program settings for the next time the program runs. All of the things you did with INI files can be done with the registry. For more exotic registry applications read up on the registry API functions in the

API viewer and relating books. They're easy to find because they all have the Reg prefix. To see an example of the setting functions in action, load the RegistryIO.dvb project file and run the Regaccess form. The form, shown in Figure 9.6, is set up to default to the application name, section, and key shown in the registry examples earlier in the chapter.

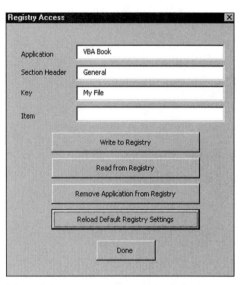

You can use the Regedit program to examine the results for your computer and experiment with keys and item data. Step through the code one line at a time to get a feel for how the functions work.

Figure 9.6: Registry Access example form

System Calls

VBA has a robust set of functions for dealing with the system's data on the hard drive, the date, and the time. You can find out information about the functions, manipulate their files and directories, and get the current time and date. What VBA doesn't supply is functions for querying the system's environment for information (other than time and date). API functions also have a robust set of function calls for the hard drive, but it is easier for most programmers to use the built-in VBA functions. Most programmers don't bother with the API calls for files and directories unless they have a feature that the VBA function doesn't—or they just like using the API calls better. Table 9.2 shows a comparison of the VBA functions with the API function calls. Blank spaces mean that the function doesn't exist for that environment.

Table 9.2: VBA and API function call comparison

Function description	VBA function name	API function name
Directory information	Dir	GetCurrentDirectory
Remove a file	Kill	DeleteFile
Copy a file	FileCopy	CopyFile
Retrieve a file's length	FileLen	GetFileSize
Retrieve a file's date and time	FileDateTime	GetFileTime
Set a file's date and time		SetFileTime
Retrieve a file's attribute settings	GetAttr	GetFileAttributes
Set a file's attribute settings	SetAttr	SetFileAttributes
System date	Date	GetSystemTime
Local time	Time	GetLocalTime
Computer's name		GetComputerName
User's login name		GetUserName
System time		GetSystemTime
Window's temporary directory		GetTempPath
Free hard drive space		GetDiskFreeSpace
System environmental variable		GetEnvironmentVariable
Format time and date data		GetTimeFormat

As the above table shows, some of the system API calls that VBA doesn't mimic are

- retrieving the computer name;

- retrieving the user's login name;

- retrieving the true system time;

- retrieving the Windows temporary directory;

- retrieving a hard drive's free space;

- retrieving a system environmental variable; and

- formatting the time and date.

We have supplied a sample project called WindowsOS.dvb to illustrate these API functions. We discuss each function call below in detail. You can load the project and run the MyComputer subroutine to see the functions in action. Step through the code to see how each one works as the routine builds a message box with all of the answers.

Computer Name

The API function call GetComputerName is used to access the computer's name stored in the registry. This function accepts a string buffer and its length and returns a long telling you how many characters are stored in the string buffer that is returned. A sample call to the function is shown in the following listing.

```
Dim CompName As String
CompName = Space$(50)
LngResult = GetComputerName(CompName, 50)
```

This API is an example of the type that stores data in the argument and returns the number of characters there.

User's Login Name

You can use the API function call GetUserName to access the user's login name stored in the registry. This function accepts a string buffer and its length and returns a long telling you how many characters are stored in the string buffer that is returned. A sample call to the function is shown in the next lines of code.

```
Dim UserName As String
UserName = Space$(50)
LngResult = GetUserName(UserName, 50)
```

This API is an example of the type that stores data in the argument and returns the number of characters there.

System and Local Time

The API function call GetLocalTime is used to access the system's time and date. This function accepts a structure object that must be defined in the user's declaration area since VBA knows nothing of API data structures. Below is the data structure definition.

```
Type SYSTEMTIME
    wYear As Integer
    wMonth As Integer
    wDayOfWeek As Integer
    wDay As Integer
    wHour As Integer
    wMinute As Integer
    wSecond As Integer
    wMilliseconds As Integer
End Type
```

The API function call fills out all of the fields in the structure; you can then process the data any way you like. A sample call to the function follows.

```
Dim sysTime As SYSTEMTIME
GetSystemTime sysTime
```

This API is an example of the type that stores data in a structure (object). Once you have retrieved the data structure, you need to format the data into the form you want. The API function call GetTimeFormat is built explicitly for that purpose. You pass it the filled data structure with a few parameters on how you want the returned data to look, and the function converts the raw data into the format you specified. It then returns it in a string buffer that you pass in.

```
strBuffer$ = String$(255, Chr$(0))
lngResult& = GetTimeFormat(LOCALE_SYSTEM_DEFAULT, 0, sysTime, 0,_
strBuffer$, 254)
```

233

The GetSystemTime API function call performs exactly like the local time function except that it returns the actual system time used by the computer not the local time using the time zone (there is an API function call for getting time zone information called GetTimeZoneInformation). You must also use the GetTimeFormat API function call to get the returned data into the format you want, just like with the local time data. A sample project called WindowsOS.dvb is supplied to illustrate these API functions. Load it and run (stepping through it one line at a time) the macro MyComputer.

The Windows Temporary Directory

You can use the API function call GetTempPath to access the Window's Temporary directory stored in the registry. This function accepts a string buffer and its length and returns a long telling you how many characters are stored in the string buffer that is returned. A sample call to the function is shown as follows.

```
Dim strTempDir As String
strTempDir = Space$(50)
lngResult = GetTempPath(50, strTempDir)
```

This API is an example of the type that stores data in the argument and returns the number of characters that are there. Notice how this function call's syntax is backward from the GetComputerName and GetUserName functions. Its string length is first, and the string buffer is second.

System Environmental Variable

You can use the API function call GetEnvironmentVariable to access the system's variables stored in the registry. This function accepts the environmental variable name, a string buffer, and its length, and it returns a long telling you how many characters are stored in the string buffer that is returned. A sample call to the function getting the Path variable from the system environment is shown next.

```
Dim strVarContents As String
strVarContents = Space$(255)
lngResult = GetEnvironmentVariable("PATH", strVarContents, 255)
```

This API is an example of the type that stores data in the argument and returns the number of characters there.

Free Disk Space

The API function call GetDiskFreeSpace is used to access the system's hard drive information. This function accepts the hard drive designation to check long buffers for returned sectors per cluster, bytes per sector, number of free clusters, and the total number of clusters. We show a sample call to the function getting the information for the C drive.

```
Dim SectorsPerCluster As Long
Dim BytesPerSector As Long
Dim NumberOfFreeClusters As Long
Dim TotalNumberOfClusters As Long
lngResult& = GetDiskFreeSpace("C:\", SectorsPerCluster,
BytesPerSector, NumberOfFreeClusters, TotalNumberOfClusters)
```

In the example above, you have more information than you really wanted, and nowhere is the number of free bytes for the drive. This is because the number of bytes available on a hard drive depends upon such variable factors as the size of a cluster and sector. For you purists out there, you might say that it is another level deeper at the hardware level and you would be right. There you need to consider such factors as cylinders, heads, physical sectors, bad block mapping, and so on. Thankfully, most programmers do not need to concern themselves with these issues unless they are working on device drivers (not a domain for VBA programmers). These numbers are good enough to work with in VBA. Once you have these numbers, it is easy to get the actual free bytes on the drive. The following code fragment shows what is needed to extract that information from the returned information.

```
TotalBytes = TotalNumberOfClusters * SectorsPerCluster * BytesPer-
Sector

FreeBytes = NumberOfFreeClusters * SectorsPerCluster *
BytesPerSector
```

While the API call doesn't give you back the exact number you want, it does give you back the numbers you need to determine the number you want. Like they say, do the math.

Conclusion

The API function calls covered in this chapter are just a tip of the iceberg. The six or seven API function calls we covered are the ones you might use on a regular basis, but there are literally hundreds of these calls into various corners of the Windows system. As your applications become more and more sophisticated, you may find that the investment in an API book is well worth your while.

CHAPTER TEN

VBA Toolbox Routines

While VBA has many built-in functions for manipulating strings and other data types, it's still up to the programmer to create support functions for those situations that the VBA language does not support. A VBA programmer must develop his or her own toolbox routines that are best suited to the application being developed. Using the basic functions supplied in VBA, the programmer creates new utilities to speed up the process of creating reports on screen or in a file, stripping information out of a string for other uses, dealing with directories and paths, and many other situations. This chapter covers several of the routines necessary for working in the AutoCAD environment. Many of the routines in this chapter are VBA versions of AutoLISP toolbox routines created for *The AutoLISP Programmer's Toolbox* (MIS Press). A special thanks to the management of MIS press is in order for granting permission to use some of the same material for this chapter.

The test functions that are supplied with this chapter on the CD show how to use the functions. We have placed a stop breakpoint in each test function so you can use the step next debug feature to walk through the toolbox functions to see how they work. Many programmers won't care:

it's enough to know that you pass in some data and the function passes out what you want—and this chapter is structured around that principle. We have documented each function as to what the syntax of the function call is and what data is returned. We have covered example situations, but they are by no means the only way you can use these toolbox functions.

Definition of Terms

character	A string with a length of one character.
control data string	A string of data passed as an argument to the routine.
data item	A string, substring, integer, or a real number.
substring	A group of characters inside a string.
control	A form control.

Toolbox Overview

The toolbox functions presented here are from actual projects and may or may not be of use to you specifically. These functions solve a variety of simple problems, and , like objects, are re-usable. That is, you can copy them into your current project and use them to help in your programming should you find a need for the same functionality.

For each toolbox entry, we have provided a description of the syntax for that function including its parameter list. We have then described the arguments supplied as parameters in more detail and have detailed conditions under which the utility is expected to function. We have also itemized the returning value or resulting action. Next, we have described, in general terms, the situation in which the utility might be used and have provided the examples on the CD that is supplied with the book.

The selections on the opposite page are presented in alphabetical order by each function's description header.

Acquiring Data Items from a Data String

Syntax: parse (string, character, integer)

Arguments: Where the *string* is the control data string to be searched.

Where the *character* is the delimiter between data items.

Where the *integer* is the position of the data item in the string.

Conditions: The string must be in string form.

The character can be any legal ASCII character in string form.

The integer must be a positive value.

Returns: A string containing the data between the delimiters or the end of the string.

Situation:

A common way of transferring data into a routine from a data file is to place the data on a line with a delimiter between each piece of data. The delimiter can be any legal ASCII character, but you want to use a character that would not normally appear in the data. Many programmers use a comma or the pipe symbol (|). Once you read in the line of data to a text string you can extract a specific data item from the string using the position in the string record. This means you must know what each position in the string is used for. The routine will return the string data item from the requested position in the form of a string.

CD Example:

To test the function, open any drawing, load the Toolbox project, and type PARSE_TEST in the immediate window of the Visual Basic Editor.

CD Example Result:

A series of message boxes showing the position and the content of each of the sub-strings being parsed.

Add Back Slashes Result to a Path String

Syntax: add_backslashes (string)

Arguments: Where the *string* is the directory path that might need extra back slashes.

Conditions: The string must be in string form.

Returns: A string with two back slashes in place of each single one found.

Situation:

Both the AutoLISP and BaseLISP (Cyco Workflow) languages view the single back slash as a flag to treat the next character literally instead of as a special character. This means that if you are creating a line that is going to one of these languages for processing, you need to fix it with double back slashes. A common situation is the string path for a file name. In VBA, it needs only single back slashes, but in the other languages, it needs two. This function takes a string and doubles its back slashes. You can then use it by jamming it down to AutoLISP or to BaseLISP through a DDE connection to Cyco's Workflow.

CD Example:

To test the function, open any drawing, load the Toolbox project, and type BACK2_TEST in the immediate window of the Visual Basic Editor.

CD Example Result:

A message box showing the results of processing both types of strings (one without any back slashes and one with).

Add Trailing Back Slash to a String Path

Syntax: adddirsep (*string*)

Arguments: Where the *string* is the directory path that might
                 need a back slash at the end.

Conditions: The string must be in string form.

Returns: A string containing the original path with a back
                 slash added at the end. When the original string
                 already has a back slash at the end, the original string
                 is returned.

Situation:

When you have a string that you know has a path in it but you're not
sure that the path ends in a directory separator, this function takes the
string and returns it with the separator added. This is typical when you
have a directory path in an INI file or the registry and you need to make
sure you can use it with a file name.

CD Example:

To test the function, open any drawing, load the Toolbox project, and
type BACKSLASH_TEST in the immediate window of the Visual Basic
Editor.

CD Example Result:

A message box showing the results of processing both types of strings.

Convert an Object's Entity Type to English

Syntax: enttype (*object*)

Arguments: Where the *object* is a VBA generic object.

Conditions: The object must contain a legal AutoCAD entity object.

Returns: A string containing the English translation of the object type.

Situation:

Each AutoCAD object in the object model has an entity type number associated with it. Autodesk has supplied a slightly English version of the number using enumeration but each type has the characters *ac* as a prefix. This function takes the entity object and translates the entity type into plain English. Instead of acCircle, you would get Circle for a circle entity object. This makes checking in your code a little easier to read and debug.

CD Example:

To test the function, open any drawing, load the Toolbox project, and type ENT_TEST in the immediate window of the Visual Basic Editor. The main work is being done in the form's btnGetObj_Click procedure. We have provided no stop in this example because it would leave you in the VBE window when AutoCAD wants a response on the AutoCAD graphics screen. It's too confusing unless you want to try it yourself.

CD Example Result:

A message box stating the entity object's entity type in plain English.

Count the Number of Occurences of a Delimiter in a String

Syntax: Syntax: count_occurrences (*string, character*)

Arguments: Where the *string* is any string.

Where the *character* is any character that is to be checked.

Conditions: The string must be in string form.

The character can be any legal ASCII character in string form.

Returns: A long number containing the number of delimiters found in the string.

Situation:

Many times you will need to determine that a path is present in a file name. Checking to see if a colon or back slash is present in the string is one way of doing it. The function can also be used to determine that a string is in the correct format for parsing. It is always a good idea to check your data before processing it. You almost never have full control of data being read into your routine. When you expect a string with five items separated by delimiters, you can use this function to double check that the line you are about to process has the correct number of delimiters in it. Then you can make a programmatic decision on what to do with erroneous data lines.

CD Example:

To test the function, open any drawing, load the Toolbox project, and type COUNT_TEST in the immediate window of the Visual Basic Editor.

CD Example Result:

A message box appears telling you the results of the test.

Create a Directory Path

Syntax:	Create_path (*string*)
Arguments:	Where the *string* is the path to be created.
Conditions:	The string must be in string form. It should be noted that this function will not create a path that uses the UNC. This is due to the limitation of the MkDir function in VBA.
Returns:	True unless the last part of the path caused an error.

Situation:

When you're manipulating files on the system it is sometimes necessary to move or copy a file to a directory you are not sure exists. There are functions to determine the existence of a path, and the MkDir function will create a new directory but only when the parent directory of the new directory already exists. This function allows you to give the whole path you want created, and it will create the whole path for you whether part of it already exists or not.

CD Example:

To test the function, open any drawing, load the Toolbox project, and type PATH_TEST in the immediate window of the Visual Basic Editor.

CD Example Result:

The path C:\TEMP\VBA is created on your hard drive whether you already had a C:\TEMP or not.

Determine the Tense of a Word

Syntax: chk_plural (*integer1, integer2*)

Arguments: Where *integer1* is a count of the number of items in a list or some other count of items in the form of 0 or a positive number.

Where *integer2* is a word code, in the numeric form of 1, 2, 3, or 4, containing the requested output to be returned.

Conditions: Both integers must be in numeric form.

Returns: A string containing a singular or plural word that corresponds to the requested word code.

Situation:

The cosmetics of your program's interface with the user counts more than you might guess. A program that gets the jobs done but does not present the solution to the user in a professional format often is judged as an inferior program. Making your program intelligent when it goes to print out a sentence can make the program seem superior. Legal word codes are as follows:

- 1 returns "s" or nothing ("")
- 2 returns "are" or "is"
- 3 returns "were" or "was"
- 4 returns "have" or "has"

CD Example:

To test the function, open any drawing, load the Toolbox project, and type PLURAL_TEST in the immediate window of the Visual Basic Editor.

CD Example Result:

A message box showing the sentence using proper tense on the words that relate to the number of items found.

Display a Fatal Error Message

Syntax: fatal_error (*integer, string*)

Arguments: Where the *integer* is a number from 1 to 4 representing the error message to display in an alert box.

Where the *string* contains the data to display in the alert box message.

Conditions: The integer argument must be in the form of a number from 1 to 4.

The string argument must be in the form of a string.

Returns: An alert dialog box containing the error code number and a message about the data. An exit function is then issued to stop processing.

Situation:

Certain situations must stop the process of your program. Many a program depends upon data from an ini, cfg, or dat file. This function issues a message box for four of those situations dealing with files and has a trap for unknown error codes. You can add your own to the function. The supplied errors are

1 - A missing file.

2 - The file could not be opened.

3 - A missing section header in an INI file.

4 - A missing key in an INI file.

CD Example:

To test the function, open any drawing, load the Toolbox project, and type FATAL_TEST in the immediate window of the Visual Basic Editor.

CD Example Result:

Message boxes showing whether the specified files were found. The file not found calls the fatal error subroutine and ends the program.

Find a File

Syntax:	Findfile (*string*).
Arguments:	Where the *string* is a file name and extension (with or without an explicit path).
Conditions:	The string must be in string form.
Returns:	The file, extension, and path in one string when found or NULL when not found.

Situation:

This function mimics the Findfile function in the AutoLISP language, which searches down the AutoCAD search hierarchy looking for the first occurrence of the file it finds. The only difference between it and its AutoLISP cousin is that a NULL is returned instead of a nil when the file is not found. This allows you to use the IsNull function to test the returned value.

CD Example:

To test the function, open any drawing, load the Toolbox project, and type FINDFILE_TEST in the immediate window of the Visual Basic Editor.

CD Example Result:

Message boxes showing whether the specified files were found.

Find a Line in a List Box Control

Syntax:	Lst_Memb_Pos (*string, control*)
Arguments:	Where the *string* is the control data string to be searched.
	Where the *control* is the listbox control.
Conditions:	The string must be in string form.
	The control must be a listbox form control.
Returns:	The index number of the string in the list box when found. Zero is returned when the string is not found in the listbox.

Situation:

When loading a listbox control with data, many programmers want to then display a default item in the listbox. You can accomplish this by storing the default line (usually stored in an INI file or in the registry) and then matching it in the listbox data once it is loaded. Should the line be missing from the listbox data, a 0 ensures that the first item in the list is displayed. This function accomplishes the task of determining what the index number of the item is or returning the default 0 when it can't find it. The more data in the listbox, the slower the search.

CD Example:

There is no example for this function. The toolbox also has a VB version of this function called LST_MEMB_IDX. To build your own example, create a form and give it a listbox control. In the UserForm_Initialize subroutine, load the list and call this function giving it a default line item. Take the returned value and use it in the Setfocus method for the listbox.

Find an Application Window

Syntax:	findwindow (*string*)
Arguments:	Where the *string* is the name found in the application window.
Conditions:	The string must be in string form.
Returns:	A long integer representing the handle of the application window when found. A 0 is returned when the application window is not found.

Situation:

When working with other applications from VBA in AutoCAD, it's a good idea to check to see if the other application is already launched before you send information to it. That way, you can launch the application when it is missing and not have your program crash. This function uses Windows APIs to search for the application's caption in its application window. There are many windows in the background, so the function has to churn though them all checking their captions for a match. The example searches for the AutoCAD Text window because it must be there for VBA to be running. You can substitute any application's caption and search for it instead. API functions were discussed in more detail in Chapter 9.

CD Example:

To test the function, open any drawing, load the Toolbox project, and type FIND_TEST in the immediate window of the Visual Basic Editor.

CD Example Result:

A message box stating the results of the search (in this case, it found the application window).

Format a Point in a String

Syntax:	FormatPnt (*string, integer*)
Arguments:	Where the *string* is a part of a point (a real number) in a string.
	Where the *integer* is the current LUPREC setting of the drawing.
Conditions:	The string must be in string form.
	The integer must be a positive value.
Returns:	The point string conforming to the supplied units setting.

Situation:

Many times you will wish to show the user a selected point on the dialog box. You must break up the point into its X, Y, and Z components, convert them to strings, then build the new string point for display. These steps are straightforward enough, but it is always nice to display the point in the current drawing precision format. This function takes the string containing the partial point and returns the point in the current drawing precision format (assuming that you supplied it to the function). The precision is supplied as an argument instead of being coded into the function to give the function more flexibility. This way you can force a precision that is not the current drawing precision.

CD Example:

To test the function, open any drawing, load the Toolbox project, and type FORMATPNT_TEST in the immediate window of the Visual Basic Editor.

CD Example Result:

The point string is built and displayed in a message box. See the test routine to view how the point was assembled.

Get the Current View's Corner Points

Syntax:	View_Corners
Arguments:	None.
Conditions:	None.
Returns:	An array containing the X, Y, and Z of the lower left corner and the upper right corner of the current view.

Situation:

Forget zoom previous. This function allows you to save the current view corner points for later use with the zoom command. This is handy for situations in which you zoom around, do some other work, then decide to undo the work but leave the zoom display in the new position. Simply grab the current view corners before working, then use the points to restore the view at any time.

CD Example:

To test the function, open any drawing, load the Toolbox project, and type VIEWCORNERS_TEST in the immediate window of the Visual Basic Editor.

CD Example Result:

A dialog showing the lower left and upper right corner points. This test routine shows you how to build string points from arrays and how the Format function comes in handy.

Get the Extension from a String

Syntax:	Get_Extension (*string*)
Arguments:	Where the *string* is the control data string to be searched for an extension.
Conditions:	The string must be in string form.
Returns:	The extension parsed out of the string. When no extension is present, Null is returned.

Situation:

Sometimes you need to grab just the extension from a string and use it to build another file. This function gets the extension for you. This function (unlike the RightToken function) returns an extension without the period.

CD Example:

To test the function, open any drawing, load the Toolbox project, and type GETEXTENSION_TEST in the immediate window of the Visual Basic Editor.

CD Example Result:

A dialog box showing the returned extension.

Get the Left Substring from a String

Syntax: token (*string1, string2*)

Arguments: Where the *string1* is the whole string to search.

Where the *string2* is a character or string.

Conditions: Both strings must be in string form.

Returns: A string from the beginning of string1 to the start of string2 (when string2 is present in string1) or the whole string (string1) when string2 is not present.

Situation:

There are many ways of getting a path from a file name. This is one of them. In many situations you already have a string containing a file name (or it's easy to obtain), but you want to get the path to the file name from another string. This function was designed for exactly that situation. One important note here is that you must assume a back slash is in the path string. There is one situation that can occur in legal data but this function can't trap. That situation is when you have a path in a string such as 'C:Autoexec.bat'. There is no back slash in the string path, but DOS will accept this path and use it (in certain situations). The simplest function for retrieving paths that covers this situation is the Get_Path function, which is covered later in this chapter.

CD Example:

To test the function, open any drawing, load the Toolbox project, and type GETSUBSTR_TEST in the immediate window of the Visual Basic Editor.

CD Example Result:

A message box showing the path.

Get the Path from a String

Syntax:	Get_Path (*string*)
Arguments:	Where the *string* is the control data string to be searched for a path.
Conditions:	The string must be in string form.
Returns:	The path parsed out of the string. When no path is present, a zero-length string is returned.

Situation:

Sometimes you need to grab just the path from a string and use it to build another file. This function gets the path for you. This function (unlike the Token function) always returns a path even when there is no back slash in it. For example, C:TEMP.DAT).

CD Example:

To test the function, open any drawing, load the Toolbox project, and type GETPATH_TEST in the immediate window of the Visual Basic Editor.

CD Example Result:

A dialog box showing the returned path.

Get the Right Substring from a String

Syntax: righttoken (*string1, string2*)

Arguments: Where the *string1* is the whole string to search.

                     Where the *string2* is a character or string.

Conditions: Both strings must be in string form.

Returns: A string from the beginning of string2 to the end of string1 (when string2 is present in string1) or the whole string (string1) when string2 is not present.

Situation:

This is another way of stripping the path off a string. The difference between this function and the Token function is that this function returns everything in the string starting from the string2 substring (a file name) to the end of the string. In this case, you know that the file name might have a path on it, and you want to remove the path and keep the file name and extension. This function was designed for exactly that situation.

CD Example:

To test the function, open any drawing, load the Toolbox project, and type GETRSUBSTR_TEST in the immediate window of the Visual Basic Editor.

CD Example Result:

A message box showing the file name.

Pad a String with Spaces

Syntax:	Pad (*string, integer*)
Arguments:	Where the *string* is the control data string to be padded.
	Where the *integer* is how many characters the final string should be.
Conditions:	The string must be in string form.
	The integer must be a positive value.
Returns:	A string with extra spaces totaling the integer argument you supplied. If the string to be padded is smaller than the requested length, it will be passed back with no changes.

Situation:

Used to create columns in single column list boxes. It's kind of crude compared with using multiple columns but handy for those times you choose to be different.

CD Example:

To test the function, open any drawing, load the Toolbox project, and type PAN_TEST in the immediate window of the Visual Basic Editor.

CD Example Result:

A dialog box showing the string before and after the padding. Try changing the second parameter to a number smaller than the length of the string and see the results.

Remove a String's Null Terminator

Syntax: StripTerminator (*string*)

Arguments: Where the *string* is the control data string to be transformed.

Conditions: The string must be in string form.

Returns: The string minus the null terminator and any trailing characters. If no null terminator is present in the string, the string is returned in the same form.

Situation:

Many API calls need a predefined string buffer. They take the string buffer and place the data into it with a null character [chr$(0)] terminator at the end of the data. Many of the string functions cannot deal with a null terminated string. This function lets you pass in the string buffer with the null terminator, and it returns a string that the string functions can work with.

CD Example:

To test the function, open any drawing, load the WindowsOS project, and type MYCOMPUTER in the immediate window of the Visual Basic Editor.

CD Example Result:

A dialog box showing your computer's settings. This example is part of Chapter 9. Try stepping through the subroutine and viewing the string buffers for each setting. Watch how they change from a fixed-length string buffer to a smaller string once they have been sent to the StripTerminator function.

Replace all Requested Characters in a String with Another Character

Syntax:	Replace_Chr (*string, character, character*)
Arguments:	Where the *string* is the control data string to be searched.
	Where the first *character* is the character to be replaced.
	Where the second *character* is the replacement character.
Conditions:	The string must be in string form.
	Both characters must be any legal ASCII character in string form.
Returns:	A new line with all of the requested characters changed to the new character. If no occurrences are found in the line, the line is returned unchanged.

Situation:

Handy for replacing delimiters with different ones. Replaces all occurrences of the search character with the replacement character in the line and returns the line.

CD Example:

To test the function, open any drawing, load the Toolbox project, and type REPLACECHR_TEST in the immediate window of the Visual Basic Editor.

CD Example Result:

Commas in a string are replaced with pipe symbols. This is shown in the message box that appears in the test routine.

Retrieve the System's Windows Directory

Syntax:　　　　　GetWindowsDir

Arguments:　　　　None.

Conditions:　　　　None.

Returns:　　　　　A string containing the system's Windows directory.

Situation:

Used for accessing data in the Windows directory from your project. This function is actually a wrapper function for the API call GetWindowsDirectory. For more API call information see Chapter 9

CD Example:

To test the function, open any drawing, load the Toolbox project, and type GETWINDOWSDIR_TEST in the immediate window of the Visual Basic Editor.

CD Example Result:

The Windows directory string that is returned to the test routines is displayed in a message box.

Show a Progress Spinner

Syntax:	spin (*character*)
Arguments:	Where *character* is the control character shown by the spinner.

Legal arguments include:

Zero-length string or a space

```
  -

  |

  /

  \
```

Conditions:	The character argument must be in the form of a single character string or nil.
Returns:	A one-character string containing the next character the spinner routine should print to the screen.

Situation:

Whether you're in VBA or AutoLISP or any other programming language, it is a good idea to entertain the users whenever the program leaves them to do some lengthy computations. This practice lets the user know that something is indeed happening and that he or she should let the program keep running. Besides giving a message before you leave, it is a common practice in AutoLISP to leave a spinner spinning at the command line. You can't do that in VBA, and the spinner control for the dialog box is used for incrementing counters—not showing a spinner. This routine takes a character and shows it on a label of the form with the word "working" before the character. The routine passes back the next character that makes it look like it is spinning. Passing the routine nil starts the routine with the default character.

Note: Most processing that needs a spinner occurs in a loop of some kind. Try to space the spinner routine so that the spinning characters appear to be evenly spinning. This sometimes means that you need to space the spinner routine in the program unevenly in the code flow to get an even look on the display.

CD Example:

To test the function, open any drawing, load the Toolbox project, and type SPIN_TEST in the immediate window of the Visual Basic Editor.

CD Example Result:

A label on a form that shows the word "Working..." with a spinner on the end.

You can check out the code in the start_click procedure of the form to see how to use the spinner in a loop.

Strip an Extension from a String

Syntax: strip_extension (*string*)

Arguments: Where *string* is a file name containing an extension.

Conditions: The string argument must be in the form of a string.

Returns: A string that has the extension removed. The path will remain when a path is included in the argument string.

Situation:

You might frequently want to process data from a file or table and write a report or some other data using the file name with your own extension attached. This function takes the path, file name, and extension and returns just the path and file name. The path is an optional part of the string. Only the period needs to be present for the function to find the extension. This function is used most when processing block table information. Autodesk stores the extension on external references when the Xref is selected using the dialog box. Since you cannot presume that the extension is not there, it is best to run each Xref obtained from the table through this function to make sure that the extension is stripped off the file name.

CD Example:

To test the function, open any drawing, load the Toolbox project, and type EXTENSION_TEST in the immediate window of the Visual Basic Editor.

CD Example Result:

The new file name is returned without the extension. The test routine shows a message box with the original drawing name and the name missing the extension.

Strip the Path from a String

Syntax: split_path (*string*)

Arguments: Where the *string* is a string possibly containing a
                 directory path and file name.

Conditions: A string must be in string form.

Returns: A string containing just the file name. When no path
                 is present, the whole string is returned.

Situation:

This is perhaps the easiest way of stripping the path off a string. The difference between this function and the others documented in this chapter is that you do not have to know the file name or path to get the file name back.

CD Example:

To test the function, open any drawing, load the Toolbox project, and type SPLIT_TEST in the immediate window of the Visual Basic Editor.

CD Example Result:

A message box showing the file name.

Verify a Control Exists on a Form

Syntax: DoesControlExist (*form, string*)

Arguments: Where the *form* is the form object containing controls to check.

Where the *string* is the control name to check for.

Conditions: The form must be a legal form object.

The string must be in string form.

Returns: True when the control is present on the form or False when it is not present.

Situation:

It is always a good idea to check to see if a control exists before you try to initialize it. If it doesn't exist, you will get an error. VBA lets you create or remove controls on the fly as the program runs. This function allows you to check before you try anything with the control.

CD Example:

To test the function, open any drawing, load the Toolbox project, and type CONTROL_TEST in the immediate window of the Visual Basic Editor.

CD Example Result:

A True result causes the test routine to show a message box.

Verify a File's Existence

Syntax: IsFile (*string*)

Arguments: Where the *string* is a file name including complete path and extension.

Conditions: The string must be in string form.

Returns: True when the file is found or False when it isn't found.

Situation:

It's always nice to know that a file you want to open is out there before you go to open it. You must explicitly supply the path and extension along with the file name to the function. There is no extended search.

CD Example:

To test the function, open any drawing, load the Toolbox project, and type ISFILE_TEST in the immediate window of the Visual Basic Editor.

CD Example Result:

Message boxes showing whether the specified files were or weren't found.

Verify a Listbox Item Exists

Syntax: lst_memb_vb (*string, control*)

Arguments: Where the *string* is the string to be searched for in the listbox control.

Where the *control* is the form's listbox control to search.

Conditions: The string must be in string form.

The control must be a valid userform listbox control.

Returns: True when the string is an item in the listbox or nil when it is not found in the listbox.

Situation:

At times you will need to manipulate data strings from one listbox control to another. Many times you will want to verify if the string is already in the listbox's list so you can avoid placing duplicates on the list. This function allows you to check the listbox first before adding a string and determine whether you should add it. Naturally, as the list grows, the speed decreases. Therefore, you should avoid using this function with very large lists unless you are willing to take the speed penalty.

CD Example:

To test the function, open any drawing, load the Toolbox project, and type LIST_TEST in the immediate window of the Visual Basic Editor. Try both a lowercase b then an uppercase B to see the differences.

CD Example Result:

A lowercase b gets a message box stating that it is not in the list (it isn't because the search is case sensitive). The uppercase B gets a message box stating that it was found in the list.

CHAPTER ELEVEN

VB versus VBA

How does VBA stack up against VB? Remember that VBA is a subset of VB (actually VB is an add-on to the VBA core). As a consequence, VBA does not have all of the abilities of VB. In this chapter, we will explore those differences and explain how VBA fits into the AutoCAD development scheme of things. We will then turn our attention to building help files for your applications. Help files are often the best way to avoid technical support phone calls for sophisticated applications. We will discuss the differences between the help systems of VB and VBA along with how to create help files.

   As you've already seen, VBA is a powerful tool, but there are others that are even more powerful, such as VB and ObjectARX. These tools are not supplied with AutoCAD; you'll have to purchase additional software and learn more skills for them to work properly.

Quick Comparison of VB and VBA

Table 11.1 illustrates some of the pros and cons of both languages.

Table 11.1 VB versus VBA

VB		VBA	
Pros	**Cons**	**Pros**	**Cons**
Runs outside AutoCAD	Runs outside AutoCAD	Runs inside AutoCAD	Runs inside AutoCAD
Easy database connectivity		Shared footprint	Limited database connectivity
Compiled		In-process application performance	Not compiled
Sophisticated UI features		Sophisticated UI features	
Database support (Enterprise Edition)	Purchased separately	Included with host application	
DAO 3.5 support		Project file encryption	

All languages have limitations and strengths. The fact that VB applications run outside the AutoCAD memory pool is both a positive and a negative. It's a negative because it is slower than VBA programs running inside the AutoCAD memory pool. But it's a positive because you can't run a VBA program interactively with the AutoCAD command line though you can with a VB program. The reverse is true for the VBA application: it's faster because it is inside the AutoCAD memory pool, but you can't use it with the AutoCAD command line because AutoCAD won't process your commands until the VBA application is finished. We cover this subject in detail in the command line workaround section of Chapter 12.

VB has data controls included with it to make it very easy to connect to a database. VBA also has data controls included, but they are more limited than in VB, and it's not as easy to connect and manipulate the data from your application.

By default, dialog boxes in VBA are modal, whereas the default in stand-alone Visual Basic is modeless. This means that a dialog box will not remain interactive with AutoCAD during the execution of a VBA program. The dialog must be dismissed before AutoCAD can respond. This limitation is imposed by VBA and will require you to rethink user interface interactions when designing programs to run in both environments.

VBA is an in-process controller, translating to better application performance and throughput for AutoCAD Release 14. AutoCAD VBA shares AutoCAD's memory and process space, significantly improving performance.

When AutoCAD is being controlled by an external VBA hosted application (such as Microsoft Excel or Visual Basic program), performance is compromised. The external application must communicate to AutoCAD through the Windows message loop using remote procedure calls (RPC). Using VBA as an ActiveX automation controller delivers performance levels bested only by native ObjectARX-compiled executables.

Multiple projects are not supported in the AutoCAD Release 14 version of VBA. However, you can have multiple modules, forms, and object files. They are supported in the VBA implementation found in AutoCAD 2000.

Visual Basic packages contain various features (at an escalating cost) that better enable you to create complex programs. Table 11.2 shows those packages and their features.

Table 11.2 Visual Basic Edition

Feature	Enterprise	Professional
IntelliSense	◆	◆
File I/O, OS Access	◆	◆
Project Templates	◆	◆
Add-in Support	◆	◆
Multiple Projects	◆	◆
Visual Inheritance	◆	◆
ActiveX Creation	◆	◆
Standard Controls	◆	◆
Application Creation	◆	◆
Learning Tools		
Database Access	◆	◆
Native Compiler	◆	◆
Active Document Creation	◆	◆
ActiveX Server Components	◆	◆
Transaction Server	◆	
Remote Data Objects	◆	
SQL Debugger	◆	
SQL Server	◆	
Visual SourceSafe	◆	
Application Performance Explorer	◆	
Microsoft Repository	◆	◆
Microsoft Visual Database Tools	◆	

Learning	Application	Control Creation	Scripting
◆	◆	◆	◆
◆	◆		
◆	◆	◆	
◆		◆	
◆	◆	◆	◆
◆	◆	◆	
◆		◆	
◆	◆		
◆			
◆			
	◆		

Which Language for Which Situation?

What does this comparison really mean? It all comes down to when should you use a given language for a particular job. Since AutoLISP is widely used, it will probably remain the most commonly used language for a while. The new VisualLISP environment will lengthen the life of AutoLISP, but as AutoCAD grows and leaves AutoLISP behind, it will be more important for even the casual user to know VBA. Getting a jump on this trend will enable you to be ready to make the switch seamlessly. The question will be whether to use VB or VBA. VB will most likely remain the language of choice for database integration because VBA does not fully support the necessary database controls and will probably be limited even in the future. VBA will be a strong contender for those jobs that are dialog-box driven and need lots of speed. VB will be the language that hovers on the edge of full-blown application development (where ObjectArx takes over). Its relative ease (compared with C++) of use will allow the

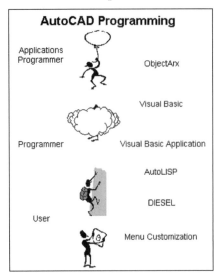

Figure 11.1: Language complexity chart

casual programmer to develop very complex products without learning the more complex C++. You are now given a wide choice of languages to manipulate AutoCAD. Figure 11.1 shows the languages and their relative position on the complexity chart.

Unfortunately, there is no clear-cut division between the lower- and middle-level languages, except maybe their database connectivity. You could even argue that AutoLISP has simple database connectivity with ASE and ASI. The short-term answer is to continue to use AutoLISP (assuming you already know it) and pick up the new VisualLISP as you develop your VBA skills. Use AutoLISP or VisualLISP when you have limited time (and it is appropriate) to get the job done, and VBA when you have the time to experiment.

Differences at the System Level

There are only a couple of differences between VB and VBA at the system level. The first is obvious: how they use memory. VB works outside the AutoCAD memory pool, while VBA works inside it. Remember that AutoCAD will use all of the memory you have available. That means that it will take up as much as necessary when it uses VBA. The speed of execution is faster because there is no need to communicate with the application through the Windows pipeline. Figure 11.2 shows the differences in the memory pool.

The other difference is slightly subtler. VBA does not have a forms load procedure, while VB does. This means that you have only the form's initialization procedure to use in VBA for preloading your form.

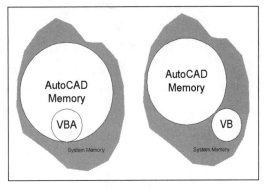

Figure 11.2: Memory differences

Porting Issues—from VB to VBA

Moving code from VB to VBA can be very simple or incredibly difficult. It all depends on what the program does. If it has a form with data controls for database integration, then it will be difficult. VBA is missing some of the more robust data controls for database integration. That means that you will need to try to reference the ActiveX controls inside VBA. Not all controls will import into VBA. Another stumbling block is the form itself. A VB form will sometimes transfer to a VBA user form, but the controls will have only VBA properties and methods associated with them. This means that a control such as a text box will lose all of its DDE linkage methods going from VB to VBA because VBA does not support those methods. You need to check each control on the VB form before transferring to make sure that you are not using some method or property that is not supported in VBA.

The two languages' terminology are slightly different and can cause some problems. VB calls its forms by the name Form while VBA calls its form a Userform. This means that any procedure that passes a form in VB must be adjusted accordingly in VBA.

Porting Issues—from VBA to VB

The same terminology problems occur when you're moving code from VBA to VB as from the other direction. The same forms issue applies to porting forms from VBA to VB as from the other direction. Going from VBA to VB is not as dramatic a change as the other direction: since VBA is a subset of VB, most of the properties and methods of a control in VBA will be present in VB. Simple database connections done in VBA will move over to VB without any problems.

Attaching Your VB Application to the AutoCAD Object Model

Should you decide to move your code over to VB from the VBA environment, you must take a few steps to ensure that the code will work in the new environment. The first step is to get the code and forms into VB. That can be difficult for certain controls. You can try to import the Userform from VBA—you might get lucky and it will import. If not, you can try to isolate the control that won't import and remove it to try again. Another alternative would be to recreate the form in VB using VB controls. Sometimes this is easier and quicker.

Once you have the code and all necessary forms, you must then reference the AutoCAD object model. You can accomplish this by attaching the AutoCAD Object Library using the References dialog in VB. The file is called Acad.tlb and is located in the AutoCAD executable's directory. Next you must have four lines of code that will attach the AutoCAD application and the current active document. Using the VBA reserved word ThisDrawing for the current active document allows any existing code that comes over from VBA that uses the word to work in VB. The following code shows no error trapping.

```
Dim Application As AcadApplication

Set Application = GetObject(, "AutoCAD.application")

Dim ThisDrawing As AcadDocument

Set ThisDrawing = Application.ActiveDocument
```

Remember that you will not have the implied reserved word ThisDrawing in VB. You will need to always use it in front of the model object. Once you use these lines of code in VB, the AutoCAD object model is exposed to you and you can use VB code just as if you were in VBA. This gives you an advantage when you need to interact with the command line or use sophisticated database controls.

The above example uses no error trapping and assumes that the Auto-CAD application is already running. This would cause an error if AutoCAD were not already running. The code below shows the proper way to check first, then try to recover before proceeding. We have shown a simple print to the debug window to illustrate that the code behaves the same in VB as in VBA once the connection is made.

```
Public Sub Attaching ()

On Error Resume Next

Dim Application As AcadApplication        'declare the application object

Set Application = GetObject(, "AutoCAD.application")'set it to AutoCAD

If Err.Number <> 0 Then    ' Was AutoCAD running?

  Err.Clear        ' No, clear the error

  Set Application = CreateObject("AutoCAD.application") ' Try to launch

  If Err.Number Then      ' Did it launch?

    MsgBox "Unable to launch AutoCAD session." ' No - tell the user

    End      ' bail out

  End If

End If
```

```
Dim ThisDrawing As AcadDocument ' declare the active document object
Set ThisDrawing = Application.ActiveDocument   ' set the active document
Dim olay As AcadLayer     ' declare an active layer object
Set olay = ThisDrawing.ActiveLayer     ' set it
Debug.Print olay.Name     ' display various properties
Debug.Print olay.Color
End Sub
```

A VB 5.0 project for testing if you like. It is called Attach.vbp. Load it into VB 5.0 and test run it from the immediate window by running the macro called Attaching.

VB and VBA Help

The Windows help engine has been available for AutoLISP programmers since Autodesk tapped into it late in the life cycle of Release 12. VB and VBA can also access the Windows help engine with the addition of context-sensitive help for a form's controls. Each language has a slightly different way of accessing the help engine, but they all use a Windows help file that you can create. You also have the ability, should you need it, to tap into Autodesk's ACAD.HLP file. This section covers accessing help in VBA, along with a few techniques you can use in VB or VBA. We have defined a project to illustrate the techniques and supply a detailed listing of all projects included on the companion CD-ROM.

VB Help versus VBA Help Both languages use the WinHelp API call to deliver help. Both have context-sensitive help for controls and forms and both can use a control's HelpControlId property to directly access a topic via the function key {F1}. The only basic difference between them is that VB has an extra control property for accessing Win95's What's This help tips, which VBA does not have on its controls. We have documented the WinHelp API call here in the same manner as the API calls in the API chapter.

Accessing VBA and VB Help

You can define a default help file for your project in both VB and VBA. You can define VB's default project help file from a dialog called from the Project/Project Properties menu item. The dialog is shown in Figure 11.3.

The VBA project's property dialog box is almost the same and it is also used to set the default help file for your project. The dialog is shown in Figure 11.4.

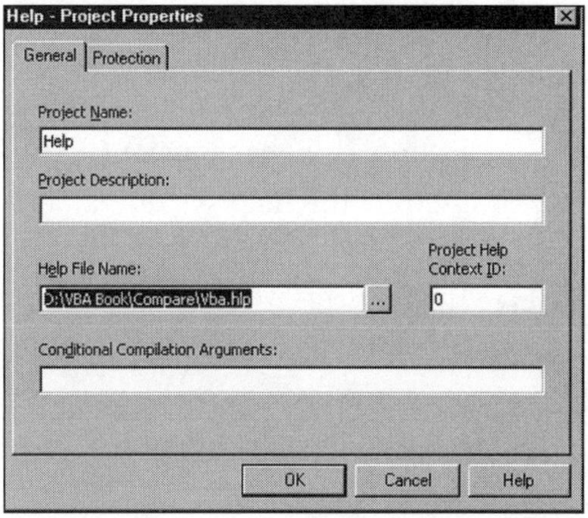

In both languages, you must select a default help file for use with the function key {F1} help, and you can set a default Context ID for the help file. This allows your application to default to a Table of Contents page should you call for help from a control that doesn't have a context ID set or has an invalid ID set.

Whether you use the context-sensitive help feature or you just want to call help, you need to use the WinHelp

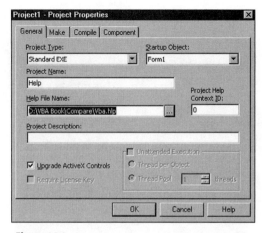

Figure 11.3: Project1—Project Properties window

Figure 11.4: Help—Project Properties window

API. This API takes a help file name and a topic and displays the help on the subject. Should the topic be missing or misspelled, you will get the default subject. This is the function declaration on one line of code that is placed in your declaration section.

Declare Function WinHelp Lib "user32" Alias "WinHelpA" (ByVal hwnd As Long, ByVal lpHelpFile As String, ByVal wCommand As Long, ByVal dwData As Long) As Long

The four parameters control what kind of help you are requesting from the WinHelp engine. Those arguments are shown in Table 11.3, below.

Table 11.3

hwnd	The window handle of the application requesting the help or the ID control or window about which help is requested when the wCommand parameter is either HELP_CONTEXTMENU OR HELP_WM_HELP.
lpHelpFile	The application's HLP file name. May have a greater than sign (>) and a window name specified after it. If so, the help is displayed in a secondary window. The secondary window name must be specified in the Windows section of the HPJ file.
wCommand	The Windows help system command. See Table 11.4, below, for details.
dwData	Additional data provided for the wCommand parameter.

The wCommand parameter tells Windows help which help command you want to use. These commands must be defined in your declaration section as global constants. They are shown in the command column used by the help system table.

Table 11.4

Command	Value	Description
HELP_COMMAND	&H102&	Executes the help topic. The dwData parameter is used to point to the requested topic in the file.
HELP_CONTENTS	&H3&	Windows 3.x command: displays a Contents page in your HJP file.
HELP_CONTEXT	&H1	Displays the topic that is associated with the context ID specified by the dwData parameter.
HELP_CONTEXTPOPUP	&H8&	Uses the topic that is associated with the context ID specified by the dwData parameter.
HELP_FINDER		Windows 95 and NT command: displays a Contents page in your HJP file.
HELP_FORCEFILE	&H9&	Ensures that the proper help file is being displayed.
HELP_HELPONHELP	&H4	Windows 3.x command: accesses the Windows help file on Windows help. Win 95 and NT users should use the HELP_FINDER command instead.

Command	Value	Description
HELP_INDEX	&H3	Windows 3.x command: accesses the Windows help file index. Win 95 and NT users should use the HELP_FINDER command instead.
HELP_KEY	&H101	Searches the help file for a matching keyword supplied in the dwData parameter. A list is supplied in a dialog when more than one match occurs.
HELP_MULTIKEY	&H201&	Searches the help file for a matching keyword supplied in the dwData parameter. Uses a pointer in the dwData parameter to point to a MULTIKEYHELP structure that contains the keyword table to search and the keyword string.
HELP_PARTIALKEY	&H105&	Searches the help file for a matching keyword supplied in the dwData parameter. The index tab is displayed when more than one topic is matched. You can force the index to be displayed by supplying an empty string as the keyword.
HELP_QUIT	&H2	Lets the Windows help system know that your application is finished with the help and closes the file and help window.
HELP_SETCONTENTS	&H5&	Sets the context ID for the topic that Windows help will display in response to the HELP_CONTENTS command or when the Contents button is selected. The dwData parameter specifies the context ID that will become the context ID for the topic.
HELP_SETINDEX	&H5	Specifies which keyword table is to be displayed in the Hlpe topic dialog box.
HELP_SETWINPOS	&H203&	Sets the size and position of the main or secondary help window. The dwData parameter is used to point to a HELPWININFO structure.

Daunting, is it? Well, the good news is that VBA does all of the work when it comes to context-sensitive help (once you've set up the context ID for the control) and you need to use only the HELP_COMMAND command and the jumpid option for your online help. We explain other techniques in detail later in this chapter.

Much of the diverse material presented above is used in writing help for C++ applications; you need not concern yourself with it since the context-sensitive help and the HELP command with the jumpid can handle any help you might want to supply to the user. The additional material is presented only so you can get a feel for the rich help environment that exists on the next level of development.

On-line Help

You usually initiate this type of help by selecting a button or menu item. You write your code to use the WinHelp API using the HELP_COMMAND option with the jumpid topic. The jumpid is simply a mechanism that the HELP_COMMAND uses to find a topic in your help file. The topic is a string with no spaces that you set up in the your help file. An example for a call to help using this syntax is below:

WinHelp 0, "MyHelpFile.hlp", HELP_COMMAND,_
"jumpid("MyTopic")"

What does it mean in English?

- WinHelp is the API call.

- A 0 is supplied as a marker for the window handle argument since the HELP_COMMAND option does not need it.

- The MyHelpFile.hlp argument is the name of the help file.

- The HELP_COMMAND argument is a constant you must define in your program. It is a long equal to &H102&. It is the only one you need to use for any help topic.

- The jumpid("MyTopic") argument is a mechanism that will find the MyTopic header string in the help file and return a long id that the HELP_COMMAND argument uses to find the topic and display it. This is the tricky part because you must use the jumpid method to get the topics id back to the API for it to find anything. It's a long way around, but it does work.

A help project is supplied for you to play with the two kinds of help. To experiment with the online help, open the Help project and run the form. Use the poplist on the form to select a topic and the Help button to see help on the topic. The poplist contains several AutoCAD topics and several topics covered by this book. The list actually has two columns. The first is the one seen by the user (the topic), the second is the name of the help file that the topic is in. When the Help button is selected, the program gets the topic and associated help file name and uses the WinHelp API to display help on the topic. Typically, you would build the topic behind the Help button and display it without any user intervention. The jumpid is built from a variable containing the topic as shown below.

param = "jumpid(" & strSubject & ")"_
WinHelp 0, strPath & strFile, basHelp.HELP_COMMAND, param

You can use the Projects poplist item List of Projects to get a list of all of the project files built for this book and descriptions on each project. Information on each project is built to illustrate how things work, and many tips on the code fragments that make up the projects are included in the help file.

Note: You will need to change the path for the help files in the supplied Help project to match where your AutoCAD and VBA help files are located. See the Help Project section later in this chapter for more details about this and other features of the supplied VBA Help project.

Context-Sensitive Help

Context-sensitive help does not use the HELP_COMMAND and jumpid topic. You register the help file with the VBA project and assign an ID (HelpContextId) to a control on the form. In the help file, you create a help topic with an associated context ID that matches the one on the control. Whenever a user sets the focus on a control with a context-sensitive help ID attached and hits the {F1} key, the help is displayed for that specific control. Since the form is considered a control, it also can have a context-sensitive help ID attached. Many programmers simply set the initial focus on a form to the Help button and allow its context-sensitive help ID to give general help about the dialog box. Controls such as buttons (other than the Help button) usually don't have a context-sensitive help ID attached since the button is supposed to do something other than call for help when it is selected. Controls like lists, poplists, edit boxes, radio buttons, and check boxes are prime candidates for HelpContextId.

Setting the help file name and location is done at design time in the VBA IDE. You must select the Help Properties... menu item from the Tools pull-down menu. The Help Project Properties dialog box appears as shown in Figure 11.5.

You then fill out the location and help file name in the Help File Name field and give the project

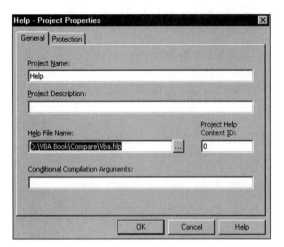

Figure 11.5: Help—Project dialog box

context ID default number in the Project Help Context ID field. This default is used whenever help is called for a subject that is not present in the help file. Usually the default is the table of contents for the help file, but you can set it to anything you wish. Unfortunately, you can do this only at design time. There is no mechanism to set the program's help file at runtime. This means that you must select the location and help file at design time, and you can't change it at runtime. Another problem is that your VBA program does not use the search hierarchy or the help file registry setting to find your help file. This means that you must explicitly give the path along with the file name in the project. That means having a standard setup for all machines in the organization to keep maintenance simple. The Help project supplied with the book has context-sensitive help IDs attached to the poplist and Help button. Actually, all of the buttons have context-sensitive help IDs of 0 (meaning the table of contents for the project help file). This is the default ID for any newly created control on the form. By creating a table of contents in the help file with an ID of 0, you automatically set up the default for any new control on your form.

Accessing AutoCAD Online Help

Autodesk states that it does not use context-sensitive help IDs in its AutoCAD help file (ACAD.HLP). This means that you cannot tie into its help file using a context-sensitive help ID from your form, but you can still tie in using the jumpid with the HELP_COMMAND method. The Help project supplied with the book has examples of this method of accessing AutoCAD help. You must build your API call using the correct path and help file name along with the correct topic for the jumpid. We have shown an example of this method in the following listing.

```
param = "jumpid(Plot)"

WinHelp 0,"D:\PROGRAM FILES\AUTOCAD R14\HELP\ACAD.HLP", HELP_COMMAND, param
```

The code shown above calls the help illustrated in figure 11.6. The topic in the jumpid is where you must guess and experiment. The few topics that are supplied in the list in the help project were simple to guess. The plot command uses a topic of plot, the line command uses a topic of line, and the arc command uses a topic of arc. You must guess because there is no documentation on the topics in the AutoCAD help file. You can see the code that builds the AutoCAD help string in the btnHelp_Click subroutine of the Help project.

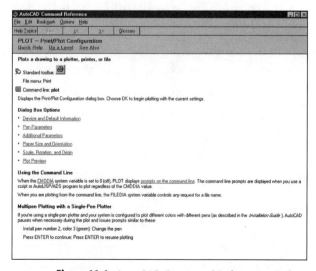

Figure 11.6: AutoCAD Command Reference window

Building a Help File Building a help file is a very complicated and tedious task. The task is made easier by purchasing a program for creating Windows help files. ForeHelp by ForeFront of Boulder, Colorado, is one such program. You can contact the company at (303) 499-9181. The help file created for this book was created in version 2.95 of ForeHelp. This is not the only program on the market to generate Windows help files, but it does have the features you need to create simple or complex files. Features included in any good help file generator are listed below:

- HyperLinks

- Context IDs

- Rich text file import

- Topic Properties

- Targets

- Alias

The VBA Help Project This project contains examples of both context-sensitive help and calling for online help using the jumpid method. It also contains help on all of the other projects included in this

Figure 11.7: VBA Help dialog box

book. Information on techniques, useful code fragments, miscellaneous tips for each project, and part of one of the chapters is included in the help file.

The VBA Help project dialog box is shown in Figure 11.7.

You need to change the path in the help project of the VBA and the AutoCAD help (if it is not at its default location) folder before using the program. The VBA help file path for context-sensitive help is found in the project's properties dialog box shown in Figure 11.8.

The steps to change the VBA help file path for using context-sensitive help are as follows:

1. Open the help project in whatever folder you placed it.

2. Select the **Help Properties...** menu item from the Tools menu.

3. Use the **Browse button**... next to the Help File Name edit box to select the VBA.HLP file from the project folder.

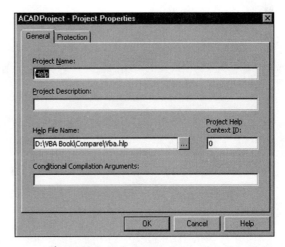

Figure 11.8: Help Project Properties dialog box

4. Select the **OK** button and save the project.

The VBA help file path must be adjusted to your system for online help to work. The steps to change that path are as follows:

1. Open the help project in whatever folder you placed it (unless it is still open).

2. Double click on the frmHelp item of the Forms folder in the project window.

3. Double click on the Help button in the dialog box.

4. In the subroutine Get_On_line_Help (beneath the btnHelp_Click sub-routine), change the string D:\VBA BOOK\COMPARE\ to a string containing your path to the VBA.HLP file (i.e. C:\HELPFILES\).

The help project assumes that the AutoCAD help file is in the default location that Autodesk places it. Should you have changed the location of the AutoCAD help folder path, you need to change the program. The steps for changing the AutoCAD help file path are as follows:

5. Open the help project in whatever folder you placed it (unless it is still open).

6. Double click on the frmHelp item of the Forms folder in the project window.

7. Double click on the Help button in the dialog box.

8. In the subroutine Get_On_line_Help (beneath the btnHelp_Click subroutine), change the object ThisDrawing.Application.Path & "\HELP\" to a string containing your path to the VBA.HLP file. (i.e. C:\HELPFILES\)

Now you can use the help project to experiment with the various help concepts covered in this section.

On-line Help There are several methods in the help project illustrating how you can use help in your project. On-line help is attached to the Help button and is controlled by the pop list. You need only to select an item from the list, then the Help button to view help on the subject. The list is set up as a double column list with the help topic column showing and the help file name column hidden. When the Help button is selected, the item is used as the topic for the help file and the hidden column entry. This technique is used to show you how you can use multiple help files from one project. The pop list contains several different help topics that exist in the AutoCAD ACAD.HLP file and the VBA Help file provided with this book. One pop list item is there to illustrate how the WinHelp API handles a topic that does not exist in the help file. Try the Missing Topic item to generate the WinHelp error message shown below in Figure 11.9.

Figure 11.9: Windows Help topic error message

The message appears, then you are put into the help file's content area. This happens because the WinHelp API makes the contents topic in the help file the default topic when a requested topic can't be found.

On line help is also behind the Linetype, Plot, and VBA Help Contents buttons, but the method coded for them does not use the pop list. This method of accessing on-line help is done to illustrate the more traditional way of accessing on-line help. The subroutines are just used to set up the topic and help file names; a generic subroutine does the work of calling the WinHelp API. Check out the code in the buttons' click subroutines.

Context-Sensitive Help Since the AutoCAD help file does not contain context-sensitive IDs, only the VBA-related objects on the form have a context-sensitive ID attached to them. You can tab around the various objects on the form and use the function key {F1} to access their context-sensitive help topics in the VBA help file.

Missing IDs are handled differently by the help file than missing topics are handled by the WinHelp API. Instead of defaulting to the content page, you are placed in the index portion of the help file. This allows you to choose any existing topic. The Linetype, Plot, and Done buttons illustrate this feature.

You'll set up the context-sensitive IDs at design time in the controls of the form in VBA and at design time in the help file. The context-sensitive ID must match for the help to be found.

VB and VBA Help Conclusion

As you've seen, help is a complex subject. However, it is a subject you need to address to make your projects as professional as possible. Users will have questions on even simple programs. On-line and context-sensitive help give you the mechanism to create concise and informative help that can reduce the calls for support.

CHAPTER TWELVE

Gotcha's and Tips

E very programming language has its quirks and special rules. VBA is no exception. Some of the ways it works contrasts with other languages you may already know; this chapter discusses some of the interesting features you will encounter. Subjects covered in this chapter are:

- Handles data types comparison

- Uses control keys to maneuver

- Creates User defined Objects

- Handles dates

- Handles Arguments

- Pointer Arguments

- Short Circuit Evaluation

- Access objects on the same level

- Creates columns and uses multiselect in the listbox control

- Deals with Variable name shortcuts

- Deals with the Command line in AutoCAD

If you don't know what some of these things are, do not despair. Some of these are advanced topics and we will endeavor to explain them as we get into the various nuances of the VBA programming environment.

Divergent Data Type Comparison

VBA variables can be declared without assigning a data type. That means it is possible to compare variables that are not of the same basic data type. VBA automatically assigns a default data type of Variant when one it not declared. It is a good idea to get into the habit of assigning the data type whenever you plan to use a variable. This is helpful from a maintenance point of view and for checking divergent data types. Before discussing a technique for avoiding problems with divergent data types comparison, a discussion of how VBA handles data types is in order. The data type of your variable should be determined by the type of data you wish to store. Table 12.1 shows the various data types you can declare in VBA.

Table 12.1: VBA Data Types

Data type	Value it can hold	Comments
Byte	0 to 255	Small positive integers.
Boolean	-1 or 0	Yes or No values.
Currency	-922,337,203,685,477,648 to 922,337,203,685,477,647	Use for money calculations when accuracy is important. Maximum of fifteen digits to the left of the decimal and up to four digits to the right.
Date	Jan. 1, 100 to Dec. 31, 9999	Data and time.
Decimal	Variant subtype	Declare your variable as a variant and then use the CDEC() function to convert the variable to a decimal data type. Behaves like the currency data type but is more precise.
Double	Approx. 4.94E-45 to 1.8E308	64-bit double precision floating point.
Integer	-32768 to 32676	Small positive and negative numbers.
Long	-2,147,483,648 to 2,147,483,647	Large whole number, both positive and negative.

Data type	Value it can hold	Comments
Single	Approx. 1.4E-45 to 3.4E48	32-bit single precision floating point
String	0 to 2 billion characters	Text
Variant	Can contain any type of data including Empty or Null	The default data type when you do not declare one. Can hold data of any type.

Most of the data types are self-explanatory, except the Variant type. Variant is very special in VBA. It can hold any of the other data types so you can use it as a general catch-all. There are some things to watch out for with the Variant, however. Since it can contain any type, you might be tempted to use it almost to the exclusion of the others. This will cause problems such as divergent data type comparison. Other disadvantages of using it exclusively are that it takes more storage space, and maintaining the code is more difficult because it is not obvious what type of data you are holding.

Despite these disadvantages, there are many good uses of Variant variables. One is for passing pointers to arrays as arguments. Since VBA does not allow you to pass an array into a subroutine or function, you pass in a pointer to the array, and the subroutine or function can then access the array through the pointer. Another advantage of a Variant variable is its ability to contain a NULL or Empty value. This is very useful when dealing with database records since the Microsoft Jet engine returns all data in variant form. Switching it to other data types and back would be a waste of time. Another good use is when you're working with listbox values. A listbox value is a variant. You need to declare a variant type to take its value and use it. If the user has not selected anything in the listbox, you could get a NULL value. You should check that you have a value before proceeding.

When you are not sure what type of data your variant might contain and you need to find out before processing it; you can use a special VBA function to determine the data type of the data stored. The function is called VarType. Pass your Variant variable to the function and it will return the data type of the data in the variable.

Two special values (Null and Empty) are used with Variant variables. To test for those special values you must use the IsNull or IsEmpty tests. Once you get a response from the test, you can then do further tests or process the data.

One advantage of the Null value is how it behaves with VBA operators. When you use an operator like plus (+) with a NULL value variable and a string or number, you get NULL as a result. But when you use the ampersand (&) operator with a NULL value variable and a string or number you get the string or number back. This is what allows you to get around the problem of divergent data types that could contain NULL values. An example is shown below.

```
Dim groupname As Variant

groupname = frmGroupNames.1stGroupNames.Value


If Len(groupname & "")>0 Then          '#1 - this works
```

In the example, the Variant variable group name is loaded with the contents of the listbox (lstGroupNames) selection. There is no guarantee that anything is selected or that a value was passed. If you were to check for the length of the variable and it contained NULL, the program would stop with an error. The Len function must have a string passed to it. Line #1 is the workaround to the problem. VBA binds the zero-length string with the Variant variable. When the variable is NULL, it returns a zero-length string that the Len function can deal with. When the variable has something in it, a zero-length string is added, but that does not affect the original string. This same method can be used with database recordsets. You can also use it with numbers instead of strings. Just remember that you must use the ampersand—not a plus sign.

Using Control Keys to Maneuver in VBA

The standard Microsoft function keys apply when you're cutting and pasting inside the IDE and function key {F1} gets you help just like in any Microsoft product. There are a few special VBA control keys sequences that can really make your life easier when programming.

Finding code in your project is one of the most difficult things about object-oriented code. Other common useful tools are the ability to shift (indent) blocks of code and the ability to step through your code one line at a time in debug mode. VBA has given you some shortcuts for accomplishing these things. These control keys sequences are

- Tab
- Shift + Tab
- {F2}
- Shift + {F2}
- Ctrl + Shift + {F2}
- {F8}

We indent our code for maintenance purposes. It is easier to read the code when it is lined up vertically. To indent code blocks you use the Tab or shift + Tab key sequence. The process is simple. Just highlight the lines of code, then use the key sequence. The Tab key moves the code block to the right while the Shift + Tab key sequence moves the code block to the left.

The {F2} key takes you to the Object browser covered in Chapter 3.

One of the most useful key sequences is the Shift + {F2} key sequence. You use this to bounce around in the module definition, variable declaration, or object browser. You place your cursor over a variable or procedure and use the key sequence. VBA will take you to the declaration of the variable or to the declaration of the procedure. When you place your cursor over an object, the key sequence takes you to that object's definition in the Object Browser.

The Ctrl + Shift + {F2} key sequence returns you to the last position of your cursor (unless you are in the Object Browser). These features are very handy for moving quickly around the code modules, checking that you have properly declared a variable within the current scope, or seeing an object's definition and getting back to where you started.

When debugging your code, the {F8} function key is of primary importance to you. It allows you to step into (through) your code one line at a time. You can place a break point on a line of code near the suspect code, and the program will halt processes at that line in a wait state. You can then use the {F8} key to move one line at a time through the problem area, viewing variables or watching the flow of your program. There are other key sequences that work with {F8}. You can see them on the Debug pull-down menu.

Class Modules in VBA

VBA has the ability to define a class similar to languages like C++ or Delphi. Classes allow you to define your own objects. They are the definition of the object. In AutoCAD terms, you could compare a class to a block table definition and an object to the block occurrence in the drawing. One class definition with multiple objects derived from it. You define properties and methods for your objects in the class module. You can then use the class definition over and over again in the form of objects within the program. Since one program can reference another program's code, you can share the object with other programs. The difference between a VBA object defined in a class module and one defined in C++ or Delphi is that the VBA object cannot inherent like in the other languages. Inherence is an import feature of higher level object-oriented languages. It allows you to define a parent object and spawn other objects (copies) from the parent. The other objects can have additional methods or properties added to the original parent object's methods and properties that are unique to the child. When a parent object's method or property is altered, all children objects' methods and properties change in accordance. In VBA, you are allowed to create instances of the original parent object (much like in C++), but the child object does not stay linked to the parent. This means that changes made to the parent object are not reflected automatically in the child objects derived from the parent. This is why VBA is not a true object-oriented programming language; although it may seem like a small difference, it can be important when dealing with large families of objects.

Still, you can create your own object with VBA. You can create a person object that has properties like age, height, weight, race, religion, and any other information you need to access about a person in a class module. That object is then available to hold information in your program. You need only declare the object in your procedure, then load the information into it. Objects can be very handy when working with database recordsets. Other uses for your own created objects include but are not limited to:

- Wrapping API procedures

- Wrapping Registry calls

- Handling reading and writing with ASCII files

- Creating new properties for forms

- Defining real world components of your designs such as structural members or survey data

- Holding standard calculations used to solve engineering problems

- Implementing individual client or government styles and standards

A form is a special class module VBA provided for us. It contains collections of controls that we can use. When you create a form, you are filling in details about the form and adding your own methods (subroutines) and properties.

To show how this all works, we have provided a small example project. Open up the Employee.dvb provided on the sample CD and call the TestEmp module from your immediate window. The module has a stop in it to allow you to step though the code one line at a time using the {F8} key. You can see the values assigned to the properties of the employee by placing your cursor over the property as you press the {F8} key. This method of stepping through the code is also useful because you see how the program moves through the class module code.

The module has hard lined an age and name into a newly created object called employee. It does nothing more than put up a message box with the employee's name and age in it to show that the object took the data. Look at the Employee class module to see the property and method definitions relating to the employee object. The declarations in the class module are the properties, and the procedures in the class module are the methods. VBA even recognizes them and uses them in the modules with the Intellisense feature. After you create a new instance of the employee object in a module and set it, you can see the properties and methods by typing in the object's name and a period (.). The Intellisense feature of VBA shows the properties and methods defined in the class module for employee.

The Special Character for Date and Format

The Date and Format functions return a Variant data type. Because of this, it is important to either use a string or to wrap a date string you wish to convert to a date with the special pound symbol (#). Otherwise, VBA interprets the separator symbols as mathematical operators. The example below illustrates the differences.

```
Dim MyDate, ADate, BDate, MyStr As Variant

Adate - 1/27/93

MyStr = Format(ADate, "Long Date")      'Line #1

BDate = "1/27/93"

MyStr = Format(BDate, "Long Date")      'Line #2

MyDate = #1/27/93#

MyStr = Format(MyDate, "Long Date")     'Line #3
```

Line #1 returns MyStr as the incorrect date of Saturday, December 30, 1899. This is because the VBA is dividing the numbers in ADate (getting 3.982477E-04), and then the Format function is converting the number to a date. Line #2 returns MyStr as the correct date with a value of Wednesday, January 27, 1993. This is because BDate contains a string value, and the Format function will handle a Variant data type containing a string date. Line #3 also returns MyStr as the correct date with a value of Wednesday, January 27, 1993. This is because MyDate uses the special date characters around it, and the Format function handles a Variant data type containing special date characters.

Collecting a date from a user on a form and converting it can cause unpredictable results unless you know the data type of the control you got the data from. A text box will return a string that works with the Format function, but a listbox value returns a variant, and it might not be in string format. It is safest to use the special date characters around data that you collect and want to convert into the date format with the Format function. You can see the example by opening the Dates.dvb project supplied on the CD and stepping through it by calling the PlayDate subroutine in the Immediate window.

Named and Optional Arguments

First a brief definition of terms. An argument is the data being passed into a procedure from outside the procedure. A parameter is the data accepted inside the procedure from the calling procedure. Most programmers use the terms interchangeably, but they really apply to the point of view you are taking when discussing the data passing. Here we are discussing passing in the data, so we are talking about arguments.

VBA allows you to pass arguments into a procedure (subroutine or function) by three methods. You can supply the arguments in the order they are declared in the procedure, by name (in no particular order), or by a declared optional argument.

Given a sample subroutine called ShowEmp you can see how to call using the various methods. You can run the sample routine by opening the Arguments.dvb project supplied on the CD and copying the samples (supplied as comments in the routine) into the immediate window. The procedure declaration is shown below and the declaration is what is needed to explain the concept.

```
Public Sub ShowEmp(strName As String, intAge As Integer, dteBirth_
As Date, , optional height as integer)
```

Passing in the Declared Order The default way to call the sub-routine would be to call it and pass the argument in the order you defined them. The call for this method might look like this.

```
Call ShowEmp ("My Name", 22, #2/3/76#)
```

Or

```
ShowEmp "My Name", 22, #2/3/76#
```

The name is a string in the first position, age is an integer in the second position, and the birth date is in the third position.

Passing by Name You can pass the arguments into the procedure by name in any order you wish. The method is to give the name of the argument in the procedure's declaration followed by a colon, equal sign, and the value. For the same procedure call to ShowEmp listed above, the call would look like this:

```
Call ShowEmp (bDate:=#2/3/76#, Name:="My Name", Age:=22)
```

Or

```
ShowEmp Age:=22, bdate:=#2/3/76#, Name:="My Name"
```

The position of the argument does not matter when you use the named argument method.

Optional Arguments The sample routine supplied for the two previous argument methods shows how the third optional argument method works. Each of the examples shown will work fine even though the height argument was not present. That is because the Optional declaration was used for the height argument. When you want to pass the height into the routine, just add it to the list of arguments.

There is only one rule for optional arguments. They must be declared last in the procedure's declarations. You can put in as many as you wish as long as they are last in the list. When you use the optional height argument, your call might appear like this:

```
Call ShowEmp ("My Name", 22, #2/3/76#, 72)
```

Or

```
ShowEmp Age:=22, bdate:=#2/3/76#, Height:=72, Name:="My Name"
```

Notice that even though the declaration had to be last in the procedure, the call does not have to make it last when using named arguments.

Using an Array of Doubles versus a Variant as an Array

VBA for AutoCAD does not allow you to pass an array to a procedure. To quote Autodesk from its 14.01 Release FAQ statement, "Support for early binding requires that all properties of, and arguments to, methods which passed data as an array must now be passed as a VARIANT. This includes all 2D and 3D coordinates, which have previously been passed as arrays."

The truth is that while VBA can pass arrays as arguments to procedures without causing an error, procedures cannot declare arrays in their declaration list. This can sometimes be a bit confusing because you can define an array in the calling procedure and pass it into another procedure—but only if you define the incoming parameter as a Variant. We have illustrated below the way to pass an array to a procedure.

```
Dim Pnt(0 To 2) As Double
Dim Ent As Object
Call GetEnt(Ent, Pnt)
```

```
Public Sub GetEnt(Ent As Object, Pnt As Variant)
```

High-level languages such as C use pointers to pass around variables and arrays. The one trap that you can fall into in VBA is thinking that you can define the array in the calling procedure and set a variant pointer to it, then pass the pointer to the called procedure (much like in C). This method simply does not work in VBA. Since there is no pointer capability in VBA, the passed-in variant is treated as the array, and the original array is never filled. This is because the variant is passed-in by reference as its own variable and not as a pointer to the array it was set equal to. This whole process exists because you cannot pass arrays into procedures imposed by VBA on the procedure's declaration list. Below we have illustrated a typical situation of passing a Variant into a procedure. The called procedure can then use variant as an array and fill it using subscripts. The filled array is then available in the calling routine after the called procedure is finished.

```
Dim Pnt As Variant

Dim Ent As Object

Call GetEnt(Ent, Pnt)

Public Sub GetEnt(Ent As Object, Pnt As Variant)
```

The Pnt variable contains an array point created by the selection object. You can access each of the elements in the Pnt variable as though it was a declared array.

The same problem exists in trying to pass the array back to the calling procedure. An array cannot be used to receive data from a procedure. Always use a variant in both the calling procedure and the called procedure in that situation. The project called Array.dvb supplied on the CD with this book has three procedures you can experiment with to see these differences. They are

- Pass_Declared_Array

- Undeclared_Array

- Pass_Undeclared_Array

To check them out, you must load the project and call each one from the immediate window in the Visual Basic Editor.

Passing an Array to an Object's Methods

Passing an array to an object's method works great, but it is different from passing one to a procedure. Some of the Autodesk object methods want an array of doubles passed to them for holding data (usually a point). Several of the model's utility object methods want an array of doubles for points. They include:

AnglefromAxis	GetAngle
GetCorner	GetDistance
GetEntity	GetOrientation
PolarPoint	TranslateCoordinates

Another AutoCAD model object that uses the array of doubles as an argument for its method is the Selectionset object. The methods are

- SelectAtPoint
- SelectByPolygon
- SelectOnScreen

There are many more examples in the AutoCAD object model. In general, when a model object's method needs a point, it needs an array of doubles. We have shown the syntax for that type of operation below.

```
Dim ptPick(0 To 2) As Double

ThisDrawing.Utility.GetEntity mobjBlockRef,ptPick,"Select a Block"
```

Collections and Procedures

Collections are similar to arrays but without all of the storage restrictions. You do not have to declare the size of a collection before using it, and you do not have to change the declaration of the collection as you add more items. The only restriction placed on you with collections is that you cannot store user-defined data types in them.

```
Dim colOne As New Collection

colOne.Add 1

colOne.Add 2
```

300

```
colOne.Add 3
Dim i As Long
For i = 1 To colOne.Count
Debug.Print "colOne(" & i; ") = " & colOne.Item(i)
Next i
```

The above code illustrates how to spin through a collection to retrieve items. Collections are indexed from 1, not 0, as in an array. You have a Count property to find out how many items are in the collection. The Item method allows you to retrieve data from a collection while the Add and Remove methods allow you to put data into and delete data from a collection. Below we have illustrated creating a collection, adding items to it, spinning through it, and printing the items.

```
Dim colOne as Collection
Set colOne = New Collection
```

Passing a collection to another procedure to be loaded is similar to passing an array, except that you do not need to use a Variant containing the collection. You can pass the collection directly, and the procedure will load it. One feature of the collection object is that you can declare it in one line and initiate it in another. The example shown above illustrates the one-line method of declaring and initiating the collection, called colOne, at the same time. Another method is shown below.

```
Dim colOne as Collection
Set colOne = New Collection
```

This ability to split the declaration and initiation of a collection allows you to pass in a declared and initiated collection or just a declared collection and let the called procedure load the collection. Unfortunately, you cannot pass back a collection, so you must always use an existing collection that is passed in, similar to the array problem. This is a minor problem and just another trait of the language. Several collection examples are provided on the CD in the Collection.dvb project. Run any of the following procedures to see how collections behave.

- Pass_Collection

- Pass_Declared_Collection

- Pass_Undeclared_Collection

- Return_Collection

You can load the project and run any of the procedures in the immediate window. The Return_Collection procedure will fail. This is done to illustrate that Collections cannot be passed back from a function.

Short Circuit Evaluation

Short circuit evaluation is the order the language deals with in a complex condition statement. In AutoLISP, the language checks the first part of the condition, then moves on to the next part of the complex statement when the first condition is valid. This is very convenient: it lets you check to see if a variable has a value bound to it before you compare it with something in the same line of code. In VBA, you can either sync the data type for comparison or do everything all on one line of code—or you can first check to see if the variable exists. Then place the code for the comparison inside the true condition of the statement. Earlier in the chapter, we gave you an example of syncing the divergence data type for comparison. That example allowed you to check on one line of code a variable that might contain a NULL. The example shown below illustrates the longer way of testing first, then continuing to process.

```
Dim groupname As Variant

groupname = frmGroupNames.1stGroupNames.Value

If Not IsNULL groupname Or Len(groupname) > 0 Then       ' #1 -
'causes an error

If Not IsNULL groupname                                  ' #2 - first
'see if its null or not

    If Len(groupname) > 0 Then                           ' #2a - now
'check if it has data in it
```

The line #1 causes an error in VBA when the variable contains a NULL because it is an example of short circuit evaluation (which does not work in VBA). VBA does not stop evaluating the line of code just because the last thing it evaluated was invalid. In AutoLISP (different syntax, same principle), it would work because the language would stop evaluating the line of code when the groupname was NULL.

Lines 2 and 2a are one way of doing it in VBA. VBA would never get to the 2a line of code because it would evaluate the line 2 code and move past the true condition when the variable contained NULL. The more elegant way of testing was shown in the divergence data type comparison section, earlier in this chapter.

The bottom line is that when you get an error on your condition statement of invalid data type, chances are that you have run into short circuit evaluation. You can solve the problem by the above example or by syncing the data type as shown in the divergence data type comparison section of this chapter.

Accessing Objects on the Same Level as Your Current Object

The AutoCAD object model has a hierarchy. The AutoCAD application is the top object, with everything in it under it. When you are working with an object and you need to work with another object on the same level of the hierarchy, you need to specify the parent object first. Under the application object are the preference and document objects. While working with the document object, you can access the Preferences object by explicitly using the application object in the call to the object. Figure 12.1 illustrates part of the object model's hierarchy.

The Application object represents the application's frame controls and path settings and provides the means to navigate down the object hierarchy. This can be confusing because the application appears to be under the special object called ThisDrawing, but it is actually the other way around. ThisDrawing is the special shortcut name for the document.

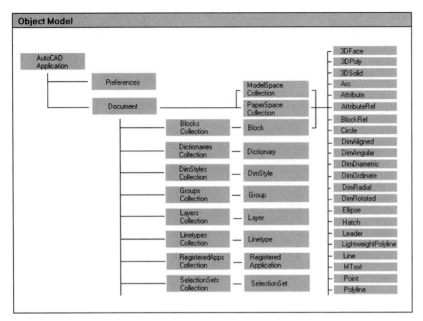

Figure 12.1: AutoCAD Object Model

Given the following code, you could access the preferences while working on the document (same level).

```
Dim preferences As AcadPreferences

Set preferences = ThisDrawing.Application.Preferences


Dim strConfigFile As String

strConfigFile = preferences.ConfigFile          'Line #1
```

The code in the example sets the AcadPreferences object to the Preferences object by starting from the document (ThisDrawing), and moving up the hierarchy to the application object, then down to the Preferences object, which is at the same level as the document object. It can then access any object under the Preferences object as shown in line #1. You can see how the object path is going up and then back down by reviewing the object model. Using the explicit definition of the whole object trail or using the With statement allows you to access any object in the object model at any time.

304

Listbox Columns

Listbox columns are one of those things that you would think obvious, but even intermediate level programmers can stumble on it the first time. It's not hard, but columns in lists are very flexible, and you can do many things with them. For example:

- You can have up to ten columns in a listbox.

- Columns can be different sizes.

- Columns can be hidden.

- You can specify which column will return a value on selection.

- You can load data into the columns or specify a two-dimensional array that is linked to the listbox and its columns.

- You can create a column header within the listbox.

Multiple columns

Creating the columns in a listbox is easy. Simply enter how many columns you want into the ColumnCount property of the listbox object.

Column Size

Controlling the width and visibility of the columns is not as obvious, even though there is a ColumnWidth property on the listbox. The ColumnWidth property uses points per inch (much like a font) to measure the width. When you set a column position to 0, the column is not shown. If you do not specify a width, the default is to split up the columns into equal sizes. The minimum size is 72 points, but you can make them smaller. A sample of column widths for a listbox with three columns is shown below.

```
ColumnWidth | 40 pt; 40 pt; 40
```

It should be noted that you could use inches instead of points in the above example. Consult your VBA online help for ColumnWidths to see a more detailed discussion of this property.

Column Visibility

To make the second column invisible the ColumnWidths property would be set as shown below.

Listbox Column Specification

One of the nice features of using columns in a listbox is the ability to access any of the columns on a selected item. You can set the BoundColumn property of the listbox to the column number you want values from when an item is selected in the listbox. This works even when the BoundColumn is set to a column that the user can't see! This allows you to build a two-dimensional array in which one element of the array is visible to the user but the other isn't. When the user selects from their visible list, you can use the invisible list to process the data item. This is a great feature for things like associating a color in English that the user sees, but processing the associated color number behind the scenes.

Loading Listbox Columns

There are three methods for loading listbox columns. Actually, only one example is a method; the other two are properties of the listbox. They are

- AddItem
- List
- Column

AddItem Method

The AddItem method allows you to add data to a single column or multiple columns in a listbox. Given a listbox called lstItemWindow with a ColumnCount of 1, the code to load an array of data into the listbox would look like that shown below.

```
Dim intI As Integer
With IsItemWindow
     For intI = 0 To UBound(SampleArray)
              .AddItem SampleArray(intI, 0)
     Next intI
End With
```

To add data to multiple columns (after changing the ColumnCount to 2) using the AddItem method, the code would look like that shown below.

```
Dim intI As Integer
With IsItemWindow
     For intI = 0 To UBound(SampleArray)
              .AddItem SampleArray(intI, 0)
              Column(1,.ListCount - 1) = SampleArray(intI, 1)
     Next intI
End With
```

Notice that the only difference between the single loading example and the one for two columns is the line of code marked in italic. You must first use the AddItem method to put the data into the first column, then immediately use the Column property to add the next piece of data.

List and Column Properties

Both of the above AddItem examples use a two-dimensional array (previously constructed and loaded). There are two different properties of the listbox that allow you to link a two-dimensional array directly to a listbox without having to load each item individually. The List property is just one line of code as shown below.

```
1stListWindow.List = SampleArray          'load using list property
```

Just setting the listbox property equal to the array is enough to access all of the data in the array. The Column property behaves the same way

307

except for the fact that it inverts the X,Y of the array to Y,X. When you have need of this feature, you should use the column property instead of the List property. The load would look like that shown below.

```
1stColumnWindow.Column = SampleArray      'load using Column

property
```

Column Headers

Column headers are available when you set the ColumnHeads property of the listbox to True. But they will work only with a rowsources attached. This is not a feature that can be currently used with AutoCAD.

To review the various column features, you can open the Columns.dvb project (supplied with this book) and run the ColumnSamples macro.

Multiselect in a Listbox

There are three types of selection you can use in a listbox:

- fmMultiSelectSingle to select a single item at a time.

- fmMultiSelectSingle to select multiple items one at a time.

- fmMultiSelectSingle to select multiple items in groups using the shift key.

Single item selection is the default, but you can select any of the three using the MultiSelect property of the listbox. The supplied sample project Columns.dvb has three list boxes on the form. The left one is a single select box, the middle one is a multiselect box, and the right one is an extended multiselect box. To review the various multiselect features, you can open the Columns.dvb project (supplied with this book) and run the ColumnSamples macro. After loading some data into the boxes, try selecting in each box to see the difference in how they work.

Variable Name Shortcuts

VBA has the ability to recognize the old Basic shortcut variable naming conventions (type-declaration characters). This is very advantageous for those programmers who already know the shortcuts but very confusing for those who don't want to dump a portion of their childhood from memory just to memorize them. The shortcuts are cryptic and hard to understand unless you know them or have a chart. An example of the type-declaration character in an Integer is the percent sign (%). This is counterproductive during programming or maintenance. It is better to spend your time working on the design of the program than trying to understand a cryptic variable data type. It is best not to use the old shortcuts for these reasons. Programmers maintain code much more than they create new code (just like editing in AutoCAD is done more than creating new geometry). Why add extra effort to deciphering the code?

Command Line Workaround

This section is provided because VBA in AutoCAD Release 14 was a younger implementation in AutoCAD, and not all objects were exposed yet. Because of this, you actually need a command line workaround for dealing with objects that are not in the VBA object model yet.

Autodesk said it couldn't be done, so naturally we had to find out how to do it. (We must give credit where it is due to Andy Baron and Mike Gunderloy of Application Developers. They researched and wrote the code that makes it possible to use the command line from a VBA application.) We also need to stress that you should not use this workaround for anything other than non-supported objects in VBA. The example provided is for external references. VBA for AutoCAD Release 14 does not have an Xref object, thereby limiting it from working with external references. It is one of the few legitimate reasons for having access to the command line from VBA at this time, and it is the main reason this section is included in this book.

The Problem

The linkage code in VBA behaves much like a DDE linkage in VB on the surface. There is no way to monitor what's happening on the command line. You are stuck with jamming a command down the pipeline and hoping for the best. To further complicate the matter, you cannot work around the problem like you can in VB because while VBA is running, the command you sent down the pipeline is not executed. It happens only when VBA is done.

In VB with DDE, a common method was to stay in a loop until a semaphore was set. You would launch the code to AutoCAD, then switch to a wait state subroutine looking for the semaphore. The launched code would set the semaphore as the last thing it did and your wait state code in VB would see the change and allow the program to continue. This worked because VB was in its own memory pool, not AutoCAD's, and it did not have to close down to run the command. Because the command will not run until the VBA macro ends, you cannot put VBA into a wait state looking for a semaphore. It would just hang there since the semaphore would never get set because the launched code would not run until VBA stopped. A perfect catch-22. Fortunately, there is a solution.

The Solution

The supplied project called Commands.dvb has a sendcommand macro definition that illustrates how you can use the workaround. The workaround in VBA is to send one string to AutoCAD to be processed and tack on the AutoLISP (command "-vbarun" "sendcommand") line at the end of whatever code you're sending down the pipeline. The result is that VBA sends the command and dies. Then the command line is executed in AutoCAD, and the last line of the stream is the call to load the 'sendcommand' macro again. To use this in production would mean that you would need to save the variable state in VBA before closing down and restore it again when starting up (a simple enough procedure using the registry or a temporary file).

This solution is not pretty and needs testing to determine if it blows the command stack or causes any other memory problems—but it does work.

Passing Forms and Controls as Parameters

A small problem arises when you want to access the information of a form or control when not in the form's module. You can't directly do it. You must pass the form or control into the procedure to access its properties and methods from any other module than the form's module. While VBA doesn't pass arrays into procedures, it does allow you to pass objects. The form and its controls are all objects. The rule of thumb is to pass the form when you want to access any of its controls or pass a specific control when you want to just work with it.

Occasionally, you may even pass in both. The project file Control.dvb (on supplied CD) has an example of this situation in the Tabs procedure of the BasGlobal module. The form is passed in to allow the procedure to spin through all of the controls on the form, but an individual control (a multipage control) is passed in for quick access to its properties. The routine could just as easily have been written to accept the form and the multipage's name. Then the code would have had to find the requested control as it spun through the various controls of the passed-in form. One technique is not any better than the other—they are just different ways of approaching the design. The syntax of the procedure taking a form and control is

```
Public Sub Tabs(Form As UserForm, Ctrl As Control)
```

One problem that arises when trying to manipulate a form or its controls from a procedure that is outside the form's module is that you don't get the benefit of the Intellisense design feature in the outside module as you design. This means that you need to know the object's properties and methods to access them (no hints as you type). One method of getting around this problem is to design the module inside the form procedure and then move it over to the support module. Naturally, you will

311

need to make adjustments after the move, but these are minor compared with trying to work without that great Intellisense crutch.

Another thing to remember about the design mode is that the Properties window doesn't always show all of the object's properties. Some properties are present only at runtime and are not in the window at design time. This little fact can drive you to distraction when designing. You know that there was a property but it is not on the list. That's why it is important to use the online help and the object browser.

Multipage Form Controls

The multipage form control has the ability to have more than one tab. You organize your various other form controls on the different tabs you create, and you can access them from anywhere in the form module. This fact allows you to be creative with controls on various pages of a multipage control. You can collect data from controls on different pages or process only pages you want. Since the multipage control is part of a page collection, you can get a count of how many pages are on the control and move around the pages by accessing the page names or the index number corresponding to the page you want. The ability to use the page name is a collection feature that arrays do not have. The Control.dvb project (on supplied CD) has examples of the techniques for using the multipage control.

Conclusion

Even if you are an experienced VB programmer, you should have found one or two tips in this chapter that you didn't know before. These solutions and tips are all based on fighting through these problems directly. We hope your adventures in VBA will be all the more enjoyable with these road hazards and features off to the side called out in advance and out of the way.

CHAPTER THIRTEEN

Programming Style

S tyle is always a difficult subject to broach because everyone
believes that his or her system is the best. Still, there are many
things about programming style that programmers can agree
upon. The reason we need a common style is so anyone trying to maintain our code can read it and understand it. Whether you write for multiple clients, or in-house for your company, or at home to make your
projects run more quickly, it is best to follow some simple guidelines for
your code. Good style code always has the following guidelines in common. Some of the important common guidelines are:

- The code is always well commented.

- The code is kept concise and simple.

- Repetitive actions are placed in their own subroutines or functions.

- Variables are defined within the proper scope, precedence, and life.

- All modules have error trapping.

We can look at these common guidelines in detail in the following
pages. Whole books have been written on the subject—and this chapter
just covers some of the more common guidelines.

Commenting Your Code

On the surface, commenting on code may seem to be a common sense practice but you would be amazed at how programmers interpret this subject. Some ignore it and do not comment at all, others comment only at the beginning of a section of code, and others comment every line. Not commenting your code at all is an open invitation to disaster. No matter how good you are, failing to comment the code will lead to confusion when you are maintaining your program later. While there is no right or wrong way to commenting (as long as you do comment some), comments can be taken to extremes. If you make too few comments, you can end up with code that looks good to you while you are writing the program, but six months later, you might be lost on why you did something. On the other hand, if you comment too much, your commenting can result in cluttered code that is difficult to read and maintain.

The comments themselves can also create clarity or confusion. There are at least two types of comments. The first is a comment on the design of the code. That is, why you did what you did or how you approached the program's design in this particular section. An example of this type of comment is shown below.

```
' Public Function Position_recordset(ByRef dcData As Control) As Long

' Note: dcData must be a control of type "Data Access"

' This function is needed because the record count is not
accurate until you do a movelast and movefirst on the

' recordset. This causes a problem when there are no records in
the set. This function passes back the record

' count as a long. An example of the function call would be:

' Data1.Recordsource = "SQL statement here"

' Data1.Refresh

' Dim Reccount As Long

' Reccount = Position_recordset(Data1)

' If Reccount > 0 Then

' do your work on the recordset here....
```

```
'  Else
'     Msgbox "No records found".
'  end if
end function
```

The above code example tells the future programmer about the incoming argument and why the function was created. It even gives an example of how to use the function in the calling program. All of the comments are placed at the head of the function and are sometimes referred to as header comments. Because of these comments, any programmer can understand the nature of the function and plug it into any program by copying and pasting the example code into the program to use it.

The other type of comment is the comment that tries to clarify the action of the code. One way to use this comment is on condition statements and loops. An example of this type of comment is shown below.

```
' The following code loops through all entries in the selection
set and assigns the xdata to each entity.

Dim ent As Object
For Each ent In sset        'For each entity in the selection set
      ent.SetXData xdataType, xdata        'assign the xdata to the entity
Next ent
```

The above comments clarify what the loop is going to do. Some programmers mistakenly think that each line in the program needs this type of comment. That isn't true (although, we sometimes do it when commenting code for a book or article). Simple coding like setting a variable or declaring a variable is so common that all programmers know what you are doing; and commenting on it is unnecessary and clutters up the code. Occasionally, you might comment on the declaration of a variable or its usage when it is not obvious why it is being used or where it was created (if it seems out of scope). It's perfectly all right to do this when this happens. However, you need to keep out of those situations as much as possible because it makes it hard to understand the code when you or someone else is in maintenance mode.

Another example of action commenting is when you are filling in some data that you feel might need better explaining for anyone who's working on the code later. An example of this type of action comment is shown below. A discussion of the scope and life of a variable is included later in this chapter.

```
' The following two variable definitions must be arrays of the
same size.

' The first variable holds integer values that define the types of
the data in the second variable. The first value

' (index 0) of one variable maps to the same index of the other
variable.

Dim xdataType(0 To 1) As Integer    'Define xdataType for the data types

Dim xdata(0 To 1) As Variant        'Define xdata for the data values

' The following variable assignments define the values for each
array.

xdataType(0) = 1001 '1001 indicates the RegApp name

xdata(0) = appName  'RegApp name string value

xdataType(1) = 1000 '1000 indicates a string value

xdata(10 = xdataStr 'Xdata string value
```

The example shown above clarifies the data type and other type of data being placed into the arrays. Notice that even in a situation where the comments are helpful, comments on every line make the code look cluttered. One way of making sure the clutter is at a minimum is to use tabs and align the comments. This is a common practice and helps a lot with the look of the code. Perhaps the single best reason to comment your code is that even though a program might be a couple of lines long, it will someday have to be read and maintained by someone else.

Keeping Code Concise and Simple

You would think that keeping code concise and simple would be common sense items, but programmers often abused them. When your code starts running on, page after page, it becomes hard to decipher and maintain. It is better to divide the code into subroutines or functions and call them as needed. This shortens the routine you're in and makes it easier to read. Some programmers argue that this method can actually make it harder to read the code. While this can happen, it is better to comment the action of the call to the subroutine and move on. With good comments, it does become easier to read the code (but not always easier to maintain). A good rule of thumb is to keep routines no longer than one paper page (about forty lines of code) long. This makes it easy to print out the code when needed for review. Younger programmers are using paper less and less as they have gotten used to the screen and the search mechanisms in the editors. Many programmers that have been around for a while still like to print out the code for review. This is a matter of convenience; however you choose to go about it, but by following the rule, your code is simple to read by either group.

Experienced programmers sometimes laugh at simple code. They seem to feel that because it is simple it is not useful or they feel the need to show off their expertise with the language. This is nice for the ego but terrible for the programmers who follow and must maintain the code. It is far better to write a simple piece of elegant code than to write code that is complex for its own sake. The average programmer can maintain simple code, and the average programmer is always the bulk of the programmers out there. An example of code differences in VBA is collections and arrays. Microsoft would rather we used the new paradigm of collections to hold lists of items, but most programmers who have been around for a long time and used VB or BASIC know how to use arrays for that type of activity. Collections have a clear advantage over arrays because they do not have to be declared as a specific length, and you do not have to re-dimension them on the fly when you add data from a data list of an unknown length (thus making them simpler than arrays). However, using an array is more common and therefore easier to maintain by a greater number of programmers. Some programmers will argue (rightfully so) that all programmers should understand the language to that depth, and they will use the collection instead of the array to do the work. The thing to remember in that situation is to comment the process for later maintenance.

Knowing when to use a complex or a simple piece of code is important and, in certain situations, it can drive how you code. The example of collections and arrays is a good illustration of this problem. A common use of arrays in AutoCAD is to hold a point. The X, Y, Z points are stored in the array and referenced by their position in the array. This process in this situation is actually more complex using a collection. Using an array (usually the more complex code) is better because the collection is more complex to code, understand, and maintain in this simple situation.

Proper Use of Subroutines and Functions

Subroutines and functions (procedures) are the mechanisms used to create concise code in your program. Subroutines and functions are treated the same in VBA except that functions return information while subroutines don't. If you have experience coding procedural languages (such as AutoLISP), you still should have been doing something like this by creating modules to make your code more concise. Whenever you have repetitive code that is going to be used more than once in a program, you should place it in a procedure. The exception to this rule is when the code is just one line of code. Then it doesn't make much sense to do it unless you are adjusting how the code returns information (a function).

An example of a subroutine that might perform a repetitive task is a routine for reading information in from a file. The routine would take the desired location, file name, and a variant pointer to a collection or array and fill the object with the information in the file. Your passing routine would only check to see if the object has any information in it after the call and before continuing the processing. The subroutine would not pass back the object; it would just fill it out when the file was found.

An example of a function that might perform a repetitive task would be a parsing function. This function would take a string, a delimiter, and a position and return the string found at the position requested from the string sent using the delimiter provided. The function takes up about twenty lines of code, but you can use it over and over again in the main program. Each call in the main program is just one line of code instead of twenty. This makes the program more concise and easier to maintain. You know that the function works the same every time: and the only problem could be that you request something that is beyond the length of the string (which should be trapped for in the function). The whole program becomes easier to understand and maintain.

Scope, Precedence, and Life of Variables

All programming languages have variables. How you work with them determines, in part, your programming style. Scope, precedence, and life of a variable are there in some form in every programming language. Scope of a variable is where that variable is available to be used. Precedence of a variable is which scope declaration wins in a given situation when VBA encounters a variable declared in multiple procedures. Life of a variable is how long that variable exists within the scope. Each language has a different way of treating the scope of the variable, the precedence, and how long it lives within that scope. The AutoLISP language 'declares' scope in the function definition. When you list the variable to the right of the slash in the parenthesis, the variable is available only inside that function. Any information bound to that variable is lost when the function is done running (that is, at the end of its life). You can change the life of the variable by unbinding it before the scope ends. Then the life is less than the scope. When a variable is not listed in the function's definition, it stays in scope as long as you are in AutoCAD (this started in AutoCAD Release 14 with the ability to define persistent AutoLISP variables) or until you exit the drawing. The variable is commonly referred to as a global variable in this situation. Precedence takes place when you declare the same variable name in both the calling routine and in the subroutine. The declaration on the local level always has precedence over any other declaration. That means that the variable inside the local routine will not change the value of the same named variable in the calling routine.

In VBA, you have even more possibilities for scope definition. VBA has forms (actually they are special Class Modules), Modules and Class Modules. Where you place the definition of the variable makes its scope, precedence, and life different. A variable defined in a form is available only to routines in that form. To make it even more complex, there are many different types of variable definitions you can make. There are Public, Global, Private, Const, Dim, and Static variable definitions. They can be placed in the declaration area of the form or in subroutines and functions of the form. To complicate things further, you can place these defin-itions in other modules or class modules and still make them available to the routines in the form! The relationship of the variable scope within modules of VBA can be illustrated using the diagram shown in Figure 13.1.

Several of the declarations shown in the diagram are illegal, and VBA will stop you from using them by stopping the compilation and telling you

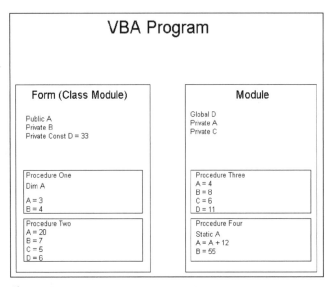

Figure 13.1. Scope, Precedence, and Life example

that the variable is already declared within the current scope. We have shown them to illustrate the scope concepts. A couple of rules for declarations are:

- Use Private instead of Dim in the Declaration section.

- Static can be declared only at the Procedure level.

- In a standard module, Public is the default scope when none is specified.

- In a class module, Private is the default scope when none is specified.

You can experiment with the concepts by opening the Scope.dvb project (on supplied CD) and running the various buttons on the form. Table 13.1 illustrates how scope is affected when you declare the variable in Figure 13.1 and how the precedence works within the scope.

Table 13.1: Scope of the variables.

Procedure	Results
Program Initiation	**D is set to 33 for any procedure in the Form.**
Procedure One	Dim A is illegal in the current scope. You can't declare it since it is already declared as a Public variable in the Form. Remove the Dim statement and proceed.
	A is then set to 3 for any procedure in the Form.
	B is set to 4 for any procedure in the Form.
Procedure Two	C is not declared in the Form. An error occurs. Declare C or remove the C = statement.
	A is set to 20 for any procedure in the Form.
	B is 7 for any procedure in the Form.
	D is set to 11 for any procedure in the Module. It is set to 33 for any procedure in the Form.
Procedure Three	A is set to 4 for any procedure in the Module but not in the Form.
	B is illegal because it is not declared anywhere in the Module and it is private to the Form.
	C is set to 6 for any procedure in the Module but not in the Form.
	D is set to 55 for any procedure in the Module but not in the Form.
Procedure Four	A is set to 12 the first time the procedure runs, 24 the second time, 36 the third time, and so on.
	B is illegal in the Module because it is never declared in the Module and is private in the Form.

To check the life of the variables, you can put a watch on the variable (use the variable in the declaration) and see how the variable changes (or doesn't change) as you move through each procedure. Each procedure has a stop placed in it so you can set up your watches, and then step through each line, one line at a time, using the {F8} key.

Error Trapping

Another critical style item is error trapping. Just when you think you have the program bullet-proof, a brain-dead user comes along and breaks it. Who's wrong in that situation, the user for trying something out of the ordinary or the programmer who didn't anticipate the potential problem? Sorry—the programmer is the correct answer. You should develop a style of programming that includes error trapping in every module. This brings up another style item. Good object-oriented programming means having only one point to enter a procedure and one point to exit a procedure. Error trapping has to be considered as part of this one-point entry and exit style. An example of one-point entry and exit and error trapping is shown below.

```
Public Sub ErrorTest1()

    Dim FileName As String

    FileName = "c:\"

    On Error GoTo HandleErr

    'all work goes here

    FileLen (FileName)

ExitHere:

    Exit Sub

HandleErr:

    Select Case Err.Number

        Case 53

            Msgbox "File" & FileName & "not found.,_
            vbOKOnly + vbExclamation
```

322

```
        Case Else
                'Call a generic last-ditch error handler
                Call HandleErrors
        End Select
        Resume ExitHere
    End Sub
```

This typical error trapping code can be installed into any routine and modified for the type of errors expected. It uses the select statement and labels to control the flow of the program after an error is encountered. Notice how everything leads to the ExitHere label whether an error is encountered or not. Situations can occur in which it seems pointless to include code of this type, but it is good practice to include it anyway as you never know when a procedure might be expanded. Notice that there is a trap for errors that are not specifically handled by the routine. That trap calls a subroutine that passes along the regular error message to the user but allows them to keep working. Certain critical errors will still bomb the program, but in most cases it is a graceful way to trap an error. It also emphasizes the fact that you must do error handling in each procedure, but you can call out to other subroutines once you have trapped the error in the procedure. An error-trapping example is supplied on the CD called 'Errors.dvb'. You can experiment with it to walk though the code and see how the error handler works.

Do You Need to Change Your Programming Style for VBA?

Whether you need to change your programming style for VBA all depends on how you have been programming up until now. If your style already includes the points discussed in this chapter, then you probably don't need to change much. This assumes that you have already been programming in an event- driven language such as VBA. If you have been writing code in a procedure- driven language, like AutoLISP, it could be a different story. You could have been doing all of the things listed in this chapter and still have to change your programming style. That is because event-driven programming requires a different programming approach than procedural-driven programming does. The differences are discussed later in this chapter, but you need to understand that the difference is enough to revisit these issues in a new light.

One common habit to avoid in your programming style is the use of global variables. This can be a very tempting trap because it is something you can declare once and then you don't have to worry about the darn things again. When you do this, the issue of scope, precedence, and life comes into play, and you have the added problem of some routine changing a value of a global variable when you don't expect it. The better approach is to use global variables to define constants but pass arguments to routines for processing. The routines can then declare variables locally and process the passed argument. This is a good rule of thumb, but like any general rule you will have exceptions where it is compelling to use a global variable. Don't be afraid to use global variable; just keep them to a minimum for maintenance's sake.

It is important to know that Error handling in VBA is hierarchical in nature. That means that an error will be trapped by the first routine that has error handling in it. If an error occurs in your routine, and there is no trapping in your routine, the error is passed up to the calling routine. If that routine does not have error trapping, the program will keep handing up the error to the calling routines until it reaches the topmost routine. If that routine does not handle the error, VBA handles it (and this is not always pretty).

Event-Driven versus Procedural-Driven Language

The biggest difference between event- driven and procedural- driven programming languages is finding your code in the event- driven program. Naturally, this is from the point of view of a procedural language programmer who has to switch to a language such as VBA. When you stop and think about it, it really is not all that different. A very complex procedural language program that has been divided into modules can be as difficult to read as any event-driven program. Procedural languages are linear in nature. The program has one starting point and continues one line after another until the end of the program. You can place calls to subroutines, but there is always a main program that drives everything.

Event-driven languages (like VBA) are different because they can have a common starting point (the loading of a form), but they don't necessarily have to start with a form. You can select from a list of subroutines to start from whether a form is present or not. Once a form is loaded, the program waits for you to select something on the form. When you select something on the form, it triggers an event and the code associated with that event. The associated code can then call other subroutines or just process and return to the wait state of the form or end the program. There are lots of options for just one event on one form.

Event-driven language is further complicated by the fact that you can place all of the procedures in the form module or you can separate them into multiple modules. This has a direct effect on your style. What is best? That is a hard question to answer. This subject is much like the layer and file naming argument that has been around for years among AutoCAD users. Everyone has an opinion and a standard; therefore there is no standard. Probably the best solution is to separate your code in a systematic fashion. Keep the form module holding any event code for the form. Create at least one support module that contains routines that support the form's routines. You can split up the support routines into multiple modules if you like. A common method of splitting support modules is to have a global module for generic support routines and other modules for supporting things like registry, database, MAPI, and Window API calls. This allows you to have support modules that you can plug and play into any project. Many of the support modules in this book follow that method of splitting support files.

The Hungarian Naming Convention

Naming conventions have always driven would-be programmers and CAD drafters to the edge of sanity. Whether they're discussing layers, file names, form controls, or variables, it is a hotly debated issue. About the only thing people can seem to agree on is that we need a standard naming convention. In VBA, it is important that you adopt some standardized way of labeling the various components in the program. This is not just for variables: but the form's controls and even procedure names should be standardized. Many programmers have adopted a variation of the Hungarian naming convention. One of the original ways of naming program components was developed by Charles Simonyi (a Hungarian, thus the name). Most programmers take the basic idea and adjust it for their own styles. As long as the standard is consistently applied to the program, it makes the program easier to read and maintain. It all boils down to making variable names, form controls, and procedures reflect their data type (for variables) and what they do. This can often lead to long variable, form control, and procedure names, but it is worth the extra effort when you go to debug a problem or maintain an old piece of code. The following section documents some of the conventions used in the example code in this book.

Variables

Tacking on the data type of the variable as a prefix to the variable name makes it easier to identify what should be in the variable when you're debugging a problem. Finding an unexpected data type in a variable can lead to solving a problem much more quickly than having to guess at something that looks correct but isn't. Table 13.2. shows a standard you can adopt.

Table 13.2: Variable prefix tags

Prefix Tag	Object Type
Byt	Byte
Bol	Boolean
Cur	Currency
Dtm	Date
Dbl	Double
Int	Integer
Lng	Long
Obj	Object
Sng	Single
Str	String
Var	Variant

Using the above examples, a few typical variable names would be:

- BolAnswer   for a true/false variable
- VarField   for a variant type
- Lngx   for a long counter
- StrLine   for a string

Use explicit data type definition at all times in conjunction with the naming conventions. Never assume that the programmer reading your code knows the short cuts or understands the implicit defaults of a variable's data type definition. Some explicit data type definitions are below:

```
Dim bolAnswer as Boolean
Dim varField as Variant
Dim lngX as Long
Dim strLine as string
bolAnswer = True
VarField = ""
lngX = 0
strLine = ""
```

Constants

Keeping track of constants is relatively easy. Tack 'con' on to the front of the constant. You can add a tag for class modules if you are worried about constants conflicting between modules. You could use 'usr' for a user class with a 'c' tacked on after for the class distinction before the constant tag.

conPi   for Pi

usrcError123   for an error handler

User-Ddefined TTypes and CClasses

Make the prefix based upon what the class or user type does. If the user-defined type is for a bitmap, you might use 'bit' as the prefix.

bitImage

Collections

The data type of the collection should be used as the prefix with an 's' following. This may seem strange at first glance but when the final name is constructed you see that the 's' makes the name reflect that the object is plural and contains many items.

intsEnties

Form Controls

Here you have two choices. You could use just the control type as a prefix or you could combine it with the data type that the control will hold. An example of the combination prefix would be:

txtstrFilename   for a text edit file containing a string filename

btncmdOK   for an OK command button

The different types of common VBA form controls are listed in Table 13.3. Many other third-party controls exist, and you can be adapt them to the naming convention.

Table 13.3: Control tags

Prefix tTag	Object tType
ani	Animation
btn	Button
hdr	Column header
ctl	Controls
frm	Form
iml	Image list
lim	List Image
lit	List Item
lvw	List View
nod	Node in treeview
pnl	Status bar panel
prb	Progress bBar
sld	Slider
sbr	Status bar
tab	Tab
tbr	Tab strip
tvw	Tree view
upd	Up down

Procedures

VBA names the event procedures for the form—and you can't change them (or the code wouldn't work). User-named procedures should have the first letter of each word capitalized:

CmdOK_Click

RightToken

Chk_Plural

Fatal_Error

Modules

Since modules are Visual Basic modules, use 'bas' as a prefix for the module names. This also solves a problem in VBA that is not present in VB programs. VBA does not allow a module called Global. By adding the prefix, you get 'basGlobal', which is legal in VBA.

basRegistry

basDatabase

basMAPI

basWindows

Conclusion

As you can see by the material covered in this chapter, style is a complex subject. Entire books have been written on it. The material presented here was designed to stimulate your interest in the subject. There are several good books on the market covering programming style in much more depth than a single chapter can.

CHAPTER FOURTEEN

Class Modules and Objects

There are objects everywhere in programming these days. Understanding the different types of objects can be daunting to a programmer who doesn't have experience with them. In general, an object is a container that is used to store data, to maintain data, and (on certain types of objects) to respond to events. This chapter will explore the use of custom classes in VBA. Specifically, we are going to show how to create our own objects, and how we can manipulate these objects into programming tools that greatly enhance our ability as programmers to produce good applications.

Not All Objects Are Equal

All the entities in the AutoCAD database are objects. There are entity objects, collection objects, and so forth. The repeated use of the term object can get confusing when talking about programming—especially if you are new to object-oriented programming in the first place. One area of confusion in AutoCAD-based programming is that there are two types of objects.

The first type is a programming object that helps you in the program by organizing data and maintaining it. VBA allows you to create programming objects inside the program using the class module. Objects created in this manner have properties and methods; however, this type of object cannot contain event trigger definitions. We will see how to create an object after we see what is different between this kind of object and an AutoCAD object.

The second type of object is an AutoCAD object that is stored in the drawing database. AutoCAD objects are already defined: all you can do as an applications developer is manipulate them as they exist. That is, you can call the existing methods to change the properties of the objects. An important difference between this type of object and program objects is that AutoCAD objects can contain event triggers. Using event triggers, the objects from the AutoCAD database can behave under your program's control but still maintain the integrity of the database system.

Objects that you create in your own programming cannot contain event triggers. That is, you cannot teach AutoCAD to respond to some new event. Instead, you can use only those event triggers that are supplied. Now, you could have an event trigger run one of your object methods, and once we learn how to create our own objects we will explore that concept a little.

The VBA Class Module

Creating a new object in VBA means that you must define a new class module. A VBA class module is a programmer-defined object that has properties (stores data) and methods (maintains the data). This is a very handy tool for programming because you can build all of the tedious programming for storing data and maintaining it into the class module (one-time coding).

When defining a class, you define all of the functions, subroutines, and data elements as either public (the default) or private. When defined as private, the function or variable can be accessed only by other routines inside the class definition. That is, when you use a copy of the class definition, the application using the class can access only those elements defined as public. Private items inside the class object definition are off-limits to the application. Instead, the private items are modular subroutines within the class definition that are used exclusively by the class routines.

After a class module (object) is defined, you use the object's definition to create instances of the object as needed. When a variable is dimensioned, one of the data types available—along with all others—will be the new class name. An application can then use the object by supplying data and manipulating it via the methods defined in the class module. The application keeps track of the instances of the objects and not the lower level of any arrays or collections that the object contains for maintaining and storing the data. This makes the application program cleaner and easier to maintain.

The remainder of this chapter presents examples of custom classes and the code used to manipulate them. The CD that accompanies this book contains the source code for the projects, and you should reference it to see the code. You are welcome to manipulate these projects further to meet your own requirements. As you will see, the development of a class module is simple. Because it allows you to better organize your data, it will also repay you later. That is, when you're updating and changing code your application may require in the future, you will find that objects make the job much easier. Most often the only thing standing between a programmer and the definition of custom classes is that the terminology is confusing. Much like recursion and other advanced programming concepts, these ideas are easy to confuse, but once you understand them, they are very basic and simple to use.

Let's look at a custom object definition. The problem is, there are no truly simple examples. So please try to keep up as we explore a couple of examples that you will find both useful and instructional for understanding how VBA can be used to customize AutoCAD. While we're exploring these examples, we will present more information about objects in general, so you should read through them even if you think the application presented is of no interest to your operations.

The first example deals with extended data. Extended data attached to AutoCAD objects is considered the domain of programmers only. AutoCAD operations cannot access extended data without a tool like the one presented in this chapter. For most installations, this project is really only of use to the developers of custom applications, although it does demonstrate how easy something like extended data can become through the use of objects. The project also demonstrates the use of tabbed forms in VBA.

The next example deals with a simple production drawing problem of creating a hole chart. This routine will accept circles as input and display a chart sorting the circle data by diameter, then the X, then the Y location. Establishing hole types and labels further refines the hole chart information. Once you update the hole data list, it can be redrawn using the drawing rules in the custom objects. This project also demonstrates how to create a drawn chart given a collection of data.

Once you understand and appreciate the concepts behind custom objects, you will wonder how you developed sophisticated applications without them.

Objects Example 1: Extended Data Manipulations

This project presents a utility for manipulating extended data in a drawing. Extended data is attached to drawing objects and consists of lists of nongraphic data. In VBA, extended data is manipulated in the form of two arrays. The first array contains a coded type stored as an integer. The second array contains variable data types ranging from strings, doubles, and integers to entity handles. Manipulating extended data in VBA is somewhat cumbersome—it involves many loops through the arrays along with other processing tricks. The idea was to create an object that manipulates extended data in a fashion that makes it easier to build an application using extended data. After that, the next question was how to present this object to readers in a fashion that was both interesting and somewhat useful. From that perspective the extended data editor project idea originated.

A word of caution is needed: Extended data is used by specific applications and normally hidden from the casual AutoCAD operator. Only under programmatic control can you get at the extended data elements. The purpose of the example project is to allow an advanced operator or programmer to explore the extended data that can be found in a drawing. When the project is run, a dialog box appears that allows you to select AutoCAD objects. When the object selected contains extended data, it is displayed in the dialog box for the operator's subsequent edits. This utility should not be provided to most AutoCAD operators, as any changes they make to the extended data will most likely end up disabling the application that uses the data.

Getting back to programming, there is no object for extended data in AutoCAD VBA. Instead, AutoCAD VBA provides variant arrays for access into the extended data. There are two arrays. The first contains group code values that help decipher the value in the same array location of the second. By using an object to both store and manipulate the extended data information we can greatly simplify our programming effort concerning extended data. Consider the fact that any application that needs to manipulate the extended data must spin through the arrays working with multiple data types. Why not program a library of general-purpose utilities that take care of these problems and allow our applications to simply access the extended data in an orderly fashion? Let's start by building a custom class definition of the extended data object.

Making a Class Module

Building your own object inside VBA using the class module is embarrassingly simple. Go to the Insert pull-down in your project and insert a class module. Name it as you would any other module (for this example it is called Xdata since it will be used to maintain extended data information) and program your subroutines and functions in the new class module code window. It is that simple.

A class module differs from the other modules found in the VBA environment in that you can assign a variable to an instance of the class. A module is a library of subroutines and functions that your program can access. The functions and subroutines in the class module are the same as those in any other module in that they exist only once in an application. Only the data gets duplicated each time a new instance of the class is used. The functions and subroutines are referenced under the same name to help keep the confusion to a minimum by allowing polymorphism. This is how the add method is used over and over again in all the objects. The code portion of a module exists only once in a computer program. It is run over and over again using different data to achieve the desired results. So don't be tricked into thinking that the code component of a VBA class module needs to be kept small. The code is not duplicated for each instance of the class that is used in an application.

The rules for programming a class module are also very simple. Any public scope variable declared at the module level is an exposed property of the object in the calling program. Any public subroutine or function in the class module is an exposed method to the calling module. All the other rules for programming using scope, lifetime of the variable, and persistence are the same as in any other module in a program. When you want to create a variable, subroutine, or function that is not exposed as part of the object in the calling program module, you just declare it as a private scope. Naturally, all variables declared using the Dim statement in the class module's subroutines and functions are considered private variables and not exposed to the calling module. You can have properties that are any legal type of variable, including collections and arrays. The system will not figure out exactly which of your components in a class are private or public—you must supply that in the module definition. By default, if neither is specific, the item in question is considered to be public.

The benefit of creating your own object for programming is to program all of the detail maintenance code as methods of the object. Then you don't have to worry about it again. You just hand the data to the object's method you created and it does the work. You can concentrate on keeping track of the object instead of its data in your program. You can also have multiple instances of the object in your program; this way, your job becomes managing the objects instead of manipulating the data over and over again. Once you grasp the true power of object programming, it's hard to imagine how to develop an application without it.

Properties

Objects are containers of data and routines to manipulate that data. As a consequence, the place to start when you're defining a custom class (object) is with the data items or properties. Designing the properties that go with your custom object is a matter of evolution. As you start you will have some relatively clear ideas as to what properties (data items) you want to associate with your custom object. Then, as you code the routines that manipulate the properties, you discover something you had not considered—or you suddenly come up with a better way to store the information based on the application requirements. Don't be afraid to change your mind as you develop the object further. Most likely, additional data elements will be added to the property list as you create the methods for maintaining the primary data elements. Remember—one of the primary strengths of objects is that they can evolve. It is not uncommon to run into objects that store the same data in several different ways, and each of them works better for a given method or group of methods. Most often this results when the object has undergone several revisions in its lifetime. Some of the data storage techniques may be used only by older versions of the object's methods but are still provided for backward support.

The properties used for the custom extended data object were no exception. They evolved while the project was developed into a working application. Adding and removing properties (mostly adding) is something that will go on during the entire life of the object development—and sometimes afterward—as additional data may be required of the objects in the future. Something to keep in mind if you are a systems programmer who still counts the bytes is that objects can use up a lot of memory. For the most part the programmer does not have to be too aware of this; however, if you have properties that are not being used after the object has been developed it is a good idea to get rid of them. Regardless, you have to start somewhere, and that place is with an initial definition of the properties you will be holding in the object. The properties used in the project are declared in the class module's declaration section, as shown below. The project's name is Xdata (short for eXtended DATA). These properties are defined as public, meaning that any module that has this object as part of the project can access these data elements.

```
Option Explicit
Public xdatatype As Variant          ' holds object's xdata code array
Public xdatavalue As Variant  ' holds object's xdata value array
Public AppNames As New Collection  ' holds application names
Public ItemsCount As Long  ' holds count of xdata value array items
Public aryXdata As Variant  ' 2d array of xdata code & value arrays combined
Public EntityType As Long  ' Xdata object entity type = 0
```

Now let's take a closer look at these variables and how they are used in the class definition.

xdatatype, xdatavalue, aryXdata

When designing your own program object's properties, you need to consider how you intend to use the object in your programs. In the case of the extended data object we desired to have the arrays (named xdatatype and xdatavalue) remain exposed or public. We also desired to be able to put that information into a list box or combo box control on a form without much difficulty. This meant creating a two-dimensional array for the object (called aryXdata) that would contain the combined arrays and could then be used to load the list control in the calling module. Loading the two-dimensional array into a list control is then simply a matter of using the .LIST method of the object. To make the programming even easier, it is now possible to add a method to the extended data object that takes a list box control pointer as a parameter and puts the contents of the extended data arrays into the control.

Now, should the situation arise in which it is needed to load several extended objects into a control, they can be combined into one master object. You can use the List method of the extended data object (or of another form control) to populate the control. The net effect is that the tough part of the programming has been left to the object, and our application only has to worry about manipulating multiple extended data objects. This is one of the more difficult concepts behind objects to understand. You can re-use objects and build objects from other objects. It may sound confusing, but stay with it and you will get it. (Remember how hard loops and conditionals were to understand at first?)

You will handle the manipulation of multiple extended data objects using a collection. The collection holds all of the extended data objects created from all of the data found attached to a drawing object. Why multiple extended data objects and not just one big object holding all the data found? Because it is easier to break up any overall extended data (that could have multiple applications inside it) into individual child objects for each application in the master object. That is the beauty of objects. We can manipulate the data into smaller or larger chunks just by using multiple child objects to store the data in and then combining them when we're done back into a master (parent) object. The object definition that we create must have the methods and properties to do the manipulations, but you have to program that only once and then use the object over and over again to accomplish the desired tasks.

Think of a master object as something that holds all of the extended data attached to an object (an AutoCAD object, group, or a Xdata object). You then pass the master object to a new extended data object along with the requested application name and tell it to get all of the extended data for that particular application name. You now have just that application's extended data from the passed in master object in your child object. The child object is added to the collection in the main program and used with all of the other children to rebuild a new master object when needed. You should be starting to see how the extended data object is being used over and over again and how it is doing all of the work for our applications. Once the object is completely defined, our applications have to manage only the collection(s) of extended data objects.

AppNames

The need to be able to break down an object's extended data into separate children objects, based upon an application's name, prompted the need for an applications name collection (called AppNames) to be exposed as a property of the extended data object. Once an extended data object fills its array with data from the passed in object, it fills the AppNames collection by spinning through the data value array and placing only application names into the collection (located using the group code 1001 in the group code array).

The isolated application names allow you to easily check how many applications were present in the extended data of the object (a master object could have no name when no extended data is attached to the object, or a name for each application attached). It also lets you loop through the collection to build all of the necessary child objects and add them to the collection in the main program.

Another benefit from storing the application names as a property of the object is that you can easily check for the presence of a specific application name. In fact, the AppExist method presented with the other methods for this object below uses its own AppNames property to check if an application name is among the collection. Then it simply passes back a true when it is found and a false when it is not (more on the methods later in this section).

340

ItemsCount

When an extended data object is loaded and the arrays filled, the program then places the upper bound count of the xdatavalue array into the ItemsCount property. This property is used for iterating through any of the three arrays in an extended data object or for checking to see if the object has any data. This property is set to 0 when there is no data in the object.

EntityType

The entity data object we are creating is able to process extended data for any legal AutoCAD object as well as another extended data object. The Entity Type is an EntityType property, just like the one used by AutoCAD objects. (By the way, AutoCAD is an integer that is enumerated [assigned] to a constant name [number] for each object type. This is a bit of a problem for VBA because you cannot enumerate your own EntityType in VBA. However, AutoCAD does not use the number 0 as an EntityType and that fact was taken advantage of in the object definition.) By declaring the EntityType property as a long in the public declarations area of the Xdata object, VBA initializes its default to a 0. The methods in our object will not really be using the number except to provide equality among the data passed to the routines. In several of the methods that make up this object's definition, a Select Case function checks for each legal AutoCAD object and then assumes that any object that made it through is an Xdata object. Here is one area where the error checking can be vastly improved. That is, what happens when an entity type that is not recognized is provided?

Methods

The methods that are in a class are the functions and subroutines that are defined as public. Private functions and subroutines can be accessed only by the other functions in the same module, while public ones can be accessed outside of the module.

341

Table 14.1 contains the public functions and subroutines in the extended data class module. These are the functions that are exposed to the application program and that do the actual work of the Xdata object. Once again, these methods evolved over the life of the project as some were added and some that were once thought to be useful were discarded.

Table 14.1: Public functions and subroutines in the extended data class module

AppExist	Returns true if the application name exists in the AppNames collection, false otherwise.
GetXdata	Retrieves any extended data found to be attached to an object and places it in the extended data object container arrays.
List	Loads the two-dimensional container array aryXdata and displays the data in a list control on a form.
SetXdata	Attaches the extended data object contents to an AutoCAD object.
Split	Reloads the data type and value arrays from the two-dimensional array data in aryXdata. Used after the list box contents have been modified along with the data in the two-dimensional array.
StoreAppNames	Stores the application names found in the extended data container arrays into the application names collection.

Now let's take a closer look at these functions and what they accomplish for the manipulation of our custom extended data object. When an application wants to manipulate the extended data, it will call these functions and subroutines to achieve the desired results. There are only a few, but they accomplish a lot.

To view the source code for these methods, open the extended data project and double click on the class module in the project explorer. The project is stored under the name XdataObject.DVB on the CD supplied with this book.

AppExists

To better control the extended data objects collection in your project, it is important to check to see if the application you are processing is already in the object. This method takes an application name and returns a true when it is already in the object, or a false when it is not. It's handy to know this when you're deciding whether you have to add an application or replace an application.

GetXdata

Several different steps are employed in the class module for the GetXdata method. It takes an AutoCAD entity object, figures out what kind of object it is by testing the object type, transfers the generic object into a specific AutoCAD object of the correct type, then does an AutoCAD object GetXdata on the object. When the supplied object is not an Auto-CAD object, the routine assumes that it is an extended data object and processes it differently. The result is that the extended data object has its properties (container arrays and parameters) filled.

There are two ways in which the program could be written. The approach taken was to demonstrate the technique of using the object type in the AutoCAD entity to assign a local variable of the proper type, thereby establishing an early binding relationship for VBA. The generic AutoCAD entity object container could have been used once we established a non-zero object type. The problem with that approach is the time of execution. The GetXdata method would not be bound to the object until the project runs, thereby forcing a late binding call. A late binding call means that the same object types test takes place, but under the control of the VBA host processor, and that takes longer. In this case, more programming results in a faster overall execution speed. Just how much faster is left as an exercise to the student.

List

This method performs two main activities. It is used to load the two-dimensional aryXdata property. It also accepts an optional argument that will list the extended data object properties to a message box, to the immediate window (the default), or to a control (such as a list box). Pass in D (for debug.print) to send it to the immediate window, M to send it to a message box, or L, Form.listbox control, to load a listbox or combobox on a form. One of the primary purposes of this method is to make life easier when you're developing routines that use list box controls and extended data, just like the object example project will be doing.

SetXdata

Much like the GetXdata method, several different steps are employed in the SetXdata method. The routine starts by taking an unknown Auto-CAD object, figures out what kind of object it is, transfers the generic object into a specific AutoCAD object of the correct type, then does an AutoCAD object SetXdata on the object. The SetXdata method for a extended data object does not write to another extended data object. Like the GetXdata method, this function uses a test of the enumerated values for the object types to establish what kind of object it is addressing. The reason is to establish an early binding relationship with that object so that the overall execution speed of the process is maximized. The decision between programmer time and operator time should always fall in favor of the operator unless the coding requirements are too extreme.

The use of the name SetXdata and GetXdata matches the name of the method used in each of the entity objects of AutoCAD. This is a classic case of polymorphism at work in the VBA system. The SetXdata method that is defined in the class module works with the custom extended data objects we are building. The other SetXdata method is associated with the AutoCAD entity objects. It is the second method that writes the data into the AutoCAD database when called from our SetXdata method. It may seem confusing to use the same name over and over again; how-ever, keep in mind that the names of the routines are associated with the objects, thus making them unique in the system. The use of the same name just saves you from having to remember a lot of subroutine names for each type of object you want to manipulate.

Split

This method is the opposite of the List method. It splits the aryXdata array property of an extended data object into its xdatatype and xdata-value arrays. It is exposed for rebuilding an extended data object from a list box control after edits have been made.

StoreAppNames

This method is exposed for rebuilding extended data objects from a form's list box or combobox control after edits have been applied to the data in the list. It takes the extended data objects XdataValue container array and stores all application names in the AppNames collection.

That concludes the public methods associated with this class definition. If you look inside the source code for the module, you will find additional private routines that have been defined to further manipulate the data and perform the dirty work associated with the extended data. The object itself does not do much other than supply a library of routines to work with and some data to place things in. When you use the objects, you create an instance or copy of the object's properties. At the same time you establish a path to the library routines associated with the object.

The Extended Data Example Project

Now let's turn our attention to using the custom object we just defined. This application is supplied in its entirety on the CD associated with this book under the name xdataObject.DVB and can be loaded using the VBAMAN command in AutoCAD 2000. There is also a drawing provided that already contains a variety of extended data on the entities in it. The name of the drawing is XdataObj Test.DWG, and it should be opened as well as the VBA project for testing the functions.

To test the extended data object project, run the Xdata macro (in bas-Global) after loading the project. Selecting the run button launches the Xdata Control application. The dialog box interface that will appear is

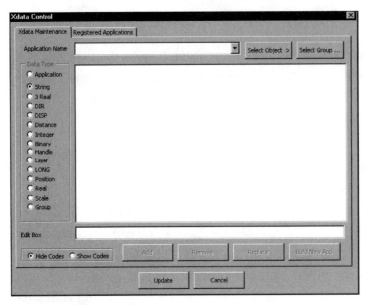

Figure 14.1: Xdata control

shown in Figure 14.1. From this dialog box you can view and edit all of the manipulation of variable objects and extended data objects. The dialog box contains two tabs. You'll use the Registered Applications tab to view all the registered application names currently in the drawing. You can also add a new registered application name in that tab area. The Xdata Maintenance tab is where the extended data located for an object or group is displayed.

The use of the application is relatively simple. After starting the entry macro (named Xdata), the dialog in Figure 14.1 is displayed. Pick the Select Object button, then select an entity object that has extended data attached to it. If the object selected has extended data, it will be displayed in the list box. Otherwise, the dialog box will be displayed again, but nothing will be in the list box.

Once data is displayed in the list box, you can select the individual items. The column of radio button matching the data type will then highlight type of data just selected in the list box. The value associated with the same selection will be presented in the edit box. If you change the value in the edit box, the updated value will be displayed in the list

346

box showing all the extended data. Use the Replace button to write the extended data back to the list selected. When finished with all the changes for the extended data of an entity object, select the Update command button to put the extended data back into the entity object.

Now let us focus more on the usage of the extended data object in the program as driven by the functions within the interface. There are a lot of openings left in this example that can be filled in as needed by your own application requirements should you choose to do so. This example also demonstrates some interesting features of VBA, such as tabs and radio column control, that may be of interest to students just learning VBA.

The application can manipulate extended data stored with entity objects or with groups—thus the Select Object > and Select Group... buttons. Whether you select from an entity object on the screen or from a group in the group dialog interface, the application loads any attached extended data from the object or group into the extended data object using the GetXData method. The particular GetXdata method used is the one for the extended data object. It will load the arrays xdatatype, xdatavalue, aryXdata, the application names collection, and the ItemsCount properties of the extended data object. The program can then verify that extended data does exist for the object or group selected by checking the ItemCount property.

Once the extended data object is loaded with data, it is used to propagate the dialog box controls. The big list box on the interface is loaded from the object using the associated List method, and then the Application Name poplist is loaded from the object (again using the List method). After that the application splits all of the data in the master object into child objects (one for each application name in the master object). The child objects are stored in a collection for later retrieval using the application name for the extended data it contains as a key. That's how it is set up when extended data is found attached to the selected object or group.

From the dialog box, the operator can add, remove, or replace extended data items from an existing application, or even create a new

347

application name and define extended data for it using this simple extended data editor application. Bear in mind that the Binary item is not editable and you cannot add new binary extended data or change any existing binary data. That is strictly the realm of ObjectARX and the C++ language. Also, the technique for adding a new extended data application and associated items is a little cumbersome. But that is because this utility is intended for editing existing extended data and not necessarily for adding new applications and data. About the only time you would need to create a new application is when you're testing an application module that wants to read existing data and you have not yet written the module to create the data .

Further usage of the extended data object is demonstrated when the operator selects the Update button to place your changes back into the selected object or group. The application has maintained child Xdata objects and has rebuilt them each time you made a change to one in the list box. It is now a matter of rebuilding a new master object from all of the available child objects and then using that master object to update the entity object or group that was selected to begin with. Stepping through the code starting in the Update button's subroutine will give you a good idea of the complexity that was programmed into the Xdata object. This is not coding you would want to do over and over again in multiple places in your application.

Extended Data Object Conclusion

That covers one practical application of a class module object in VBA programming. When building your own, remember that it is important to design your object to store the data you need in the form you need and to develop methods for handling that data based on the use you are going to put the object to in your program. These are simple rules for creating the object but the programming of the object's behavior will be as complex as you need to make it to do the job.

Classes are a way to store both data and program functions. In this example, there were several exposed properties and methods. But if you look at the source code for the class module there were also several private (non-exposed) functions defined. These functions were used internal to the object and are not available to other modules. Our next example is different in that all the properties are considered private, and the only way to access them is through the methods provided.

Objects Example 2: Hole Chart

Our next example project demonstrates how objects can be used to keep the clutter in the main application to a minimum and to allow for expansion of the system with minimal changes in the base application source code. This example demonstrates how one object can contain another object. In this example, we are going to have a base object and then a collection of these objects as another object. There will be methods for manipulating each object type, allowing the application to treat the collection or the individual objects as singular items.

The application is to create a hole chart. A hole chart is a table of locations for holes to be drilled or machined in some way. On the drawing, each hole (or circle) is labeled with a letter or number. A hole chart is the table that contains the label, coordinates, radius, depth, and type of operation. This chart is typically used by the drill operator or to develop a CNC program or for a coordinate measurement system to verify hole locations and sizes. The goal of this program is to allow the user to select circles in the drawing, then label them and build a hole chart graphic. This example is greatly simplified since the real goal is not to develop a complete hole chart application but to use the concept to demonstrate how object classes can contain references to other object classes.

Like all applications involving objects, the object presented in these pages represents the result of an evolutionary process. It is not uncommon to start with a group of properties and methods and then add more as the project evolves. And if you find that this application is useful and want to expand it, then you will most likely be adding to the methods and properties of the objects. That's okay. Objects that we define for our own use in our own applications are not used by other processes and are

349

thus under our complete control. Only when an object definition (class) is shared among several applications can it become hazardous to change objects. And then the problem is only if the base functionality of the object is changed or if items inside the object, such as properties or methods, are removed. Normally one does not remove a component from an object once the object is shared among several applications. And so long as new items are the change, then modifying the base object will not change the operation of the other applications at all.

The Holes.DVB project contains the source code for the hole charting example. This project consists of two class modules named Holes and Hole, a form named HoleChart, and a code module containing the start-up macro. Most of the code is documented to allow other programmers interested in seeing working examples of the VBA system to explore it. In the next few paragraphs we are going to discuss the concepts behind the code.

An Object in an Object

Absurd as this concept may at first appear, it makes good sense from a data organizing point of view. The innermost object is one item. It can be manipulated by itself as a singular element. Multiple objects can be kept in a list or collection, and that can be thought of as a singular object as well. This allows our programs to reference just one member or the whole group of members and do things with them. In VBA, when you create a collection, you are defining an object that can contain other objects. But if you need to do more than just the operations provided by the collection object, you need to create your own form of collection. From an object programming point of view you are deriving a new collection object using the existing collection object as a base from which to start.

So what doesn't the basic collection object do for us already that we could possibly want it to do? That answer is found the first time that you try to organize previously unorganized data in some way. The hole chart application demonstrates this in the Holes class module definition. We want the hole chart organized as follows: sorted by diameter first, then the X ordinate value, then the Y ordinate value. The add() method does not do this normally, so we need to write our own version as seen in the class module source code definition.

There are some other confusing aspects of this source code for those who are relatively new to VBA. The class module name is Holes. In the class module is a collection defined as public by the same name. That is not a mistake and not something that is to be removed. This code is a class definition. The class we are defining is a clone of the collection object. We didn't have to use the same name in the public variable as the class, but it makes the code easier to work with at the applications level and easier to code internally as the name Holes is now mapped to a collection. That makes all of the methods that are normally found in the collection object available to the new class we are defining.

Note the other methods inside the definition of the Holes class have simple access to the collection methods to accomplish their own tasks. For example, the count method accesses the count method of the collection Holes. In the class definition source code, the name Holes is associated to a standard collection object. When the application program references the name Holes, it is talking about the class Holes that includes the collection. When creating a cloned object of this nature you must redefine all the methods that will be used in your application or use a double nested named access to get back to the basic object type. For example, if we didn't provide a count method for obtaining the number of Hole objects inside the holes collection, the application would first access the class and then the collection to obtain the count. As it is coded, an application gets the count as "normal" directly from the Holes object. Internally, the Holes object gets the count from the collection to pass back as a result.

The Holes object, since it is our object, can also contain methods not normally found in the collection object. The method Draw_Holes is an example of that sort of programming. The routine Draw_Holes loops through the collection of Holes, extracting each Hole object one at a time and calling the draw method for that hole object.

The application module can now make a single call to the holes collection and have all of the holes drawn on the screen with the labels and centerlines added according to the hole's object drawing definition. Between the addition of the matching methods for the collection and the new methods added on top of the class, Holes provides an easy way for an application to manipulate an entire collection of Hole objects. More methods can be added to the Holes class such as resorting the collection based on another key sequence (such as the label or name) or placing the collection contents into a list box control, and so forth.

The Inner Object

Our next stop is to look at the Hole class module. This is another class definition, but it is different from what we've seen before since all of the variables are defined as private. That means that if we want to allow the operator to access any of the properties, we must provide a function or method that accomplishes that task. By shielding the data in this manner we can make sure that the information is legitimate at all times. That means that the radius is not 0 and that the operations that can be performed at the hole (such as drill and tap) are of a finite number so that our other processes (like a CNC program generator) can make sense of the selections.

The choice of public or private is one of programmer preference. Some applications may actually dictate that the data be public by the nature of the object and how it will be manipulated. In most cases it is actually better to write small routines to handle the data. This allows for future expansion as the object is evolved into a more advanced piece of coding.

For example, the Hole object contains methods that set and retrieve the X and Y values as well as another set that sets and retrieves the center point. What is the difference and why provide both options in the first place? The reason is to provide the application with the options of addressing the same data in multiple ways. The application may not need multiple calling options, and in that case the object should provide only those that are really required. Another reason to use methods instead of allowing direct access to the properties is to allow for future expansion of the module. Suppose this application was to screen out values less than 0 for the X ordinate or it was needed to apply a variable offset to the numbers provided. These enhancements can be made to the object and not affect the application that uses the object. When the object (class module) is updated, the application continues calling the methods it always has and continues on its way.

The Hole class module contains other methods used to manipulate the individual Hole objects. There are routines to transfer data from the AutoCAD circle object into the Hole private properties as well as routines that draw the labeled hole on the drawing. The hole label and draw routine is the most complex of all the routines in this class as it not only draws a new circle, but it also places centerlines through it, then attaches a label to a leader that points at the newly created circle. This function is an excellent beginner example of drawing slightly more complex creations under the control of VBA.

The Hole object can be used by the Holes collection object as well as by the application. In the application, an assignment is made through the SET statement to a variable defined as type Hole. With the reference to a specific hole, the methods can be called to draw it or change the properties internally.

The Holes and Hole objects are intended for use by other applications and not just the hole chart drawing utility. These objects can be expanded as needed for the creation of CNC code (simply add a method to the Hole object that creates the CNC statement to drill the hole) or other reports and drawing utilities that would use the hole chart information. The ability to expand objects is important in the Hole object's case. The module as presented here draws hole representations for drilling and tapping only; it does not include anything for counter-boring, reaming, counter-sinks, and so forth. If you need those representations, you can add them to the object definition without forcing the change of any of the applications. Instead, the applications just got smarter.

Table 14.2: Hole object private properties

Lbl	String	Label at hole.
Dia	Double	Diameter of hole.
X	Double	X ordinate of center of hole.
Y	Double	Y ordinate of center of hole.
Z	Double	Z ordinate of center of hole.
Typ	Integer	Hole type code number.
Default_Typ	Integer	Default hole type code number.

Table 14.3: Hole object public methods

Get_Label	Returns the label string value for the hole.
Get_Dia	Returns the diameter value of the hole.
Get_Rad	Returns the radius value of hole.
Get_X	Returns the X ordinate of the center of the hole.
Get_Y	Returns the Y ordinate of the center of the hole.
Get_Z	Returns the Z ordinate of the center of the hole, also considered the depth of the hole.
Get_Point	Returns a variant that is the center point of the hole.
Get_Operation	Returns an integer that is the operation code for this hole.
Put_Label	Stores a string into the label value for the hole.
Set_Dia	Stores a double as the diameter of the hole.
Set_Rad	Stores a double as the radius of the hole.
Set_Point	Stores a variant array as the center point of the hole.
Set_X	Stores X ordinate of the center of the hole.
Set_Y	Stores Y ordinate of the center of the hole.
Set_Z	Stores Z ordinate of the center of the hole.
Set_Operation	Stores integer code value for operation.
Set_Default	Sets default code value for operation when adding new items.
Load_Circle	Converts circle object data into hole object data.
Draw	Draws the circle with label and center lines.
Round	Rounds all the doubles found in the hole object.

When you compare the Hole object's private properties as shown in table 14.2 with the public methods available, shown in table 14.3 you'll notice that there are more methods for setting the properties than there are properties. That is because this object provides the option to set the diameter or the radius value. If the application supplies the radius and uses SET_RAD to store it in the object, the value is doubled and saved as the diameter. It's the same in reverse when the radius is requested. This saves the application program from having to double or halve the value as it can be retrieved as needed—that is, in the context of the application.

Objects provide a powerful way to store and manipulate data and data collections of multiple data types. The use of private properties and public methods for setting and retrieving the data allows the data to be secure and to conform to the way the application needs it. Although it may appear as if we have stored a lot more information than is really needed, we have reduced the amount of overall system requirements by not storing both the radius and diameter as well as the point plus the individual ordinates. As the Holes collection grows, the methods are not copied for each of the Hole objects inside, just the properties. Thus, not storing all the versions of the data—instead just storing the methods to access the data in different ways—results in less storage needed by the system to house large collections of holes.

The Hole Charting Example Project

Running the hole chart example project that is provided with this book is very easy. First copy the Holes.DVB file from the CD to your AutoCAD VBA applications directory. Then load the application using the VBALOAD or VBAMAN commands in AutoCAD. Select the Macros option or use the command VBARUN, then select the Chart macro to run. Chart will immediately request that the operator select circles. Use any valid pick mechanism to select the circles including windows and individual selections. After selecting the holes, press the Enter key to continue to the dialog box as seen in Figure 14.2.

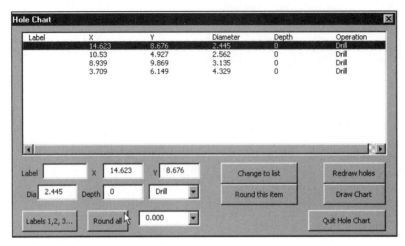

Figure 14.2: Hole chart dialog box

The circle data found will be presented in the list box of the display. The X, Y, Z, and Diameter values are taken directly from the circle objects selected in AutoCAD. The holes are sorted in order by diameter, then X, then Y.

When circles are first selected in this application, they have no label and are assigned a standard default operation code. To change any of the values, select the line to change in the list box. Then change the values in the edit box windows provided. After making changes to an item in the list it is important to remember to select the Change to list button to write the values in the edit boxes back to the list display.

Other buttons to press include Round all, which will round the values of all real numbers (X, Y, Z, and Diameter) to the precision set in the popup list box next to the button. Labels 1,2,3... will automatically label all holes with a sequential number starting with 1 and incrementing by 1. Redraw holes will erase the selected circles, then redraw them using the label and centerline inclusive method from the Hole object. Finally, Draw Chart will accept the input of a point, then generate a chart from the data in the list box using the current default text height to control the size of the chart rows and columns.

Hole Chart Application Conclusion

This application does a lot, but it could do a lot more with some more refinements and tweaking on the behalf of the student programmer. If you find the application appealing, you should invest the time in the source code to add the features needed for your operations. Obviously the Hole object can be expanded to support other Hole types. That means the draw method must be updated to accommodate the changes as well as the Set_Operation and Set_Default methods.

This project does demonstrate that if a basic collection is not enough, it is simple enough to clone it and create your own version. Custom objects in programming allow for future expansion as well as simplification at the application level.

Creating Your Own Object

Do you have an idea for an object? Try writing down the list of properties (both public and private) that your object would include. Then list and describe the methods needed both internally (private) and externally (public) for your object. You will notice that the list of properties and methods may change while you define the methods more thoroughly. That's normal since one often recognizes the need for more of one or the other as the method definitions are refined. At the same time it is normal to remove things from the original list as better ways are uncovered to handle the problems or store the data.

After getting a handle on what the object properties and methods are going to be, select to insert a new class module into the project that will first use this class. After developing the class module to a level desired, export it to a CLS file (CLS is the file extension and is considered a Class file). Use the Files menu in the VBA editor or Right-Click in the project window on the class to be exported. The export option will appear in the menu presented.

For later projects, the CLS (class module) can be imported using the File menu option for Import. This will bring the class definition into your new project. One thing important to note is that if you change a class in a project and save the project the class definitions in the other projects will not be automatically updated. Instead, you must export the revised class module, then import it back into the other applications. As these applications are saved back to disk, the updated class modules are stored with them.

We can't stop saying this again and again: once you master the concepts behind objects it becomes difficult to imagine developing advanced applications without them. At first they may seem like a fancy way to store a library of subroutines, and in a way they are, but objects allow you to think differently at the application level. They help isolate items down to the bare essentials so that the details are covered. And they are expandable into new ways of doing things. If you need to change an object to add a new extension to it, then that change does not affect the other applications that use the same object. By allowing for the referencing of both data and program code under the same structure, you can create building blocks from which you can create even more advanced blocks and applications.

Index

Also available from 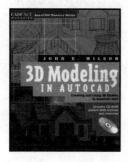 Miller Freeman Books
in partnership with CADENCE

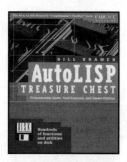
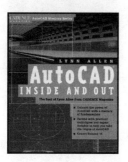